Praise for *When Parents Hurt*

"*When Parents Hurt* is a wise and helpful book that I recommend if you are a parent struggling to make peace with one or more of your children. Dr. Coleman writes in a gentle and humble manner that is clear, easy to follow, and full of helpful suggestions and compassionate understanding."
—Frederic Luskin, Ph.D., director, Stanford Forgiveness Projects, and author of *Forgive for Good*

"Joshua Coleman's book is a gift, offering extraordinary wisdom coupled with practical advice about how you can come to terms with your own and your child's imperfections, rebuild a relationship with your grown offspring, and learn how to accept that which cannot be changed. If you are estranged from an adult child, if you regret the way you treated your daughter or son, if your divorce harmed your relationship with your kids, this book is for you."
—Steven Mintz, Center for Advanced Study in the Behavioral Sciences, and author of *Huck's Raft: A History of American Childhood*

"Most parents today invest more time, energy, and resources in their children than ever before, in part because young people get less from other adults and institutions than in the past. In his exceptionally perceptive new book, Joshua Coleman explains how this social dilemma multiplies the risk of disappointment, resentment, and guilt, offering practical advice to help parents cope with these intergenerational tensions."
—Stephanie Coontz, author of *Marriage, a History: How Love Conquered Marriage* and *The Way We Never Were*

"I LOVE this book. It is a necessary book that is written from such a realistic and compassionate perspective that it is heart-warming. It deals with a real problem that is far more pervasive than all the warm/fuzzy hype about family would have us believe. The heartache of parents who don't get along with their grown children has to be the pain that keeps on giving—in both directions. I don't imagine it does wonders for the grown children and the architecture of their lives and their approach to parenthood to be chronically at odds with their parents. This book shows families a new way to think about and structure their conversations with each other."

—Hara Estroff Marano, editor at large, *Psychology Today*, and author of *A Nation of Wimps*

"A unique, no-nonsense, insightful guide for parents who feel guilty or deeply disappointed by their relationships with their adolescent or adult children. An especially healing, practical resource for divorced parents and for anyone exhausted by strained, hurtful relationships with their adolescent or grown child."

—Dr. Linda Nielsen, professor of Adolescent Psychology & Women's Studies, Wake Forest University, and author of *Embracing Your Father: Building the Relationship You Always Wanted With Your Dad*

"In this desperately needed book, Joshua Coleman addresses the issue of estrangement, difficulties, and pain between parents and their teen and grown children. We all know of it. We all hear our friends talking about it. But for a therapist to write from the parents' point of view . . . ground-breaking. This is a book for, maybe, everyone with children. If your children are still young, it is a chance to be proactive in terms of staving off future problems. If you are in the midst of difficulties, it is timely and comforting and full of great suggestions for how to take care of your own peace of mind, and perhaps make some positive changes with your children. AND even if your relationship with your children seems great, it is worthwhile to think more deeply about why that is, and whether there might be some hidden problems which, if thought about, could make things even better. In short, it is a truly great book for parents, and a great book for therapists who work with families."

—Heather Folsom, M.D., author, and adult and child psychiatrist

"This is an incredibly insightful and sensitively written analysis of a difficult subject. . . . As a practicing psychologist, I have recommended it to many of my clients who are struggling with their relationship to their adult children, and have consistently received rave reviews from them . . . . I highly recommend it to all parents who hurt."
—Jan Levine, Ph.D., coauthor of *Why Do Fools Fall in Love?*

"[A]n important book that can help parents heal . . . Coleman offers parents a step-by-step way to cope and to carry on with hope for the future . . . . And his book poses the question at the heart of many relationships between boomers and their young adult children. What is this relationship supposed to look like? What do we owe each other? How are we supposed to treat each other? How do we avoid hurting each other?"
—*Baltimore Sun*

"A superb treatment for parents wounded emotionally or psychologically by their children . . . an accessible, hopeful exploration . . . a unique and groundbreaking approach . . . an eye-opening read for anyone."
—*Library Journal* (starred review)

"Taking a refreshingly different viewpoint from many psychologists, Coleman does not blame parents alone for a lost relationship. Instead, he explains the many factors that can cause the parent/child relationship to go wrong . . . and what can be done to make amends."
—*Greater Good Magazine*

When
Parents
Hurt

Compassionate Strategies
When You and Your Grown Child
Don't Get Along

JOSHUA COLEMAN, Ph.D.

WILLIAM MORROW
An Imprint of HarperCollinsPublishers

To the reader

WHEN PARENTS HURT. Copyright © 2008 by Joshua Coleman, Ph.D. All rights reserved. Printed in the United States of America. No part of this book may be used or reproduced in any manner whatsoever without written permission except in the case of brief quotations embodied in critical articles and reviews. For information, address HarperCollins Publishers, 195 Broadway, New York, NY 10007.

HarperCollins books may be purchased for educational, business, or sales promotional use. For information, please e-mail the Special Markets Department at SPsales@harpercollins.com.

FIRST COLLINS PAPERBACK EDITION PUBLISHED 2008

Designed by Joseph Rutt

Library of Congress Cataloging-in-Publication Data has been applied for.

ISBN: 978-0-06-114843-9

17 18 ID/RRD 20 19 18 17 16 15 14 13 12

CONTENTS

Contents

PARENTS
ON THE FIRING LINE

Dear Mom,
I have decided that I don't want to have any contact with you ever again. Please don't write or call me anymore. I can't stop thinking about all of the ways that you were never there for me when I was growing up. Whenever I see or talk to you, I just end up feeling depressed, angry, and upset for weeks afterwards. It's just not worth it to me and I need to get on with my life. Please respect my wishes and don't contact me again.

> *Letter from Clarice, 23,*
> *to her mother Fiona, 48*

Fiona sat on my couch in her first visit without looking at me or saying anything. She reached into her purse and handed me the letter from her daughter as if to say, "This says it all." And it did. As a psychologist, I've counseled many adult children like Fiona's daughter; in some cases, I've helped them to craft letters just like hers, or supported them in cutting off contact with a mother, a father, or both. I know the finality that these letters can portend. It's a deadly serious business and the stakes are huge—a therapist has no business giving advice in this arena unless he or she has carefully thought about the long-term implications of these decisions.

I felt for this desolate mother sitting in front of me because I knew that the letter *could* be the last contact that Fiona would ever have with her daughter. A flood of questions were already circulating in my mind. "Why is her daughter so angry at her? What has Fiona done to try to repair it? How capable has she been of taking responsibility or listening in a non-defensive way to her daughter's complaints? How receptive will she be to my recommendations for how to respond?"

"I'm sorry," I said, handing back the letter. "That must be so painful."

Fiona looked relieved, as though she had expected me to blame her. "I worry about her all of the time and can't stop wondering what horrible thing I did to make my own child turn against me? I'm sure I made my fair share of mistakes, but I wasn't that different with her than I was with the other three." She started sobbing. "Clarice was always the hardest of my four children. Even when she was young, she seemed so impossible to please. We did everything for her: individual therapy, family therapy, medication, you name it—nothing seemed to make her feel happy or connected to us. My other kids resented her because she sucked all of the time, energy, and money out of the family that should have gone to all four of them. She won't talk to my other kids, either, except for the youngest. It's really heartbreaking," she said, grabbing for the Kleenex. "*It is so goddamned heartbreaking!*"

ARE PARENTS TO BLAME?

Not that long ago I would have assumed that Fiona must have done *something* terribly wrong to cause her daughter to respond in such a dramatic way. My training as a psychologist taught me that the problems of the adult child can always be linked to some form of mistreatment from the parent. While this is often true, it doesn't hold for all families. And when it is true, it's often a far more complex picture than most therapists and self-help authors realize.

As I worked with Fiona over the next few months, I came to understand that she had been a reasonable and conscientious mother. As her story and others illustrate, it is possible to be a devoted and conscientious parent and *still* have it go badly. You can do everything right and your child can *still* grow up and not want to have the kind of relationship with you that you always hoped you'd have. You can do everything right, and your child may *still* end up with a drug problem that costs you thousands of dollars and endless heartache. You can do everything right and your child may *still* choose the kind of friends or partners that you never imagined she would have chosen because these people seem so lost and are dragging your child into losing more. You can do everything right and your child can *still* fail to launch a successful adulthood despite being gifted and talented or possessing an IQ that most people would kill for.

Very few of us escape feeling guilt toward our offspring. It may be part of our evolutionary heritage, a way that nature hardwires us to stay sensitive to them, even after they're grown. And some parents *are* responsible for transgressions that are harmful to their children: child abuse, incest, neglect, and alcoholism are a few of the more egregious examples. However, whether the parenting mistakes are subtle or serious, real or imagined, today's parents are completely confused by their children's failures and accusations. They need guidance and support for *themselves*, not more advice about their children.

WHO IS THIS BOOK FOR?

This book is written for:

- Parents who carry enormous feelings of guilt, shame, and regret about how they treated their children.

- Parents raising children with a diagnosis or temperament that makes them harder to parent, and maybe harder to love.

- Parents whose divorces have created a profound change in the quality of their relationship with their child. This includes children who are rejecting or blaming them, refusing contact with them, or seem to be damaged by the divorce.

- Parents whose current or ex-spouses are dedicated to bringing them down in the eyes of their child.

- Parents who were devoted and conscientious, yet their adult child refuses contact with them.

- Parents whose partner (parent/stepparent, boyfriend/girlfriend) makes it difficult to provide the kind of safety or nurturance that they want to give their children.

- Parents who are mismatched in some important way with their child: for example, a successful and driven parent with a learning disabled child; a vulnerable, insecure parent with an aggressive and rejecting child; a depressed parent with an active/risk-taking child.

- Parents who are wounded by their grown child's inability to launch a happy or successful life.

THE WOUNDS CAUSED BY TEENS AND ADULT CHILDREN

Since parenting a child at any age has its challenges and provocations, I could have started with childbirth and continued through each developmental stage. However, I have chosen to limit my topic to the wounds caused by teenagers and adult children: I start with teenagers because adolescence is the place where some of the hardest confrontations begin to be waged between parent and child. While many parents hope or pray that their young child will one day outgrow her problems—her trapeze-like mood swings, her difficulty "fitting in," her defiant and insufferable temperament—most begin to realize by adolescence that their soon-to-be adult may be no different and no easier than the very same child was at ages two, five, and ten; it's only the hair and clothing that have changed.

Adult children are another story. Financial strings aside, a young adult has almost total discretion to spend time with you, or not. The only time younger children have similar latitude is in divorce where the courts or living arrangements enable the child to have much more choice over how much time he will spend with a noncustodial parent.

In other words, adult children are even *freer* to launch salvos against the parent's happiness and well-being, to have their own versions of how they were raised, and to state those claims with authority. It was *their* childhood, not yours; *their* experience, not yours; and now, in case it wasn't perfectly clear, *their* adulthood! With adult children, closeness or distance is negotiated on an equal playing field—a field with rules unheard of before in history.

NOT A PARENTING BOOK

For all of its glory and gut-busting work, parenting is a dangerous undertaking. You put in long hours, examine every decision and action, do the best you can, and yet the child who once adored and needed you can come to reject, shame, or belittle you. The youth who was to be your greatest source of joy and pride can become your greatest source of worry and disappointment. The sweet kid who wrote you love notes and gave you hugs has written you off, or gives you the finger instead.

This book is written for parents who have concluded, after years of therapy, medication trials, soul searching, or family interventions that they should stop listening to all of those other parents, pediatricians, psychologists, and talk-show experts who say that if they only do steps one through seven, they too can have the relationship with their child that they always wanted. They have decided that these well-meaning advisors are naive, misinformed, or plain ignorant and wrong, because frankly, they are. Their advice is based on a parenting model that offers little to those who are greeted by pain, guilt, or disappointment every time they open the door to their teenager's room or try to get their grown child to return their calls.

UPCOMING CHAPTERS

Chapter 2 will help to provide clarity about where you are right now with your child and will help you understand how you got there. It outlines the many ways that you can become hurt as a parent, and will provide questions to help you begin to think about how you got there and where you need to go.

While all parents experience feelings of guilt, some parents are chronically plagued by the belief that they have damaged their children, sometimes without any corresponding evidence. Chapters 3 and 4 are written to provide guidance for parents who feel guilty about their behavior in the past, or who need help dealing with their child's accusations in the present.

Our current ideals about parenting and children are historically unprecedented; most of our ideas about what children need and who parents are supposed to be are flawed in many, many ways. These ideas greatly contribute to parents' feelings of shame and failure. They contribute to children and others feeling entitled to blame parents for the children's problems, inadequacies, or poor relationship with the parent. "Parents" and "children" are constructs whose definitions change with every century, if not every few decades. Chapter 5 seeks to place today's parent in a historical and economic context.

Chapter 6 examines the shame that so many parents feel when they have strained relationships with a child. We'll examine the basis for your vulnerability to shame and provide guidelines and exercises for working through those feelings.

Chapter 7 details the problems that occur when a parent and child are temperamentally mismatched. A mismatch occurs when what comes naturally to the parent is completely at odds with who the child is, and sometimes at odds with what he or she needs. We'll look at how temperamental mismatches can create long-term conflict in the parent-child relationship and provide recommendations and solutions.

Teenagers can cause parents to feel inadequate, enraged, scared, and hopeless. Today's parents of teens face special challenges because of the peer group's increasing power to supplant the parent's authority. Chapter 8 is written to help parents manage the thorny cluster of emotions provoked by difficult teenagers and to provide guidance on how and when to intervene.

Chapter 9 looks at the guilt, disruption, and loss that parents feel with divorce. It will also examine the ways that ex-spouses and stepfamily issues may contribute to the alienation divorced parents sometimes feel with their children. Guidelines and exercises will be provided.

While divorce can strain the relationships between parents and children, a difficult marriage can do the same. In Chapter 10 we look at the wounds that occur when your spouse or partner makes it harder for you to be a good parent. Some common situations are spouses or partners with poor communication skills, anger management problems, abusive behaviors, psychiatric disorders, or addictions. Guidance and exercises will be offered.

In Chapter 11 I will provide help for those parents whose hurt comes from having a teen or grown child who can't get his or her life developed and launched. This will cover those children who have already moved out of the home and those who are still living there.

One of the most painful experiences for a parent is to have a grown child who refuses to have a relationship, or who makes that relationship extremely difficult. Chapter 12 is written for parents whose adult children have rejected them, either through constant blame or by completely cutting off contact. Guidelines will be given about when to pursue, when to back off, and how to gain serenity.

Part of what makes parenting difficult is the way that children can trigger painful feelings from our own childhoods. In Chapter 13 we'll consider how your own childhood history affects your parenting and your response to your child's treatment of you. Recommendations, exercises, and guidelines will be given.

WHO IS THIS BOOK FOR?

This book is for you if you have lost something important during your years of raising children: your bearings or your self-esteem, the opportunity to be the parent you desperately wanted to be, or the potential to repair the damage from your own painful childhood. While there are thousands of books telling you how to better raise your children, there are none written on a topic that is just as important: healing the wounds of the parent. If this is your goal, this book is written for you.

TWO

GETTING IT WRONG ABOUT PARENTS

Defining the Problem

I am often consulted by a mother or father who has, just the night before, scolded his or her toddler for some disagreeable behavior such as biting his sister on the nose or kicking the cat while it was en route to the litter box. These parents ask if they should start saving up now for the inevitable trip to the therapist's office. They envision this child recounting to a nodding therapist the time mother cruelly and unjustly scolded him for innocently playing with his sister or sweetly petting the family cat. "Mom was such a *bitch*. No wonder I have intimacy issues!"

While some parenting behaviors *can* create problems in children, I believe we need a much more nuanced and complete picture than the one currently being provided by therapists, politicians, and talk show hosts. A larger picture is necessary because influences such as genes, economics, peer groups, siblings, culture, and personality can cause some kids to make their mediocre parents look and feel pretty great while others make their exceptional parents look and feel pretty awful. Some children, just by *their* nature, create a lot of parental error and heartache. Some environments create problems in children that have little to do with whether mom and dad are following the latest and greatest parenting advice to a T.

Since parenting is a science of approximations, there is often no perfect outcome or intervention for every single child. In an attempt to make a sensitive child feel safe, we could be accused of being excessively protective and not providing an environment where she could learn to tolerate anxiety and fear. In an effort to make a defiant child more compliant, we could be blamed for being overly restrictive and for missing those times when he's cooperative and interested. These "mistakes" may stem from our attempts to be loving, or from being worn down, intensely worried, or just incredibly irritated by having to provide feedback to a system that is constantly in need of rebalancing.

While parents are expected to love all of their children equally, parents *don't* feel the same way about all of their children, both when they're young and when they're grown. And is it any wonder? A child who radiates affection and love toward his affection- and love-starved parent is going get a lot more response and tenderness than one who is inconsolable, defiant, and withdrawn.

Difficult children of any stripe tend to bring out behaviors and emotions that we would prefer to avoid seeing in ourselves or letting the rest of the world know about. They make us lose our tempers and say stupid, hurtful things that we could never imagine saying and pray no one overhears at the grocery store or at our in-laws' dining room table. Difficulties with children of any age can make parents feel depressed, shamed, and jealous of all those other parents who have it so easy.

PERFECTING PARENTING

Research psychologist Diana Baumrind has influenced many parents and psychologists with her theory of authoritative parenting. It's a useful concept and one that I often suggest to parents who are looking for general guidelines. From this perspective, there are three types of parents: authoritarian, permissive, and authoritative. Authoritarian parents are characterized by using too much control and showing very little affection. Permissive parents are characterized by showing a lot of affection and very little control. Authoritative parents show a lot of affection and a lot of control. Her findings reveal that, all things considered, authoritative parenting is the best predictor for successful development.

"So," one can easily conclude, "if you're authoritative, then presto! Mold the perfect child into a healthy adult by providing a healthy mixture of affection and control." But it doesn't always work that way. Part of what makes parenting so confusing, and therefore so treacherous, is that what works for kid A may be useless for kid B. Some parents are great with certain types of kids and clueless with others; better with boys than girls; better with girls than boys; better with cats than either.

And some kids are just easy to raise. I met a couple of these well-behaved youths a few years ago when I went to visit a childhood friend in Los Angeles. After introducing me to his wife, we sat down in his living room. Other than the radio turned quietly to a classic rock station, the house was eerily quiet.

"Oh, darn," I said, looking around at his suspiciously well-kept home.

"What's the matter?" he asked.

"I was hoping to meet your daughters. I thought you said they'd be here."

"Oh, they're here. They're playing together in the next room. I think they're probably reading together or just hanging out. 'Emily, Elyse, come out; I want you to meet somebody.'" His daughters, aged nine and thirteen, came into the living room in the way that kids on TV walk into a room: smiling, peaceful, well-paid. "I'd like you to meet my friend, Josh."

"Hi, Josh," the older one said. "Hi, Josh," the younger one said in the same way, only younger. The girls sat down in front of us on the floor while Kenny and I talked for an hour and a half without interruption. An hour and a half. Um, an hour and a half.

"Man," I said, "how do you get them to do that?"

"Oh, they're always like that. They're really good kids."

Aha! There it was. They're good kids! But aren't mine good? Does practicing World Wrestling Federation takedown moves in the checkout aisle of the grocery store make them bad? Does the fact that they constantly interrupt me when I have friends over, despite my calmly asking them to wait a second, wait a second honey, you're interrupting, okay, one second honey, okay, can you, CAN YOU LET ME FINISH A FREAKING THOUGHT?! make them bad kids?

"Yeah, mine are good too." I said. And, they *are* good. It's just that they're not easy. They're not remotely easy.

In fact, my boys are loud, rowdy, and constantly in motion, and because of that, a larger percentage of my parental reserves go toward containing and corralling them so they don't disassemble our house and build a skateboard ramp out of the spare parts. I was far more patient with my daughter than I am with them; her nature was calm and introspective, which freed up time for playing, talking, or reading. What a concept.

Because my boys are fraternal twins, I have my own ad hoc science experiment going, and can observe how reasonably consistent parenting results in radically different fifteen-year-old boys. For example, one of them seems wired for immunity to parental intervention. If a conversation is going to finally and gracelessly end in "because I said so," it will be with him. I adore him and admire his strength of character. However, he has trouble understanding the consonant and vowel combination that forms the word "No," and that means that we're going to tangle more than I wish. Authoritative parenting characterized by calm and clear limit setting? Sure, after a few martinis.

The other twin is the opposite. When I'm feeling impatient, I can see the shadow of my mood inhabit him like a low-grade fever. Where the first one seems oblivious to my behavior, this one tracks it like sonar on a shifting ocean floor. It makes him sensitive and thoughtful and vulnerable to taking things much more personally than I would ever wish for him.

My grown daughter lives temperamentally between the two. She is adaptive like the latter twin, but her nature bends and bends only to whip back up and smack you in the face if you aren't paying attention. She was easy when young, but reclaimed every inch in adolescence and early adulthood that she ceded in childhood.

It's through my relationship with my daughter that I decided to write this book. I was married and divorced in my twenties and remarried nineteen years ago—ergo, the twins. While my daughter and I are now very close, we went through several years when she was a young adult where she hardly returned my calls and expressed little interest in seeing me. Those were hard and disorienting years. Scratch that. Those were the most painful and confusing years of my life.

We all expect to let go of our children at some point. In many ways, we start grieving the loss of them as they take their first wobbling steps away from us. But no parent wants it like that. Not years later, when you find yourself staring at a 3 x 5 photo of her when she was sitting on your shoulders at the age of three, her head happily and innocently inclined against yours, smiling at a blue, cloudless sky. Never when you want so badly to be a good, loving parent and reap the rewards that seem so obvious and secure in a world where, increasingly, so little seems guaranteed. Never anticipating a future when you would have to constantly try to stitch *something* together: a weekend, a day, a letter, a phone call to try and mend the torn tissues of connection caused by the bomb crater of divorce and its unexploded shells. Never, never, never.

Yet whether you're divorced or married, it can happen. And, as judged by my clients and friends, it happens a lot. I constantly hear from mothers and fathers who are carrying deep feelings of loss and longing, guilt and grief, anger and shame. Regret about how they treated their kids. Regret about how their kids treat them. Regret about how all of their lives turned out. *Regret, regret, regret.*

And they all want to know: What are you supposed to do with those feelings? Who is supposed to understand your waking and sleeping sorrow about the life your child is living with or without you? Or the worry that your child may never, ever get it together and become a full-functioning adult? Or the prospect of never again seeing or being close to one of the most important people in your world?

How do you admit what you're feeling to others when doing so risks inviting more shame from their well-meaning, but often hurtful or disorienting advice; advice generated from the premise, however inexplicit, that you must have done *something* wrong to create distance or problems in a relationship that most assume is inviolate.

I can write about this because those years seem safely behind me, or so I hope. Whatever needed to be bridged has been bridged and the water beneath my daughter and me runs relatively clear. Fortunately I had a few friends who had been through similar ruptures, or were going through theirs at the same time: friends whose teens or young adults were struggling with addiction, eating disorders, anxiety, depression, cutting themselves, suicide attempts, school failure, or just pushing them away. Having other parents to offer their own wisdom and guidance—who can calm you down when you want to launch an outraged letter to your child, a payback for withdrawal, a deluge of unwanted advice—is priceless.

As a result of my own experience, I feel nothing but compassion for the parents I work with who show me the self-righteous, guilt-tripping letter that they just mailed to their son or daughter detailing all of the ways they feel so worried, so mistreated, so devalued, so *abandoned*. Parents who, in desperation and anguish, write some version of "screw you, you ungrateful brat! I'm tired of being treated like the bad guy. If you want to see me or change our relationship, you can reach out to *me* for a change!"

My response is almost always the same: "I can totally understand why you would write that. It makes complete sense to me. However, I think you now have to write your kid a different letter."

Much of this book will be about that different letter. To be clear, I'm not as interested here in your child as I am in you. Your child, however precious, can get into therapy if he or she needs to. My focus is on you and your well-being. If I offer you parenting advice, and I occasionally will, it has less to do with my desire for you to be a good parent and more with my wish to get you back on your feet.

You need a guide because there aren't a lot out there on this subject. The internal world of the parent is almost a taboo topic except where it relates to marshalling the resources to create a perfect child.

IT'S NOT JUST THE PARENT

In case I haven't made it clear, there are many outside influences affecting how you feel and how your kids turn out other than your behavior as a parent. The parent-child relationship does not occur in a void. New findings in the field of behavioral genetics, for example, suggest that children are equally likely to affect how *parents* behave. Despite decades of research in child development, many of us are still oriented somewhere between Jean-Jacques Rousseau's view of children as total innocents and John Locke's belief that they are blank canvasses for parents to paint their ambitions and desires upon. This book seeks to reframe that view.

The recent findings in child development and genetics are relevant because they show that children come into the world spring-loaded for action far more than anyone previously thought. They're checking us out and seeing what works, pretty much from the moment they pop out of the womb. This research shows that about *half* of the way that children behave has nothing to do with the quantity of affection and active listening and stimulating environments that we provide, and a lot to do with what that body builder, DNA, tells it to.

Moreover, when most people, psychologists especially, talk about nature vs. nurture, we assume the nurture part is parenting behavior. It turns out that a more accurate calculus is 50 percent genes and 50 percent *environment*, with environment defined as a bunch of players in addition to mom, dad, and a cruel older brother. From this perspective, a well-rounded view of environment has to answer the following questions:

- How does the parent respond to the inherited temperament of the child? For example, we now know that an aggressive temperament in a child greatly increases the chance for an aggressive reaction in the parent (behavioral geneticists refer to this as *child-to-parent effects).*

- How do the genes of the parent affect the parent's behavior and reactions to the child?

- How do the siblings respond to the child or to the child's relationship with the parent? Studies show that children constantly compare how their parents treat their siblings with how they are treated, and that this perceived difference in treatment can affect their development. In addition, studies in genetics show that siblings are incredibly different from each other and that these differences may affect their perceptions of the parent as good or bad, fair or unfair, loving or neglectful.

But wait. There are more factors affecting child development!

- Which peer group does the child choose and why?

- From which is she excluded?

- What positive experiences does he have with teachers or other significant people that move his life in a particular direction?

- What negative experiences does he have?

- How much is available to the developing teen or young adult in terms of employment or meaningful activities outside of the home?

These factors are important in providing the stepping stones to successful adulthood, regardless of what parents provide.
And that's not all!

- What are the culture's prescriptions for parental involvement in managing their child's behavior?

- What is the economic status of the parents, and what advantages and protection does it offer? How does the parent's economic status affect the availability and choice of peer group or educational opportunities available to the child?

- How much insulation does economic status provide against the more destructive aspects of the culture?

- How much institutional and governmental support does the culture provide for parents and children?

- What are the culture's prescriptions about how involved a community should be in raising children?

CHILDREN VS. PARENTS

As if all of these weren't enough, children themselves from the very beginning have their own agendas for their best interests—interests that are often in conflict with those of the parent. You may feel at odds with your child now, but if you're a mother, the battle between you began in pregnancy. As soon as the embryo was formed, it began sending out powerful hormonal messengers to build a placenta and lay out supply lines for food, space, and a comfortable womb. It took control of your pituitary gland and caused it to synthesize large amounts of chorionic gonadotropic hormone to insure that the pregnancy was protected and maintained. Over the course of your pregnancy, it was your budding baby, not you, who was in charge of your body.

In most pregnancies this orchestration proceeds in a cooperative manner between mother and soon-to-be-child. But sometimes it goes awry, such as when mom's body can't counter the fetal demand for sugar-rich blood, and gestational diabetes develops as a result. In other words, well before there was a teenager to talk back to you, there was a fetus with its own agenda and strategy to insure that it got a full serving of what it needed to survive and thrive, including potentially endangering the well-being of the very person who was giving it a place to live. Sound familiar?

And that's just the pregnancy. After childbirth, the contest between what is good for baby and what is good for mom (and dad) continues. Human infants require the most protracted period of dependency of any primate. As a result, they require a huge investment of parental time and resources—resources that may threaten the very survival of the mother, father, or clan.

From the very beginning babies are checking us out to see what causes us to turn toward them and what results in our turning away. Infants as young as one year have been shown to reassure mothers who appear distressed, or to try and soothe other children who are upset. By the age of thirty-six months, children are active at getting their mothers to turn their attention away from their siblings and back into the orbit of the developing toddler.

From the child's perspective, their very survival depends on an ability to obtain as many critical resources as they can from the parent in time, nutrients, and emotional investment while trying hard not to alienate that parent who is their lifeline. Because infants and small children are relatively powerless, they have to use whatever talents they have to get what they desperately need. As evolutionary biologist Robert Trivers writes, "An offspring cannot fling its mother to the ground and nurse at will." It has to use whatever means it has at its disposal. These mechanisms include being adorable, screaming loudly, and in general being a squeaky wheel and outmaneuvering siblings for a larger slice of the parental pie.

In this way, the goals of the parent and of the child can be at odds because the parent, in addition to nurturing any particular child, has to spread her resources across her children, herself, and other family members in as judicious a manner possible. We don't have as much control as we may think over how our children turn out in part because it's not necessarily in their best interest to cede that much control.

"Okay," you're probably thinking. "There are other factors, but it still doesn't show me how to deal with all of the pain I'm going through."

I know, I'll get there. Help is on the way. Let's start by finding out where you are right now by answering a few questions.

"Defining the Problem" Questionnaire

Choose the items that best describe you or your experience. You may circle as many items as you wish for a given question. You may find it helpful to take notes as you go along, keep a journal of your thoughts and feelings, or write about the themes that you find particularly useful or upsetting. This section is provided more to define the problem than to solve it. Solving it comes next.

What were your hopes and dreams when
you became a parent?

- My child and I would be best friends or very close.

- I would be able to be a better parent than my parents or to give my children what I never received.

- Parenting would be one of the most meaningful experiences in my life.

- I could help my child excel in school, sports, popularity, and other areas.

- I would be able to experience a deep and profound love.

- _____

- _____

How have you been disappointed in those dreams?

- I feel as though my child hates me.

- I often dislike my child and wish I'd never become a parent.

- I feel disappointed in who my child has become and the kind of life he or she has chosen.

- I have made many of the same mistakes that my parents made with me.

- I have been a much better parent than my parents, yet my child makes me feel like a failure in my role.

- I believe that someone else could have done a much better job raising my child than I have, and that makes me feel sad and ashamed.

- _____

Which emotion do you find the most burdensome
in regards to your child?

- Guilt

- Anxiety

- Fear

- Anger

- Worry

- Sorrow

- Regret

- Frustration

- Disappointment

- All of the above

- _____

- _____

What do you think is the biggest cause of that emotion?

- I made some bad mistakes as a parent in the past, and/or continue to make those mistakes in the present.

- My child thinks I wasn't a good parent in the past, even though I believe that I was.

- My child thinks I'm not a good parent in the *present*, even though I believe that I am.

- My divorce has created problems in the quality or quantity of time I get with my children.

- My ex's behavior has alienated my child from me.

- I have a hard time relating to my child's temperament.

- My child is very rejecting.

- My child doesn't seem like other children. This makes me constantly worried about his future.

- My partner or ex is causing problems in my child.

- The stress in my marriage or relationship makes me over-react to my children.

- My own personal problems cause me to be less effective as a parent than I'd like to be.

- I worked out of the home too much while my child was growing up and I carry deep feelings of worry or regret.

- I have guilt for using physical punishment.

- _____

- _____

How has your role as a parent affected the rest of your life?

- I feel depressed and overwhelmed most of the time.

- I have a hard time focusing on the rest of my life.

- I feel guilt-ridden and worried most of the time.

- I feel as if my identity and self-esteem have been damaged.

- I feel overcome with feelings of sadness and grief.

- I feel angry, bitter, and resentful.

- I feel scared for my child's future.

- My marriage and my other relationships have been negatively affected.

- My work has suffered.

- I feel preoccupied with my child or my relationship with her all of the time.

- _____

- _____

HOW TO USE THIS BOOK

Every parent has her own individual challenges; there are no one-size-fits-all solutions to these dilemmas. Depending on your situation, I may advise you to simply wait and be patient. Or I may recommend that you continue to reach out to your teen or adult, no matter how unrewarding it is or how crappy it feels. In some situations I'll advise you take a lot of responsibility for the rift in the relationship, and at other times to correct a very distorted view of yourself that's being projected onto you. A parent who was abusive will need a different set of responses than a parent who was not abusive but is being accused of being that way. A parent whose child is rejecting them at sixteen may need a different response to that child if she is twenty-one, twenty-eight, or forty. In addition, a teen who is mouthy and obnoxious will need a different set of responses from the parent than a teen who is bulimic or suicidal.

I have organized this book with the idea that exercises are useful for some readers and not for others. Some people can't stand cognitive-behavioral exercises; others are loath to have events constantly referenced back to own childhoods. Some find guidelines useful, while others do better with education, information, or practical advice. Therefore most chapters will have some mix of all of the above.

There are certain principles that are essential to your healing. These principles are based on hundreds of studies about what helps people recover from emotional injury and maintain immunity to future emotional and physiological stress. I have summarized them below. You don't need to commit them to memory. We'll be developing them in detail as we go along.

THE ESSENTIAL PRINCIPLES

Your healing will be strengthened as you begin to:

- Fearlessly take responsibility for whatever ways that you have contributed to the problems in your relationship with your child or your children

- Make amends for the ways that you were wrong

- Move toward forgiving your child for how he or she hurt you in the past or in the present (this doesn't mean condoning or excusing bad behavior, or minimizing your hurt)

- Move toward forgiving yourself for your mistakes as a parent

- Develop compassion for your child

- Develop compassion for yourself

- Move anger, guilt, shame, and regret into the background of your life and move hope, gratitude, and optimism into the foreground

- Develop an identity and life story based on your strengths and achievements as a parent and individual, instead of a story about your suffering or failures

- Get and maintain support from friends, family, or your faith

- Give something back to society

I know those are a lot of steps and each step requires work. However, the strength that you'll get from working on these essential steps will radiate positively into the rest of your life. One of the most important steps for any parent to get a hold of is managing guilt. This is where we turn next.

~~~~~~~~~~

THREE

PARENTAL GUILT

Healing the Real or Imaginary Mistakes of Parenting

Parents who believe that they have damaged their children carry huge feelings of guilt, shame, and regret. In some families, these parents behaved in ways that truly *were* harmful and injurious. However, even subtle parenting mistakes, or those caused through good intentions, can leave parents with lasting scars. In addition, many parents wrongly believe that they caused injury because they have no calculus by which to measure their children's accusations. These beliefs may be particularly troublesome because they can make the parent behave in ways that create *new* problems.

Being a good parent today means being sensitive to our kids' complaints in a way that would have been unheard of in prior generations. While this sensitivity increases the potential for a closer, more fulfilling relationship, it also increases the chance that the parent will be made to feel inadequate, shamed, or guilty in the process. Consider the following examples and watch how the accusations become increasingly confusing in terms of what is required of the parent:

- A toddler falls on the sidewalk and gets mad at his mother for not preventing it.

- A toddler falls on the sidewalk and the *father* gets mad at the mother for not preventing it.

- A teacher of a ten-year-old calls the parents and says that she suspects their son is having problems at school "because of what's been going on at home, lately."

- A thirteen-year-old tells her mother that she hates her because she's "so self-centered," and adds, "No wonder Dad wanted to divorce you!"

- An eighteen-year-old tells her parents that her cocaine addiction was a cry for help and demands to know why didn't they see it earlier and get her into treatment.

- A twenty-year-old drops out of college after the second year and tells his parents, "It's your fault because you've always put so much pressure on me to succeed! You never cared about what makes me happy!"

- A thirty-year-old refuses to have any contact with his mother because he says that she has never taken responsibility for the ways that she was a bad parent.

Prior to the second half of the twentieth century, fewer parents would have been confused about how to handle these scenarios, especially with children still living in the home. They were insulated by the belief that it is the child's obligation to demonstrate his worth to the parent, and not the other way around. Old-school parents would have responded that the kid was being disrespectful and needed to be properly put in his place. While this wasn't always the better approach, this philosophy protected parents from the kind of guilt, self-doubt, confusion, and anguish that greet today's parents when confronted with their children's complaints.

This chapter looks at the role of guilt in creating parental suffering, and the thorny terrain of living with children's criticism and rejection. It is written for parents who made serious mistakes in their parenting and for those who were relatively innocent in their behavior; it is also written for those parents in that common and confusing area lying somewhere in between.

THE COSTS OF DENYING GUILT

Connie is a single mother of a fourteen-year-old girl. When Connie began therapy, she had been in recovery from her alcoholism for two months. Like many people in early recovery, she wanted to use the therapy to discover the issues that had kept her returning to the comforts of alcohol for the past ten years. One of her themes was understanding how her father's rages undermined her feelings of confidence and safety.

While she didn't say so directly, I suspected that Connie's feelings about her own parenting were also a source of distress. I came to this conclusion because whenever I would inquire about her daughter, she'd say things like, "She whines a lot about me not being there for her as a mom, but, Jesus, I'm not drinking now; you'd think she'd be glad for that," or "Well, it wasn't half as bad for her as it was for me growing up, so she needs to get over herself." It was clear that behind these protests and criticisms of her daughter lay a great deal of guilt and regret for how she had behaved as a parent over the many years of her drinking.

Why would Connie be so dismissive of her daughter's complaints? She was desperate to reduce the unconscious guilt, sadness, and regret she felt about her mothering. One of Connie's childhood wishes was to one day become the kind of parent to her children that her parents had never been to her. She had vowed that she would never rage like her father, nor be neglectful like her mother. Like many people who are raised in troubled homes, she ended up doing both. When Connie was drinking, she would often stay out late after work and come home after her daughter was asleep. When her daughter complained, she yelled, "The world doesn't revolve around you, little miss. I deserve to have a little fun in my life. It's not all about you and your needs!"

GUILT VS. SELF-COMPASSION

I knew that in order for Connie to begin to heal from her guilt, she would need to gradually accept some responsibility for her behavior with her daughter. However, she would *first* need to develop compassion for herself, so that she would understand why she made the choices that she made. Why is self-compassion so important? Because ongoing feelings of guilt and regret cause people to feel awful about themselves. When people feel awful about themselves, they lose perspective; they try to manage those feelings by either overreacting to or denying their pain. They get so mired in feeling betrayed, misunderstood, or guilt-ridden that they're not any good to anybody—themselves *or* their children.

In Connie's case, her need to suppress her guilt about her behavior toward her daughter caused her to under-react by minimizing her daughter's complaints. In effect, she put her hands over her own eyes and pretended her daughter couldn't see. This caused her daughter to escalate her behavior in an attempt to *be* seen. Her daughter was clearly building to a crisis that, in the long run, would only worsen Connie's feelings of guilt and self-loathing.

BUILDING SELF-COMPASSION

Connie had problems with the concept of self-compassion. Many people do. I often have to struggle with my clients around this. But struggle I do, because it is one of the most important foundations for healing from the wounds of being a parent. Some common resistances are:

- "I'm just feeling sorry for myself."

- "I was a bad parent, so it's appropriate that I feel bad about myself."

- "I have no right to a happy life if I'm at all responsible for my child's suffering or failings."

- "I have no idea what having compassion for myself would feel like."

These are common obstacles. Let's look at them more closely.

"I'm just feeling sorry for myself."

Self-compassion is not the same thing as self-pity. Self-compassion is the ability to believe that, no matter how terrible your mistakes, love and forgiveness are part of your birthright and your humanity. While you are not owed love and forgiveness by your *children*, you should seek compassion and forgiveness from other members of your family (if they're capable), your friends, a counselor, your faith, and yourself.

Let me highlight that there is healthy support and unhealthy support. Healthy support is not only well-deserved comfort, but also feedback about what you may need to change in yourself or in your life. Studies have shown that people who seek and receive support that rubber-stamps their views without helping them develop an alternative or healthier perspective don't benefit as much because the "support" keeps them in a victimized position.

"I was a bad parent, so it's appropriate that I feel bad about myself."

Guilt is a predictable and understandable reaction to the awareness that we have hurt someone we love—especially a child. Admitting to your mistakes and making a commitment and a plan for change is crucial to your healing. However, *continuing to punish yourself should not be part of your program.* It doesn't help your child and it doesn't help you. It impedes your growth and inhibits your ability to give to others who also need your love and attention. It makes it harder for you to receive love and support from those who are willing to provide it.

> ### "I have no right to a happy life if I'm at all responsible for my child's suffering or failings."

Self-compassion is not the same as making excuses. It is an attempt to move toward a position of self-acceptance for being human. I have worked with parents whose children committed suicide, had severe problems with alcohol or drug addiction, consistently failed at or dropped out of school, or were inadequate at managing adult life. In every case, those parents who were able to gain some serenity, despite their severe guilt, loss, or disappointment, were people who could develop compassion, not only for their child, but also for themselves.

Part of developing self-compassion is understanding why we made the mistakes that we did as parents. For example, as Connie was better able to understand that she had unconsciously behaved with her daughter as her parents had with her, she was able to feel less shamed by that behavior. As her shame decreased, she was able to take more responsibility for her actions. As she took more responsibility for her actions, she was able to better her relationship with her daughter.

"I have no idea what having compassion for myself would feel like."

Some of the most compassionate people I have ever met are hopeless when it comes to feeling compassion for themselves. Sometimes they were raised in homes where they were supposed to give a lot and expect little in return, or they were raised without empathy, support, or nurturance. Having experienced little support, they don't know how to provide it to themselves. They feel self critical and undeserving. Self-compassion is intimately tied with the capacity to forgive yourself, forgive others, and allow positive feelings into your life and awareness. A key aspect of this is the decision to make amends.

HOW TO MAKE AMENDS

- Make a fearlessly honest admission of your mistakes to your child. Leave out the reasons, justifications, or any other detail that makes it sound like he or she has no right to complain.

- Express heartfelt empathy for how your child may have felt in response to your behavior.

- Avoid responding to your child's anger or sadness by defending yourself. There are times to provide the reasons for your behavior or choices, but not in the act of making amends.

- Express gratitude to your child, both at the beginning and at the end of making amends, for taking the time to hear you out.

- Let your child know that you are open to talking about this again whenever he wants in the future.

Using these guidelines, Connie wrote the following letter to her daughter:

Dear Nancy,

I know you've been talking a lot lately about how I wasn't there for you growing up, and I've just gotten mad at you whenever you have. You're right. I wasn't there for you nearly as much as you deserved, and you have a right to be upset with me. I want to apologize for that. It must have felt awful for you. Because I love you, it's painful for me to face how much pain I might have caused you during the years when I was drinking. That's why I've gotten so angry and defensive whenever you've said anything about it to me. But I'm willing to listen now if you want to tell me. I also want you to know that the door is always open whenever you want to talk about it now or in the future.

Love,
Mom

After some initial distrust and hesitation, Connie's daughter began to respond positively to her mother's openness and change of attitude. As a result, she began to talk more about her own self-destructive behavior, and allowed Connie to help get her into therapy. In other words, as Connie was able to face up to her mistakes as a parent, her daughter grew closer to her, not more distant as Connie had feared by potentially opening the floodgates of her daughter's anger or disappointment. This is because her daughter took her mother's admissions as a statement of strength and dedication; because she saw her mother as stronger, she was better able to lean on her as a parent.

"YOU WERE A TERRIBLE PARENT!"

Irrational accusations, or accusations based on incomplete portraits of us, can generate as much guilt, shame, anger, and confusion as accusations founded on reality. Part of what makes being a parent confusing is that our adolescent or adult children may accuse us of doing things that we didn't do; they may take our behavior completely out of context, or may interpret behaviors that were intended to be loving and protective as selfish, hurtful, or ruinous. They may blame us for how their lives turned out in ways that are at odds with our perspective or recollection. They may be unable to give us credit for how hard we worked, or to recognize the monumental effort it took to be good parents given our own unhappy childhoods. They may not understand how difficult our own marriages or divorces were, or how their own temperaments made them tough to guide.

Developing and maintaining your serenity requires having one foot in your own experience and one foot in your child's. Let's look at what it feels like on the other foot.

FOUR

A CHILD'S VIEW

I know that you have probably tried everything you can think of to heal your relationship with your child. I know this because a parent's ongoing feelings of sadness, regret, abandonment, guilt, and worry are some of the most burdensome, disorienting, unshakeable feelings that an adult can encounter. Out of love or desperation, most parents would do anything to rid themselves of those emotions. However, despite all of your efforts and regardless of your innocence, we have to start by accepting your child's view that you could have done it differently: loved more, pushed more, or worried less. A sensitive child may wish that you could have found a way to make the world a less painful place. An aggressive or defiant child may wish that you had been more patient and kind. And even though you tried as hard as you could, read self-help books, and consulted other parents, pediatricians, learning specialists, social-skills consultants, your therapist, or your kid's therapist, your children still have a *right* to complain that you didn't do enough.

One of the cruelest ironies of parenting is that we can do harm even when we are trying to be the most conscientious. An example of this is when parents hurt the relationship with their children by trying to avoid the mistakes their parents made. One of my colleagues grew up in a commune in the 1960s, and he put it like this: "I was given a ton of freedom because my parents were rebelling against their parents' conservatism. They were worried

that discipline and limits would destroy my innocence and creativity. I remember asking if I could smoke pot with them when I
was ten, and they said 'You decide. If you think that it's a good
idea, then it's a good idea.' I was ten years old! How would I
know what a good idea was? Now that I'm a parent, I'm super-
strict. My kids practically need permission to blink, and they
resent me for it, but it's better than what I had."

Maybe. But adopting a parenting style at the opposite extreme
of our childhood experience can prevent some problems while
creating others. One couple, for example, risked their lives to
come to America so that their children could take advantage of
opportunities they never had. They relentlessly pushed their children to excel, and loudly criticized their efforts and even their
achievements. If the children performed poorly in school, they
berated them. As a result, their kids became adults burdened with
feelings of worthlessness and guilt. These parents did the best
they could, given what they knew. But their terror that their children would suffer in poverty, as they had, made them blind to the
harm they were causing. They felt bewildered and betrayed when
their adult children criticized them for their harsh parenting.

Should their children, now adults, forgive and forget? Sure, if
they can. But there is so much pressure in our culture to "get over
it" and "move on" and "grow up" that many people aren't allowed to look back long enough to grieve what they didn't get
from their parents without someone calling them immature. They
end up blaming themselves for their inadequacies and conflicts
without understanding how those problems came to be.

Remember in Connie's case how self-compassion helped her
accept herself as well as her daughter? It's no different with our
children. If children are blaming themselves for all of their problems, they may not be ready to forgive their parents. Forgiveness
sometimes comes only when they know that they didn't deserve
to be treated "badly," no matter how noble their parents' intentions. As parents, we have to accept that we may have created

problems for our children, even when we were making sacrifices and trying to do our absolute best. You should have compassion for yourself for doing the best that you could, and you should try to have compassion for your child's complaint that it wasn't enough.

As a therapist I've learned that something that may look trivial from the outside can be suffocating or hurtful to the child who lives inside that family. "My mother had a pretty low standard of parenting," a client once told me. "Tell your children that you love them and don't beat them. My father didn't beat us, so he was a success in her eyes. And everybody loved my father because he was really funny and outgoing. They never saw his subtle, day-to-day humiliations of us."

It's common in psychotherapy to hear people berate themselves for feeling hurt and angry over childhood wounds they are barely able to identify. "It's not like I was beaten or anything," is a frequent refrain. "So my parents were distant and never told me that they loved me. Lots of people have worse problems than I. That's not a reason for me to be depressed." But sometimes it *is* a reason that people get depressed and then feel alienated from their parents. Parents who can acknowledge their children's complaints without excessively defending themselves have a better chance of repairing their relationship. It's not a guarantee. It's just a better chance.

When I'm working with a couple that is considering divorce, I tell them that they need to do everything possible to work on their marriage if they have children. I tell them this because I know one day their kids will ask when they are getting back together or why didn't they try to save the marriage. Parents who have tried everything can feel more at peace if and when that time comes.

The same can be said of doing everything possible to repair your relationship with your child. If your kid complains about you, or if you recognize ways that you blew it as a parent, you want to be able to say to yourself, "I am trying everything that I can," or "I tried everything that I could and it hasn't worked. Everyone makes mistakes in life. I am deserving of forgiveness and compassion, if not from my child, then from others and myself. I need to stop punishing myself."

DIFFERENT PERSPECTIVES

It is crucial to understand that every person in a family has a unique and individual experience and perception of that family. Think of it this way: in a family of four, there are four different plays going on simultaneously. While each person has a partial view of what is occurring on the stage they share, their view is partially obstructed by a curtain behind which another play is going on, which is obscured by yet another curtain and so on for every other member of the family. This is why siblings can have wildly disparate opinions of their parents, parents can have wildly disparate opinions of their children, and spouses can have wildly disparate opinions of each other.

Akira Kurosawa's movie *Rashomon* features four narrators describing the same crime from each of their unique perspectives at Kyoto's Rashomon gate. In Michael Dorris's novel *A Yellow Raft in Blue Water* three generations of Native American women, Rayona, Christine, and Ida, tell the story of their lives together from their very different perspectives of overlapping conflict.

Amy Tan's novel *The Joy Luck Club* shows the lives of four women born in China prior to 1949, and the lives of their American-born daughters in California. In discussions with her "aunts," the young narrator begins to realize the tragic lives their mothers lived in China, leading her to understand their desires to see their children maintain a connection to their pasts. She says, "In me, they see their own daughters, just as ignorant, just as unmindful of all the truths and hopes they have brought to America. They see daughters who grow impatient when their mothers talk in Chinese, who think they are stupid when they explain things in fractured English. They see that joy and luck do not mean the same to their daughters; that to these closed American-born minds 'joy luck' is not a word, it does not exist. They see daughters who will bear grandchildren born without any connecting hope passed from generation to generation." Tan's novel shows the often-tragic dimensions, the gaping gulf of perception between what the child sees and experiences and what the parent often feels and intends.

WHAT ARE THEY UP TO?

Even though it feels like your child's goal is to bruise and injure, it's usually far more complicated. Children sometimes gain their bearings by blaming us and seeing how gracefully we accept that blame: in that moment they get a glimpse of our innocence, our conflict, and our commitment. One of the ways that teens and young adults learn how to respond to stressful situations is by behaving toward us as others behave toward them, and seeing what they can learn from the interaction.

For example, the social world of the adolescent is often a hell-hole of shame, rejection, and contempt. Hmm, you may be saying, those are just the feelings that my teen has subjected me to. Why do they behave in this way toward a parent? In part, because they're trying to learn how they should respond when they're similarly rejected or taunted at a weekend party, in the school hallway, or hanging out after school. Ideally, we can maintain our balance when they "mistreat" us so that they can call up our com-paratively more poised behavior as a model when they next en-counter that treatment from others.

Often, too, kids need to blame us so that they don't blame themselves. Children who are burdened with a difficult tempera-ment or with some other malady can carry huge feelings of shame and self-loathing. For better or worse, criticizing the parent for not doing enough or for getting it all wrong is one strategy for reliev-ing themselves of this burden. It may not feel fair, but parenting isn't a fair exchange of effort for reward. It's more like an exchange of effort for seeing what the hell happens next.

Richard was a twenty-three-year-old man whom I saw in family therapy with his parents and younger sister. Richard suffered from a form of social anxiety so severe that it prevented him from dating or obtaining more challenging work. While intellectually gifted, he dropped out of college after the first year and delivered pizzas to support himself in the Tenderloin district of San Francisco.

I worked with the family for several months and made progress. Much of the progress, however, came from allowing Richard to accuse his parents of letting him down and not being more helpful in providing him with the kind of experiences that would increase his confidence and self-esteem. Observing Richard's mother and father, it became clear that they were loving and devoted. While they had made some mistakes as parents, their mistakes were certainly within the normal range and far from pathological; dad could be accused of being a little too involved with work and mom could be accused of being too much of a worrier. But all things considered, it seemed unlikely to me that Richard's social anxiety stemmed from lousy parenting. With his sister, those parental behaviors weren't even blips on her radar.

Here is, perhaps, where the greatest amount of nuance is required of wounded parents: There *may* have been more that Richard's parents could have done for him. It's possible, had they known everything there was to know about highly sensitive children, that Richard *may* have gotten a firmer leg up into adulthood. But that doesn't mean that they were bad people or bad parents. In another era, there would have been other sources of support for children to develop themselves and to launch an adult life other than through their parents' sophistication and subtlety. Looking at what parents could have done differently does sound blaming, but that isn't the purpose.

So, try not to be too freaked out or bummed out by your children's blaming you for your "mistakes" or for how they've turned out. Let's look again at Richard: His parents could have responded by telling him how good he had it and the many ways that they were helpful and virtuous, but where would it have gotten them? As their therapist, I could have said to Richard, "It seems like your parents made some mistakes but on balance, they were reasonably good parents. I think you suffer from a biochemically derived form of social anxiety that will respond well to medication and individual therapy."

I didn't take that position because it would have been counterproductive. The biological aspects of our personalities are the skin through which we sense the world. A child born with a temperament inclined toward severe shyness, anxiety, or social withdrawal may experience relationships, family included, as potentially threatening, uncaring, or burdensomely demanding. If Richard's parents had read everything there is to know on this topic, then perhaps he would be doing better by now. But, like the vast majority, they didn't know what was out there by way of help.

But isn't that the whole problem with this culture, that nobody wants to take any responsibility for anything, everybody wants to blame everyone else? I wish it were so simple. The problem with this culture is that parents are being made culpable for their children's problems during a time in history when they have the least amount of support from extended kin, neighbors, businesses, and the government. Whereas the family once existed in a rich ecosystem fed and nourished by a community of supports, families now stand alone in the barren wilderness by themselves. The problem with this culture is that the marketplace has created a separate world for children and adolescents that greatly reduce the influence and power of parents at the same time that politicians and pundits blame them for Columbines, drug addiction, and every known disorder of adolescence and adulthood.

But that conversation isn't happening in the mainstream, so it's certainly not happening in the home. Therapists emphasize the importance of parents' mistakes because, for better or worse, parents are the front line. My first goal as a psychologist is to help my clients begin to reduce the self-hatred that mires them in anxiety, depression, and goal inhibition. Discussing their families is the logical place to start because it's one of the most important contexts where the child's self evolved. Parents are not the only influence, nor are they always the most important influence, but they're still important (and that's why there's a chapter on how your childhood affected you later in this book).

TRY TO NOT TAKE IT SO PERSONALLY

Stanford University psychologist Fred Luskin discovered that the ability to find the impersonal in an event or relationship is critical to our ability to feel insulated from the potential hurt in that event or relationship. His research shows that people who have been deeply hurt often develop a "grievance story" that causes them to spend a large amount of time reviewing the past, resulting in their feeling victimized and unhappy.

Luskin has found validation for his theory and method in a variety of settings. Perhaps the most compelling example is the work that he did with Irish Catholic and Protestant mothers who each had a son who had been murdered. Clearly, if anyone has a right to feel both aggrieved and victimized, it is someone who has had a child taken in this way. Yet each of these mothers was able to move to a far greater degree of serenity using the techniques summarized in his book, *Forgive for Good: A Proven Prescription for Health and Happiness*. Luskin's research and the research of others such as Martin Seligman at the University of Pennsylvania shows that the ability to forgive yourself and others, and to rid yourself of poisonous feelings of blame of yourself or others, is linked to a host of positive psychological and physical outcomes. For example, people who are better able to forgive themselves and others have happier lives and are less at risk of heart disease or heart attacks. In addition, they are better able to cope with loss and illness when they occur.

WHAT DOES FORGIVENESS MEAN?

Forgiveness *doesn't* mean that you turn a blind eye to being mistreated by your children or others, or that you never get angry. It doesn't mean that you are required to have a relationship with the person who hurt you (though if it's your child, I will encourage you to try for a significant period of time, but more on that later). Forgiveness doesn't mean that you have to accept, condone, or respect the behavior of those who have caused you to suffer. Forgiveness also doesn't mean letting yourself off of the hook for harm that you have caused without first making a heartfelt and significant effort to repair and make amends to the person you have hurt.

Forgiveness of yourself and others is important because it is a way of taking back your power, taking responsibility for how you feel, and focusing on your own healing. Luskin summarizes the steps of his research with the acronym HEAL: *Hope, Educate, Affirm*, and *Long-Term Commitment to Your Well-Being*. Below is a summary of his steps; I have reformulated them with parents in mind:

Hope

Hope is restating your original ideals and aspirations as a parent. For example, let's return to the questionnaire at the end of chapter 2:

What were your hopes and dreams when you became a parent?

- My child and I would be best friends or very close.

- I would be able to be a better parent than my parents or to give my children what I never received.

- Parenting would be one of the most meaningful experiences in my life.

- I could help my child excel in school, sports, popularity, and other areas.

- I would be able to experience a deep and profound love.

- _____

- _____

The items that you circled speak to your core values and strengths. These are values that are key to your beliefs about who you are and what you believe is important in life. We'll return to this shortly.

Educate

Luskin and other researchers have discovered that having rigid beliefs about how you or others should behave increases a vulnerability to ongoing distress. In the step of _education_, you are encouraged to examine what Luskin calls the "unenforceable rules" you have about how you or others should behave. Unenforceable rules are those over which you have little or no control. For example, here are some unenforceable rules that are common to parents:

"I am entitled to my adult child's respect, no matter what."

"My adult child should be able to balance out whatever mistakes I have made with all of the good that I have done as a parent."

"My adult child has no right to refuse to see me or to want to see me far less frequently than I would like."

"If my adult child rejects or mistreats me, then I must have done something terrible to deserve it."

"My adult child has no right to hurt or reject me because I dedicated my life to her and made huge sacrifices on her behalf."

An Exercise on Your Rules

Write out as many of your rules as you can think of. Then write out a counter to them based on the principle that you cannot control another person's behavior. Here's what this looks like using the above examples:

Rule: "I am entitled to my adult child's respect, no matter what."
Counter: "While I can do some things to increase the likelihood of my child treating me respectfully, he is his own person with his own temperament and view of things. I have little control over that." (Obviously, with a teen you have *somewhat* more control over how you're treated, but it diminishes each year they get older.)

Rule: "My adult child should be able to balance out whatever mistakes I have made with all of the good that I have done as a parent."
Counter: "While I *wish* that my child could see all of the ways that I have been dedicated, I can't make her. She either sees it or she doesn't. It is unfortunate, but it is not a tragedy that has to ruin or dictate my life."

Rule: "My adult child has no right to refuse to see me or to want to see me far less frequently than I would like."
Counter: "While I miss my child and wish that I could see him much more, he is a grown person with his own commitments.

He gets to decide whom to see and how frequently, even if I don't like it. I have very little control over that.

Rule: "If my adult child rejects or mistreats me, then I must have done something terrible to deserve it."
Counter: "There are many, many reasons that children reject or mistreat their parents. Assuming that it's all my fault keeps me feeling upset. She is her own person with her own view on things; however, I am not required to buy into her view of me."

Rule: "My adult child has no right to hurt or reject me because I dedicated my life to her and made huge sacrifices on her behalf."
Counter: "I am or was a dedicated parent and I take great pride in that. I do not need to have it validated by my child's treatment of me in order for me to know this. While I wish that I could benefit from my commitment to her by having a closer relationship, it is not an entitlement."

Do you see how this can be useful? In each case you look directly at the belief that is at the core of your suffering and then modify the belief to something that is more likely to generate acceptance and serenity. I'll show you more of the details as we go along, so don't worry if it isn't completely clear yet. It takes a little practice but the benefits are powerful.

Replacing pain-generating beliefs with healthier beliefs is crucial to your healing because sometimes life is just one damned thing after the next. Healthy beliefs operate like shock absorbers on a car driving over potholes, where the potholes are the inevitable disappointments, rejections, injuries, and losses of living. You can't avoid the potholes; but you can get shock absorbers that provide a lot more cushioning.

Seligman's research has shown that how you think about the past directly affects your feelings about the present and the future. Much of the pain that parents experience has to do with events that have occurred in the past, such as divorce, not being available to their children, being too critical or too much of a perfectionist, being verbally or physically abusive, and so on. "Frequent and intense negative thoughts about the past are the raw material that block the emotions of contentment and satisfaction ... and these thoughts make serenity and peace impossible," Seligman writes in *Authentic Happiness: Using the New Positive Psychology to Realize Your Potential for Lasting Fulfillment.* "The only way out of this emotional wilderness is to change your thoughts by rewriting your past: forgiving, forgetting, or suppressing bad memories." Rewriting the past doesn't mean acting like you didn't do harm if you did. It means developing compassion for yourself so that you can understand why you made the decisions that you did.

Seligman discovered something very important: your experience of the past can be transformed by focusing on feelings of gratitude and forgiveness of yourself and of others. Developing your feelings of hope, optimism, and faith can change your feelings about the *future.* Don't feel discouraged if this seems impossible given where you are right now; these feelings can be built, even if your nature or past experience has taught you to be wary of feeling gratitude, hope, or optimism. I'll come back to Seligman's research shortly, but let's return to Luskin's last two steps, *affirm* and *long-term commitment.*

Affirm

Here, you examine the first step, *hope,* and affirm the positive intentions that you have had about your child or about yourself as a parent. You affirm regardless of how things have turned out for you or your child. Why? Because we don't always get that much say about how things turn out. We only get a say over how we feel about our lives and ourselves. Your goal here is to move out of feeling victimized by your child's treatment of you and into feeling more positive about your intentions.

Let's take an example of a common parental hope:

"My child and I would be best friends or very close."

Reba, a nineteen-year-old, sided with her mother after the divorce from Geoffrey, her dad. As a result, Geoffrey has had very little contact with Reba for the past year and a half and is treated with distance and disdain by Reba when they do see each other. While Reba has made it very hard on him, he continues to reach out to her, helps pay for her college, and has made amends for the mistakes that he made with her in the past. Geoffrey needed help affirming his core value, which was to take pride in being a good father. In order to do that, he not only had to look at his original hopes, he had to affirm the ways that he had been a good dad in the past and continues to be in the present, despite getting little in return.

It is crucial to stay in touch with your positive intentions or core values as a parent by remembering what you have done positively. As an exercise, write out your strengths or core values as a parent:

My Value as a Parent

Healing Exercise on What I've Done Right

Choose the sentences that apply to you.

- I love my child (yes, you get credit for that).
- I have tried to make amends for the mistakes that I have made.
- I have been very dedicated.

- I have gotten counseling for myself so that I didn't put the pain of my past onto my child.

- I have read parenting books and magazines, received parenting consultations, or talked to my pediatrician so that I could help my child.

- I made financial sacrifices for my child.

- I made other sacrifices for my child.

- I was a better parent than my parents.

- I remained in an unhappy marriage in order to protect my child from a divorce.

- I left my marriage in order to protect my child from the harmful effects of my marriage.

- I have restrained myself, or am working to restrain myself, from saying harsh things about my current or ex-spouse, despite his or her attempts to poison my relationship with my child.

- I was a good role model of success, creativity, healthy lifestyle, intelligence, hard work, discipline (and other examples).

- _____

- _____

- _____

- _____

- _____

- _____

Write out the affirmations that apply to you on a 3 x 5 card.

Carry the card with you and read it twice a day, or more when you're feeling sad, guilty, or regretful. Why? Because your mind is capable of thinking of only so many things at one time. If you are actively feeding it positive facts or memories, it has less time and space for the negative.

Seligman and other researchers such as David Burns at Stanford University and Aaron Beck at the University of Pennsylvania have found that actively disputing negative beliefs is instrumental to feeling happy. Seligman recommends that you address negative thinking as if you're defending yourself to someone else— your child, for example. However, disputing negative beliefs is something that you say to yourself, *not* to your child; I'll get into what to say to your child later. Here, I want to help you with the battle that's going on inside of you. Part of disputing the negative is to critically address the evidence. This links to Luskin's ideas on educating yourself about your unenforceable rules, since these are based on beliefs founded on weak evidence.

Long-Term Commitment to Your Well-Being

In Luskin's final step, you commit to making amends to those you have hurt. For Geoffrey, it was to try to stay connected to his daughter and open to doing whatever it took to keep her in his life. For Connie, it meant making amends for her past mistakes and learning how to communicate with her daughter in a way that allowed her daughter to trust her. It also meant staying sober and remaining in a 12-step program. This final step often requires making a long-term commitment to develop new skills such as working on anger, pessimism, healthier lifestyle, communication skills, meditation, stress reduction, and so on. It involves making a commitment to do something every day to heal the past and look forward to the future.

AN ATTITUDE OF GRATITUDE

Researchers have found that cultivating gratitude increases your enjoyment of life and inoculates you to prior hurts and future injuries. Why should the practice of gratitude have such a powerful effect?

- Gratitude keeps you in touch with what is right about you and your life. It invokes feelings of well-being and relaxation.

- Gratitude is a present-centered activity. It helps you to focus on the here-and-now as opposed to events that are out of your control.

- Gratitude increases your feelings of resourcefulness because you focus on what you have instead of on what you haven't.

- Gratitude can increase your feelings of pride, which are crucial to combating feelings of shame.

- Gratitude can increase your energy since you're forced to attend to the joy of the moment instead of draining yourself with regret about the past or with worry about the future.

- Gratitude is at the core of almost all spiritual practices. Having a spiritual life has been shown to increase health, happiness, and longevity.

Loyola University researchers Fred Bryant and Joseph Veroff have developed a technique to work on gratitude that they call *savoring*. Savoring is taking a positive experience and wresting every drop of goodness that you can from it. This is counterintuitive to most of us raised in a materialistic culture that promises that something better is just over the horizon; whoops, not that horizon, must be the next. No, not that one; it's the next one for sure! Savoring is useful to a happy life because it promotes your capitalizing on small, positive achievements and experiences that have occurred in the past or are occurring in the present. The directions for savoring are as follows:

Share your positive experience with others: Sharing with others allows you to put your experience into a relational context. When others take joy or pleasure in our positive experiences, those experiences are made more real to us.

Build your memories: Two easy ways to build memories is to look at photos that were very pleasurable or to write about pleasurable experiences in a journal. For example, look frequently at your photos from a favorite vacation or achievement. Savor the memories or the feelings in those events. Use only those memories that are clearly positive. Avoid photos or memories that you have mixed feelings about.

Congratulate yourself: Pride is the best antidote to shame and, often, to depression. Remembering and savoring your past or present achievements is key to your self-esteem. Brag to yourself or to others who are interested in you. People who care about you want you to feel happy and to take pride and pleasure in yourself.

Become absorbed in the moment: This step requires putting out of your mind all of the things that you should be doing, should have done, or need to do tomorrow.

Exercise:

Your Savor List

Write out a list of achievements, memories, or events that bring you pleasure to think about. Assemble photos from your favorite vacations or events. Use only memories or photos that are unambiguously positive. Use the guidelines above. Do this twice a day.

SOME GENERAL GUIDELINES FOR RESPONDING TO BLAME OR CRITICISM

There is a reasonably good chance that your child will criticize you for how you raised him or her. Some of the grievances will be small; others may be substantial. Some may bring you closer together; others may drive you apart. Navigating a child's criticism is a challenge for every parent. Parents who can hear their children's criticisms (even those that aren't true) without becoming too undone are more likely to end up with closer and healthier relations than those who maintain the "I did the best I could so deal with it" stance.

Below are some general guidelines for responding to blame and criticism. These are provided for those times when it's clear there's been a significant problem in your communication or behavior with your adolescent or adult child. I am not suggesting that every familial hiccup has to be discussed or negotiated at the level suggested. Younger children, for example, sometimes have to do things because we say so, like it or not. In addition, you may have experienced years of feeling manipulated by your child's guilt trips and, as a result, feel closed down to the possibility of a positive outcome gained through a change in communication. I understand, but as Einstein said, "The significant problems that we face cannot be solved by the same level of thinking that created them." Bearing that in mind, consider the following suggestions:

If you find yourself feeling too upset or defensive about what is being said to you, tell your child so in a gentle way:

Accusation: "You were never there for me when I needed you as a kid. It was always about you!"

What you're tempted to say: "You ungrateful brat! Do you know how much I've sacrificed for you?"

What you should say: "I didn't realize that you felt that way and it's painful to hear. But I know what you're telling me is really important, and so I'm glad you came to me."

If you feel too provoked to have a productive conversation, tell your child that before it escalates:

Accusation: "I felt that you were really neglectful as a parent and I'd like to talk with you about what that was like for me."

What you're tempted to say: "I'd rather drink gasoline than have that conversation with you."

What you say: "It is hard for me to hear that right now without getting defensive. How about writing it out in a letter? I think I'll be able to digest it better if I could sit with it for a few days."

Don't sugarcoat it if you blew it as a parent. The more honest you are, the more credibility you have to repair the damage:

Accusation: "You never protected me from Dad's rages. I feel betrayed by both of you. It's made it impossible for me to have a healthy relationship as an adult."

What you're tempted to say: "Quit feeling sorry for yourself. You want to see an angry father? Try living in the house *I* grew up in! Compared to my childhood, yours was a cakewalk. At least you had a mother who loved you. It's not my fault you can't find a healthy relationship."

What you say: "You're right. I didn't protect you enough from your father's abuse and I feel terrible about that. You deserved better from me."

Take the initiative for bringing up the subject again within a few days after your child raised it:

What you're tempted to say: "If you never raise this topic again, it will be too soon. There's no way in hell I'm going to raise it again. Do you think I like having two tons of rotting sewage dumped on me like that? I don't think so."

What you say: "I wanted to check in to see how you felt about what we talked about last week. I really appreciate that you took the initiative to tell me what you'd been feeling. I'm sure it wasn't easy for you to talk with me about that. Have you had other thoughts about it since then? Let me know if you want to talk more. The door is always open."

Validate your child's reality as much as you can, even if there's only a small part you agree with:

Accusation: "You're always so impatient!"

What you're tempted to say: "Oh, poor baby. I'm sorry that I can't be more perfect for you."

What you say: "Yeah, I can be really impatient. I can see how that comes across (or came across) as uncaring."

Or,

"You may be right about that."

Or,

"I'm sorry."

If you're unable to agree with anything that's being said,
empathize with his emotions without saying that
he's wrong to feel what he feels:

Accusation: "I feel like you really don't give a shit about me!"

What you're tempted to say: "Is this is what I get after all I do for you, drive you everywhere, buy you whatever you want, give you all of the things I never had?"

What you say: "I'm really sorry it comes across that way. The last thing I want is for you to feel like I don't care about you. Nothing could be further from the truth. What makes you feel like that?"

Realize that your child may be raising issues as a way to be
closer to you, even if they are being expressed
in a way that's hurtful:

Say something like the following: "I'm sure it's not easy for you to tell me these things. I'm glad that you're willing to open up with me about this." Of course, we both know you're not going to *really* feel glad; you'll probably feel betrayed, hurt, or guilty. However, you have to approach these interactions from the perspective that your child's purpose isn't to hurt you but to potentially have a better relationship.

As you can tell, the interactions around your child's blame and criticism require a lot of restraint on your part. There may need to be an ongoing dialogue for a long time in order for change and for healing to occur. Don't avoid revisiting these topics just because they're painful territory. Show that you want to keep the conversation open until there's resolution. If there is no resolution, make it clear that you value your child's attempt to bring the issues to the table and that you're open to talking more in the future.

One of the most important steps in healing comes from your ability to reduce your burden of guilt and worry. The kind of dialogue that I'm encouraging you to have with your child is probably quite different from any dialogue that you ever had with your parents. Today's parents are required to possess a degree of sophistication rarely seen in history. Understanding how parenting standards of the current era contribute to that pressure is critical to gaining a healthy view of yourself.

In the next chapter we'll step away from the intra-psychic world of the parent for a moment and into the social and historical environment where parents live.

FIVE

BRAVE NEW PARENTS OF THE TWENTY-FIRST CENTURY

A common topic in today's parenting magazines is advice about how to worry less. Here's my advice: Stop reading parenting magazines. Stop watching the news.

Stop listening to the radio, get off of the Internet, don't buy a newspaper, don't watch any talk shows, and don't go to any bookstores. Ignore the sounds, images, experts, pundits, priests, politicians, and advertisers broadcasting all of the news that's fit to reveal that death, injury, low self-esteem, and academic failure are lurking around every corner of your child's life! They're all sending the same message: that only through your constant vigilance, dedication, and education will you be able to protect your child and provide her with all of the care she needs and deserves. That is, if you care. You *do* care, don't you?

Here's an example of a question from a reader and the response from an expert in a popular parenting magazine:

Q: Since I grew up hearing negative comments about my looks, I often tell my three-year-old how beautiful she is. My friend says I'll give her a big head. Who's right?

The expert answers by cautioning the reader that she shouldn't overdo it because she risks sending the message that "appearance is more important than anything else," and she should therefore compliment her beauty only "now and then." Mom was also advised to balance it with praise about her personality: "Encourage her to be smart, funny, strong, and brave ..."

Now, I've written a parenting and marital advice column for years, so I'm not one to talk. But this is a common interchange where a reader poses a rather benign concern and the expert's response ends up raising more questions than answers. For example, "It's okay now and then to tell her she's beautiful." How often is "now and then," and how do you know when you crossed the line from increasing her self-esteem to producing a full-blown narcissist? What is a "swelled head" anyway, for a three-year-old?

"Encourage her to be funny, strong, and brave." All right, the mother said she was worried about complimenting her little girl too much; she didn't say that she was completely clueless as a parent. Even so, you have to wonder what the strategies are for encouraging a three-year-old to be funny. "Honey, stop combing your hair and work on your stand-up routine!" "Joanie, remember when you're at preschool today to do your Sarah Silverman imitation for the other kids, but leave out the offensive parts. I'm spending $20,000 a year to send you there and we need a glowing recommendation from them to get you into a good kindergarten! Now go practice. No, not in front of the mirror! It will give you a swelled head!"

While the twentieth century has seen unprecedented improvements in the quality of children's lives, today's parents are freaked out. They obsess over the slightest error in parenting and worry that they may have forever blighted their child's life with a comment made in anger or exhaustion. New mothers act like their husbands are practically committing child abuse if they don't share their obsessive reading of every available book on pregnancy, early childhood development, and acing the SATs. Both parents worry that if they don't closely monitor the academic implications of every grade from preschool through high school, their child will get crowded out of the increasingly tight bottleneck of available colleges and the ever-shrinking opportunities for employment.

Today's parents feel burdened with guilt about being gone at work, putting their kid through a divorce, or having too little time or money to spend on their child. Because of the likelihood of divorce, many believe that their relationships with their children may be the one relationship they can count on. As a result, many parents create a self-fulfilling prophecy by putting all of their energy into their children and letting their marriages wither on the vine. Where did all of this parental worry, guilt, and uber-standards come from?

A NEW MODEL OF THE FAMILY

Since the 1920s, there has been a radical change in the boundaries between parents and children as family models have shifted from authoritarian to democratic. On the positive side, this has created new opportunities for intimacy and friendship between parent and child that would have been far less likely in prior generations. Aside from economics, many of today's young adults move back in with their parents after college because they actually like spending time with them. Imagine.

While changes in parenting attitudes have partly been a boon to children, it has also left both parents and children confused about what constitutes a proper use of authority and boundaries between parent and child. The democratic climate of the family, the popularization of parenting advice, a cultural view of children as fragile, the ability of the media and the marketplace to generate a separate world for children, and an increase in parental guilt have all combined to increase the power of children in the home. This has had the effect of leveling the playing field, placing children in a position to judge, reject, and shame their parents in ways unheralded before in U.S. history.

THE FAULT OF THE PARENT

By the mid–1930s, most mothers reported that they had read at least five parenting pamphlets or books a year, and most subscribed to at least one child-care magazine. Common issues discussed were similar to those that adorn the headlines of parenting magazines today, such as solving moodiness, managing sibling rivalry, curing bedwetting, and addressing sleep problems.

While parenting advice has existed for centuries, there was a significant shift in the twentieth century toward blaming the parents for the problems of the child. This shift in perspective radically changed parenting advice, and parenting advice radically changed parents by eroding confidence in their own ideas about parenting and encouraging them to defer to medical and psychological experts.

Sigmund Freud was one of the most significant contributors to link adult psychological problems to faulty parenting. Many of his ideas remain part of our everyday language to this day. (For example, when someone says, "That guy is so *anal!*" they're using a Freudian concept rooted in the idea that overly restrictive potty training causes an uptight or obsessive personality, which, by the way, it doesn't.)

As Freud's theories gained popularity, there was an increased move toward cool-headed professional advice that stood in contrast to the sentimentality that characterized the Romantics' views of children. In 1928, behaviorist John Watson gained national prominence with his statements that parents could shape their children, with proper techniques, into whomever they chose by implementing his scientific approach. His bold proclamations caught the attention of millions and brought beliefs about parental omnipotence to new heights. Watson wrote:

Give me a dozen healthy infants, well-formed, and my own specific world to bring them up in, and I'll guarantee to take any one at random and train him to become any type of specialist I might select—doctor, lawyer, artist, merchant-chief, and yes, even beggar-man and thief, regardless of his talents, penchants, tendencies, abilities, vocations, and race of his ancestors.

Watson's ideas had their philosophical underpinnings in John Locke's theory that children come into the world as blank slates to be molded by parents and others. Yet Watson was Locke's *blank slate* run amuck. In order for parents to achieve his ambitious requirements, they were counseled to adopt a rigid feeding schedule and provide only a minimal amount of love and attention. Watson believed that with the right amount of reward and punishment, children could be taught not to cry or have tantrums (if only!). He was an important figure in increasing parental insecurity and undermining their confidence because he, along with Freud, counseled that the success or failures of their children lay solely in parents' hands.

Dr. Benjamin Spock caught the wave of resistance that parents felt against treating their children with the kind of systematic detachment advised by Watson, and argued for a much more loving and tender methodology. In 1946, Spock sold 750,000 copies of his book *The Common Sense Book of Baby and Child Care* in the first six months after publication. As historian Steven Mintz writes in *Huck's Raft: A History of American Childhood*, "Unlike Calvinists who considered children the fruit of original sin, or behaviorists who told mothers to 'never hug and kiss' their children, Dr. Spock urged parents to trust their instincts, talk to and play with their infants, and shower them with love." While Spock's perspective appealed to a public hungry for a more tender view of child rearing, he did little to deflate the theory that children could be ruined beyond repair by small failures in parenting behavior.

CHILDREN AT THE BARGAINING TABLE

With the notable exceptions of the Quakers and Native Americans, strategies that relied on guilt, shame, or pain dominated American parenting attitudes up through the Victorian era. During the twentieth century, these gradually gave way to approaches that emphasized negotiating with children to help them understand their behavior and motivation. The emphasis on helping children develop a greater "internal locus of control" was deemed critical to the kind of self needed to navigate the multifaceted social environment of bureaucracies, large corporations, and management—a self quite different from that required in the social isolation and independence of rural life.

However, this focus on the child's inner life had a downside. Parents began to feel terrified that experiences in and out of the home could be deleterious to their child's well-being, and during 1950s and the 1960s started demanding that schools act in a more cooperative way to protect the self-esteem of their children. Under this pressure, grades began to inflate: Ds became Cs, Cs became Bs, Bs became As. As of 2001, 94 percent of Harvard's college seniors were graduating with honors (pity the poor 6%). Some California schools by 2001 had as many as forty class valedictorians, as opposed to the traditional *one*. This was ostensibly as a salve and a buy-off to the other parents who were worried about their children's feelings.

Coaches of children's sports activities began to give children trophies at the end of the season, regardless of whether they were on the losing or winning team. While parents prior to the twentieth century believed that the rigors of competition and strain would strengthen their children, contemporary parents began to fear that comparison with other children would leave them feeling insecure, discouraged, or damaged. Parents increasingly worried that they weren't doing enough to develop and protect their children's self-esteem.

THE PATHOLOGICAL MOM

As the twentieth century pushed forward, more theories evolved that blamed parents, often inaccurately, for creating disturbing behaviors in their children, adolescents, and adults. The influential child psychologist Bruno Bettelheim stated that mothers of children with autism caused the disorder with their consistently distant interaction with their children. He referred to them as "icebox mothers" because he saw that they rarely smiled or interacted with their autistic children. However, since we now know that autism is a genetically based disorder, often characterized by a lack of emotionality and social responsiveness, it's more likely that the mothers failed to respond to their children because the children provided less to which they could respond.

Similarly, mothers of children with schizophrenia were held accountable for this malady that typically surfaces in adolescence. Gregory Bateson's theory that mothers caused schizophrenia by engaging in *double bind communication* was very popular and influential when I was an undergrad in the 1970s. The *double bind* theory argues that the parent, typically the mother, literally causes the child to go crazy by issuing one directive while simultaneously issuing another that is incompatible with it. For example, "Go away/stay close." While this kind of parenting could certainly produce anxiety, we now know that it would be insufficient to produce schizophrenia, a condition that has a large heritable component. A highly stressful family environment *may* be more likely to trigger the expression of schizophrenia in someone who has the genetic vulnerability to it, but that's very different from a parent causing it.

Other disciplines, too, weighed in with the parental blame assumption. Anthropologist Margaret Mead wrote that culture is "the systematic body of learned behavior which is transmitted from parents to children." While this sounds reasonable, we now recognize that parents are only one of the *many* ways that children assimilate cultural values. In older children, peers seem to have a far more powerful effect than parents in transmitting culture.

DANGEROUS HOUSEHOLDS

During the early 1900s, a new slew of household dangers came into prominence. The hazards of electricity, refrigerators, and other home appliances resulted in thirty thousand deaths a year by the 1930s, a disproportionate number of them involving children. Once again, mothers took the hit. For example, a Red Cross official wrote in 1947, "Prevention of accidents in the home is largely the responsibility of the homemaker." During the same time, safety campaigns about traffic dangers caused many parents in urban areas to restrict their children to the home. By World War II, accidents were the leading cause of death among children. As historian Peter Stearns writes in *Anxious Parents: A History of Modern Childrearing in America*, " ... the ideas of risk and accident were also being redefined in favor of a nearly explicit position that accidents were not really accidental, they flowed from parental fault." He observes that while nineteenth-century manuals counseled parents about health and character, accidents were viewed as largely unavoidable.

RADIO, TELEVISION, AND THE CRIMINAL NEXT DOOR

Concerns about radio's capacity to corrupt in the 1930s, 1940s, and 1950s bear striking resemblance to contemporary fears of television, movies, and the Internet. For example, Stearns cites an article that appeared in *Scribner's* magazine in 1933 stating, "I should like to postpone my children's knowledge of how to rob a bank, scuttle a ship, shoot a sheriff, the emotional effects of infidelity, jungle hazards, and the horrors of the drug habit for a few more years at least." In 1945 only 5,000 families in the United

States had televisions, but fifteen years later seven out of eight families were plugged in and gathered around.

Television, despite its entertainment value, brought a new way to immediately telegraph disturbing information about dangers to children and the need for good parents to be alert. It contributed to a growing awareness that there were forces outside the family home that could influence children and thereby undermine parental authority.

The business of the media has had a field day with parental insecurity. Talk about finding a niche and filling it. There is no better way to get someone to not switch channels than to ask questions like: "Is your neighborhood safe from a chemical that has been linked to cancer in children? Find out when we come back." "Do you know what to do to prevent teenage obesity? Stay tuned." "Is the Internet exposing your teen to the risk of sexual predators? More after the break."

In magazines, television, books, and radio, these are often preceded by The Top 3s:

"The Top 3 Ways to Increase Your Child's Self-Esteem," or "The Top Three Things You Need to Know about Today's Colleges." I would like to propose one titled "The Top Three Most Annoying Top Threes."

The media are often wrong in their facts and have been responsible for perpetuating some of the most troubling urban myths. For example, most adults of my generation remember Halloween as a time of great independence. The candy bars were huge, I mean, HUGE! But best of all, Halloween was something you did without adults, and that was what made it so awesome.

As much as I hate to admit it, there's no way I would let my kids trick or treat alone when they were younger. During Halloween, we and other parents in the neighborhood shepherded our children from door to door like herders of mendicants in Harry Potter robes. Why? Maybe because in 1982 reports began circulating about apples with razor blades buried inside them. An increasing view was emerging that the outside world, even our neighbors, could no longer be trusted. Parents, in order to be *good* parents, needed to be watchful and vigilant. The famous razor-blade apples were never discovered (though there were a few apples found with pins stuck in them). However, with the long arm and lightening-fast reach of the media, rare events could, and continue to, create epidemics of parental fear and blow rare events all out of proportion.

Another example: Most parents are terrified that kidnappers and child molesters lurk around every playground. Perhaps this is because campaigns in the 1970s claimed that fifty thousand kidnappings occurred each year when the actual figure was between two hundred and three hundred. The media and some well-meaning child advocacy groups have been involved in fanning the flames of moral panic about pedophile rings and child pornography in the mid–80s, daycare scandals and satanic cults in the 1990s, and sexual predators in the present.

I often see couples teetering on the brink of divorce because they are so worried that a potential babysitter is going to either kidnap, molest, or violently shake their child that they never get out the door to spend any time together. "I'm just being a responsible parent. It could happen and I could never forgive myself if anything like that were to ever happen." And that's my point: today, a responsible parent is a worried and guilt-ridden parent.

THE PERILS OF PLAYTIME

Parents feel guilty that they can't offer their children many of the joys and freedoms from extended parental supervision that were available to so many of them, such as Halloween. In most neighborhoods today, if a parent told another that her ten-year-old was out all day with his friends riding bikes, but she wasn't sure where, she'd be reported to Child Protective Services for child endangerment.

Not only have parents become more worried about the dangers of their children being away from home, but the availability of places to play is rapidly disappearing. In the short period between the early 1980s and late 1990s, there was a 40 percent decline in outdoor activities and unstructured play. Many of the fields, woods, and lots have vanished as a result of businesses, housing developments, and the decrease in safety of the neighborhoods. The fact that the United States population doubled between 1900 and 1950, and almost doubled again between 1950 and 2000, has also significantly contributed to a decrease in space.

As public space grows scarcer and more dangerous, children and parents are forced together under the same roof as never before in our country's history. In addition, the decline of large extended families means fewer family playmates within or outside of the home. Parents have become more responsible for entertaining their children. They also feel more obligated to do so because they feel guilty that their kids' lives have become so managed and regimented. In many homes, parents have stopped requiring chores of their kids in order to make more time for entertainment and leisure. And today children don't just play, they have *play dates*. What the heck is a play date? Is it like a dinner date, only with Legos?

Parents' capacity to provide their children with entertainment has also become a yardstick by which kids can judge their parents. Unfortunately, it's also a yardstick for parents to judge themselves in comparison to other parents. For example, in the Bay Area where we live, winter brings a buzz of talk among families and advertisers about the joys of going up to Lake Tahoe to ski. Having spent most of my formative years in the un-hilly terrain of southern Ohio, I am an intermediate skier at best. However, my teenage boys constantly hear from their peers about weekend ski trips, vacation homes on the slopes, the newest in snowboarding equipment, and fathers who spend long days with their children, endlessly traversing the groomed trails of a Sierra mountainside.

I feel the pressure. My children are hardly persuaded by my argument that I moved to California, in some measure, to forever be parted with winter and snow. Nor are they sympathetic to my growing middle-aged fear that the next sprain or fracture will forever end my ability to walk, jog, or join a conga line.

From their perspective, I am not only depriving them of a fun activity, but closing their entry into a peer group engagement built around mogul conquests, half-pipe rotations, and catching air at fifteen feet (I don't know what it means, either). They would feel inadequate if prevented from being able to participate in these pleasures. As a result, I would feel inadequate as a parent for depriving them of the opportunity to be on equal footing with their peers.

So, we take the four-hour drive to Tahoe, in no small measure because I don't want to look like a slacker dad in a community of fathers who are—ostensibly—not. Yes, it's fun to be in the snow, and there *is* an awful lot to be said for building memories with your children. However, failing to entertain children to the standard that they believe they're entitled to is not child abuse.

Still, the claim "I'm bored," rather than being a statement about a subjective experience, ends up being a statement about the parent's adequacy and worth. Children can now judge parents by how well they provide opportunities and therefore how deserving they are of the child's love and respect. They can later, rightly or wrongly, blame them for the ways that they turned out, or failed to turn out. They can attribute the failure to provide "formative opportunities" as being far more central than it may have been.

This also extends to the level of parental involvement in their children's many activities. For example, in Steven Spielberg's movie *Hook*, a remake of *Peter Pan*, Captain Hook attempts to curry favor with Michael by arranging a baseball game. When Michael is up to bat, Hook motivates him by saying, "This is for all of the baseball games that your father never attended!" The child snarls in righteous anger and hits a home run.

This is a major reversal in polarities. Where prior generations of children were expected to earn the *parents'* love and respect, today's parents are worried that they won't have their *children's* love and respect because they're not *enough*: not psychological enough, not sensitive enough, not fun enough, not "there" enough. They're worried, often correctly, that their real or imagined mistakes in parenting may one day come back to haunt them.

THEIR OWN WORLD

Paradoxically, at the same time that parents were being made to feel increasingly responsible for their children, children were being increasingly affected by influences outside parents' control. As Mintz writes, " ... the most important development was the growing influence of extra-familial institutions in socialization. Schools, churches, television, and the commercial marketplace fostered separate worlds of childhood and youth in which certain cultural references and experiences were shared by peer groups and from which parents and even older siblings were excluded." Historian Stephanie Coontz observes in *The Way We Really Are: Coming to Terms with America's Changing Families* that there was little difference between the games that teens played and those played by their parents in preindustrial societies. That has all changed.

THE CHILD AS CONSUMER

The economic potential for a marketplace feeding frenzy by product-hungry, cash-rich children and their guilt-ridden parents was increasingly realized over the twentieth century. In the United States, $15 billion a year is spent on marketing to children, and children see 110 commercials a day. Half of all children between the ages of seven and sixteen have cell phones, and 25 percent of two-year-olds have television sets in their bedrooms. Girls between the ages of ten and nineteen spent $75 billion of their own money in the United States in 2001, and that doesn't include what their parents bought for them. Children between the ages of four and twelve spent 400 percent more in 2002 than they did in 1989.

WATCH WHAT YOU EAT!

Increasing information about the effects of pesticides and poor nutrition caused parents to become alarmed that they weren't doing enough to protect their children's health. Fears that one small error in judgment could have a lasting impact on their children's development persist and are constant topics in the media.

Worry about children's nutrition has now reached fever pitch. Recently, the producers of Sesame Street changed the nutritional habits of "Cookie Monster," a character greatly admired by children everywhere for his uninhibited passion for cookies. A newspaper recently reported that he would now take the position that "A Cookie is a Sometimes Food." As the show's vice president of research and education states it, "We're teaching him moderation."

Please.

Changing Cookie Monster into a moderate eater isn't going to improve children's diets. As one columnist noted, since the blue Muppet dines upon *anything* that's shaped like a cookie, perhaps young viewers should be advised to avoid garbage lids, Frisbees, and platters too.

THE ROLE OF DIVORCE

As divorce rates began to escalate in the 1950s, 1960s, and 1970s, and women began returning to work in record numbers, parents began to feel more guilty and anxious about the quality of life they were offering their children. This remains an ongoing source of guilt and anxiety for many parents, and for working mothers in particular.

In the 1970s there was a big spike in the rate of divorce. This was fueled by the liberalization of divorce laws, the de-stigmatization of divorce, a greater acceptance of alternative arrangements of living together, women's increased economic power, and a newer ideology that emphasized the importance of personal happiness and fulfillment in marriage.

While divorce has been a positive for children in high-conflict families, the increase in divorce rates brought forth new ways for children and parents to be separated and alienated from each other. As will be discussed in chapter 9, children sometimes form alliances with one parent over the other or blame one parent more for the divorce. All of these factors can contribute to a child's decreased feelings of attachment, loyalty, and respect toward the parent.

MONEY WORRIES AND THE WOUNDED PARENT

Parents in poor communities grieve, not only for the lack of an economic future for their children, but also for their inability to protect them from police and gang violence. As historian Coontz writes, "Lower class parents are especially ill-served by an overemphasis on parental responsibility for children's outcomes, since research shows that the social dynamics of poverty and low status give them less influence over their children in relation to peer groups than parents in other classes."

Dedicated parents in poor neighborhoods both fear and despair as they watch their children growing up in an increasingly competitive society with increasingly fewer opportunities. Their kids are asked to compete for jobs and in college applications (if they make it that far) against students from well-funded public schools or private schools where the preschools cost upwards of $20,000 a year. Economic stressors can also affect the quality of parenting, which may make parents more susceptible to feeling guilty in the present, and vulnerable to later accusations that they were too critical, angry, or preoccupied. Accusations of being a lousy parent, whether from our children or ourselves, can create intolerable feelings of shame. Understanding and navigating those feelings are the subjects of the next chapter.

SIX

CONFRONTING PARENTAL SHAME

Easing a Lonely Burden

"The more you know about shame,
the less trivial seems comedy."

DONALD NATHANSON,
Shame and Pride: Affect, Sex, and the Birth of the Self

Nice days were a rarity with Tommy, though Polly hoped they'd start happening more often. After a series of evaluations, Tommy had recently been diagnosed with Explosive Personality Disorder, and Polly looked forward to learning new ways to deal with him that would make for smoother sailing. Today, though, she was just grateful to have made it through the day, so far, without a blowup.

Polly was almost out of the grocery store when it happened. She was rounding the aisle from the produce stand, heading to the checkout counter like an Olympic runner just steps away from the world record, when he screamed, "NOOO!! You didn't get me any chips!! I want chips!!"

"Oh God, no, please, not now," she thought. "Please let me just get the hell out of this store before you do one of your 9.1 Richter Scale meltdowns. I just can't take it. Not today."

"Chiipss! Momma, I want chips!"

"Honey," she said calmly, looking around to see how many horrified onlookers would get to judge her today, "We have chips at home, remember? We got chips *yesterday* at the store."

"NOO! I hate that kind. I want the good kind. YOU PROMISED WE'D GET THE GOOD KIND!" he screamed in a voice that would have made Linda Blair proud.

"Tommy, we have the good kind at home." Polly said, faux calmly, the panic rising in her throat along with a desire to squeeze the circulation out of his hand. "Remember, you picked them out yesterday. C'mon now. We have to get home to make a nice dinner and you can help."

"NOOO! THOSE CHIPS ARE STUPID, YOU'RE STUPID! YOU'RE A BIG, FAT IDIOT! I WANT MY CHIPS!!!"

A phalanx of shoppers passed her wearing tight masks of scorn, contempt, and pity.

"Tommy," Polly said calmly through her humiliation, heading for the aisle where the provocative chips and their triglyceride-ridden counterparts sat, "You can't call Mommy names. Remember what we talked about with Daddy? No name calling."

Harriet had the fortune and misfortune of raising her eighteen-year-old daughter in Hillsborough, a wealthy suburb of San Francisco. Now that her daughter was college age, the inevitable conversation of her women's group dinners revolved around obsessions over SAT scores, college apps, and of course, who was going where.

"Liona got accepted to Brown and Yale. She can't decide," said Marlene, an old friend of Harriet's from college.

"Wow," said Harriet, pulling out the ruby-encrusted saber from her ribs. "That is fabulous! You must be so proud!"

"Well," Kathleen, another friend, said, "Rick applied to five schools but he only got into one—Berkeley!"

"Berkeley? That's nothing to be ashamed of," Harriet said, pouring a fourth glass of wine as the conversational lazy Susan began to dizzily spin in her direction. "I hear Berkeley's impossible to get into these days."

"Bobby got into Berkeley, too," said Constance, a friend from Harriet's book club. "He and Rick are talking about rooming together. He got into Amherst and Oberlin. He's thinking about Oberlin because they're supposed to have a good music program."

"What's happening with Becky?" asked the mother of the daughter who was accepted to Yale and Brown.

"Oh, she didn't get in anywhere," Harriet said, with a 'Whaddya gonna do?' shrug.

"Aw, I'm sorry," said the friend whose son got into Berkeley, Oberlin, and Amherst.

"Yeah, her SATs weren't great, her grades weren't great, and she refused to apply to more than one school, even though we tried to get her to apply to a bunch."

"Oh, she can apply again next year," one of the friends offered.

"Yeah, there's a lot she can do in the meantime to increase her desirability," said another.

"Of course she can," Harriet thought, "except for the fact that she has absolutely no ambition, she's chronically depressed, and she possesses a learning disability so pronounced that she would practically need a live-in tutor to keep track of her homework, just like I've been doing since she was in the third grade."

While her friends knew that Becky wasn't an easy kid, they had no idea how much shame and heartache Harriet had experienced with her daughter, especially in such a high-achieving community. Becky's failure to get into college was just one more in a long line of failures that Harriet, despite her dedication and commitment, struggled with as a mother.

• • •

Because today's parents are held to such a high standard of perfection, parental shame has become far more common in the past thirty years. Parents whose children act out, misbehave, fail, or behave oddly cause their parents to feel embarrassed and humiliated when they compare themselves to others, especially those with seemingly more successful or better-adjusted children. In addition, children's increased power in the home has created the conditions whereby parents are far more vulnerable to being shamed by their own children.

Shamed parents carry around a secret and lonely burden, because talking about their shame means opening the door to critical feedback and thereby experiencing further feelings of alienation. This chapter is written to provide empathy and guidance on this topic.

GUILT VS. SHAME

Guilt is the belief that we have done something wrong, such as berating a child, or failing him in some way such as not attending some event that was very meaningful to him. However, it is possible to feel guilty about an action and still believe that you're fundamentally a good person. In addition, guilt suggests an opportunity for repair: "I'm sorry for what I did. What can I do to make it up to you?"

Shame, while interwoven with guilt, isn't so much a belief that we have done something bad, but that we *are* bad. Occasional feelings of shame are not only normal and expectable, but also necessary from an evolutionary perspective. As social animals, the capacity to feel shame evolved as a way to remain oriented to surviving and thriving in a group; those who lacked this ability were more at risk of behaving in ways that were at odds with group norms, and as a result placed themselves in greater danger of punishment and ostracism. To this extent, shame often has a social component—that is, it involves looking or feeling flawed in the eyes of others.

For many, parenting may have been the one opportunity to love and be loved unconditionally—fearlessly free of the inhibiting shackles of shame. It may have also been the one chance to partially repair the ways that our own childhoods left us disfigured with feelings of defectiveness, unlovability, or fear. Part of the pleasurable merging that people experience with their infants is the opportunity to experience an existence unmarred by feeling separate and isolated from another. The innocence and dependence of an infant mirrors a reflection of us as perfect, needed, and worthy.

However, parenting becomes more treacherous as children grow because their capacity to reject, shame, and humiliate the parent increases in weight and power as they get older. While a toddler's tantrum may cause us to feel flummoxed and helpless, it is nothing compared to the way a teen or young adult can penetrate our most vulnerable areas and flay at the core of our identity and self-esteem.

THE SHAME OF SEPARATION

For example, it is not uncommon for teens to reject their parents in order to cut the tidal pull of connection and dependence. One of their more effective strategies is to make the parent feel inadequate. In this act, the teen says, "You have no value, so why should I remain so attached and dependent on you?"

Marriage researcher John Gottman has found that spousal contempt is a strong predictor of divorce. This is because contempt from one spouse induces powerful feelings of shame and inadequacy in the other. Being shamed on a daily basis, apparently, is not most people's idea of a good time. Psychiatrist and researcher Janet Kiecolt-Glaser has shown that marital partners who are the objects of ongoing disdain are far more at risk for decreased immune function. When these spouses say, "You make me sick," they're not exaggerating. While both researchers' data is based on marriage, it seems very likely that these findings would carry over into parenting, even more powerfully. After all, what could be more stressful than experiencing your child's ongoing hatred or contempt of you?

I have seen the most grounded and healthy of my friends, colleagues, and clients completely undone when faced with their children's ongoing disdain. They find themselves locked into a relationship where the daily message is that there is something really, really screwed up about them. While some parents are able to parry these assaults with relatively little injury, many parents feel bloodied and bruised by the battle. As one mother put it, "My son makes me feel like the most stupid, ineffective person in the world. I walk away depressed from every interaction we have. I'm just counting the days until he moves out!"

This unhappy dynamic can continue, however, even after children leave home. While prior generations—pre-telephone, pre-cell phone, and pre-email—could have reassured themselves that they haven't heard from their children because it takes a while to hear from them, that's all changed. Now, a lack of communication means something entirely different: a child who refuses to return a call, an e-mail, or a letter sends a strong message: "Of course, I could've contacted you, but I didn't." Other adult children may remain in contact, but spend so much of the interaction criticizing, ridiculing, or raging that the parent is left stunned and disoriented. Message sent: "Your love is worthless and you are worthless." Message received.

There are many ways that parents' and children's needs are at odds, and individuation from the parent can be one of the biggies. Even when separation isn't aggressively wrought, the very fact of it can feel shaming, especially to a parent who already carries feelings of inadequacy or worthlessness. I have watched more than one parent get tripped up by the sudden loss of intimacy that comes as the peer group supplants the parent as the gravitational center of intimacy and authority. Unfortunately, as with any relationship that may have been close and confiding, the parent may further alienate the teen or young adult by shaming back, or by acting so victimized that the child is driven further away. As one mother said, "We were once so close and now I get treated like a piece of crap. Screw her. If she wants a good relationship with me, she can come to me." Don't hold your breath, Mom. She's working on learning how to *not* come to you—and the more victimized you act, the longer it's going to take for her to come back.

THE LENGTHENING OF ADOLESCENCE

Parent/teen and parent/young adult relations have become especially complicated because adolescence has been extended much further than in prior generations. University of Pennsylvania sociologist Frank F. Furstenberg and colleagues observe that the definition of adulthood, "traditionally defined as finishing school, landing a job with benefits, marrying and parenting," has been extended by a decade. Using this standard, 65 percent of men reached adulthood by the age of 30 in 1960, while only 31 percent had by 2000. For women, 77 percent met the standard of adulthood by age 30 in 1960, but only 46 percent by the year 2000.

This shift has had a huge effect on parent/teen relations. For example, if children are remaining younger longer, then they may need to extend the kind of rebellious, shaming and devaluing behavior—long associated with the thirteen-year-old to seventeen-year-old set—into their mid-to-late twenties (if not later). Why? Because your adult child is still working on separating from you. It's love, not hate, that causes her to mistreat you. Now, don't you feel better?

The consolidation of identity, long the hallmark of successful adolescence, also appears to be taking longer to achieve than in prior generations. One reason is that the current culture of parenting prevents children from experiencing just enough hard knocks to train them in weathering the stormy transition from living at home to living independently. Our current view of children as precious and fragile may cause us to advocate for them so aggressively and diligently that they view themselves as being overly vulnerable to the inevitable slings and arrows of life. This is part of what psychoanalyst Carl Jung meant when he wrote that "neuroses are the avoidance of legitimate suffering."

Writer Hara Estroff Marano describes this as "hothouse parenting"—the notion that children are being raised with the philosophy that they can only thrive under conditions that are warm, close, and carefully nurtured. Another writer coined the term "helicopter parents" to describe the phenomenon of constantly and busily hovering over one's children, always at the ready to swoop down and rescue them from any insult or injury.

Hothouse or helicopter parenting may partially explain why today's college counseling centers are groaning under the weight of students with severe mental health issues. One survey found that the severity of psychological problems seen in college counseling centers has been rising since 1988. Of course, this may also be occurring because earlier diagnosis, and a de-stigmatization of therapy, has meant that people are more likely to seek help or remain in college when they would have dropped out before. Colleges are also more aggressive in seeking out at-risk students and helping them get treatment.

In addition, years eighteen to twenty-five are especially vulnerable to the emergence of mental illnesses such as schizophrenia, anxiety disorders, bipolar illness, depression, and personality disorders. Some of these illnesses may remain hidden until unleashed by the kind of stressors that the highly competitive and socially stressful environment of college can create.

A further source of potential shame for both parent and burgeoning adult has been the winnowing of financial opportunities that once allowed teens to emerge into adulthood, confident that they could support themselves on a decent wage. As a result, many young adults in the United States and abroad don't leave home until later in life, or return home after a brief sortie into the adult world.

This extended adolescence can seriously strain teen and adult relations. Contemporary perspectives of children as fragile may cause parents to be unable to do the type of "tough love" limit-setting sometimes required to force a child out of the warm though stifling comfort of the nest into the cold but fresh air of an independent life. Teens who can't leave home or adult children who return can create shaming dynamics for both themselves and for their parents.

For example, Kyle lived with his mother after his parents divorced when he was seven. He moved in with his father at the age of sixteen after his mother moved to Chicago with her new husband. When Kyle graduated high school, he asked his father if he could continue to live with him, go to a community college, and save money until he could move out on his own. His father reluctantly agreed.

Unfortunately, Kyle didn't hold up his end of the bargain, continually dropping out of classes so that he didn't progress very far in college. He also wasn't disciplined enough to save enough money from his part-time job to move out on his own.

Kyle's dad still blamed himself for the divorce, and for the depression that Kyle appeared to develop in response to it. As a result, he felt too guilty to set limits with Kyle, such as telling him that he would have to move out by a certain date, or if he didn't maintain a full schedule of classes. The father's difficulty in setting limits, and the son's difficulty in striving for independence, was a volatile dynamic fueled by Kyle's shame and guilt over his failings, and dad's shame and guilt over the divorce. As a result, they both shamed and blamed the other and perpetuated a difficult and destructive spiral. These dynamics will be addressed more fully in chapter 11, "Failure to Launch."

THE COMPASS OF SHAME

People respond to feelings of shame in different ways. Psychiatrist and shame researcher Donald Nathanson proposes that there are four strategies to deal with shame: *attack the other person, attack yourself, withdraw from yourself, or avoid others.* Attacking the other person is a way to decrease their power to judge you or make you feel bad about yourself. This can be done through belittling, criticizing, ridiculing, or gossiping about that person to others. Some of the shaming that children do to their parents is an attempt to relieve themselves of shame by devaluing the parent in the way that Kyle did with his dad.

The desire to attack those who would shame us can sometimes assume murderous proportions, as evidenced by the Columbine and other school killings. As Judith Rich Harris writes, "Most school shooters are kids who were picked on or rejected by their peers. They have been badly hurt and made to feel puny and powerless. They want to get even and they want to feel powerful. Guns in their hands make them feel powerful." Nathanson describes it similarly: " ... the thoughts that cause the most pain are those of weakness, smallness, incompetence, clumsiness, and stupidity ... In a burst of rage we prove our power, competence, and size." While parenticide is rare, many teens and young adults attempt to make their parents feel worthless because of the many ways that they feel worthless. Many parents return or initiate attacks as a way to defend themselves from their own poisonous feelings of shame.

Attacking yourself is an entirely different strategy. Here, the goal is to reduce the other's power to shame you by getting there first. For example, I sometimes have to tell my patients in the dating world to refrain from listing all of their inadequacies on the first encounter. "They're going to find out anyway, so I might as well get it over with" is a common refrain. Their goal is to avoid the horrible sensation, familiar to all who struggle with the shame, of having their imperfections revealed. So they proceed to tell their would-be suitors all of their failings, insecurities, and problems—which they discover, lo and behold, isn't a big turn-on. For wounded parents, attacking yourself often takes the form of conscious self-loathing and self-sabotage.

Another strategy common with wounded parents is to *withdraw* from yourself in an attempt to hide feelings of shame, humiliation, anguish, and inadequacy from the world. Parents' feelings of shame make it hard to be open with others about their struggles or to seek support for fear of revealing their defectiveness. As a result, they feel isolated and alone with their problems.

The final strategy is *avoidance*. With avoidance we deny that the problem exists. Avoidance is much like denial in the sense that the person lies to themselves to avoid the painful feelings of shame. "I really don't care what she does anymore," said a father. "Frankly, I've put her out of my mind." The desire to avoid shame can also cause parents to deny the harm that they've done because the feelings of shame evoked by the memory are too painful.

THE PROBLEM WITH EMPATHY

Empathy is the ability to experience what others experience. It is the key to good relationships and social success because it gives us insight into what others think and feel. This *theory of mind* allows us to be helpful to others and to avoid situations with them that could cause us problems. It also appears to be a capacity that we're born with.

Empathy is a necessary and almost unavoidable part of parenting. It is through empathic reflection that an infant begins to develop a sense of self. For example, when a baby smiles at a parent and the parent smiles back, this causes the child to "be seen" and to feel effective and related. Similarly, the constant mirroring and responsiveness of a parent to a child's expressions of pleasure or discomfort helps the infant begin learning how to regulate her emotions, and later in life, her thinking.

But what happens to the empathizer when their empathy is frustrated or meets a dead end, as happens for parents with difficult children or children who attack and reject them? In the same way that children are hard wired to need an empathic response in order to regulate their emotions, parents may be hard wired to feel shamed and inadequate when their love proves futile.

Contemporary culture makes parenting sound like it has the potential to be a one-stop shopping center for all of your emotional needs, and this increases the parental risk of feeling shamed. Despite the fact that only about one-third of mothers describe parenting as "very fulfilling," most people feel like there's something really wrong with them if they feel burdened by their children, or if they don't find parenthood to be the wellspring of satisfaction that others claim it to be. Of course, parenting is especially burdensome if your kids don't cooperate in making it fun, or if your past mistakes make it hard to get back what you once had. In those cases, parenting becomes the central wellspring of your suffering. As with spouses in unhappy marriages, wounded parents often have to reconcile their powerful needs to love and be loved by someone who is unwilling to play.

Occasionally a friend or client will say to me, "I could never do what you do, listen to people's problems all day." It's hard for them to imagine experiencing ongoing feelings of empathy for others without feeling burdened by its demands. But peoples' expectations of themselves as parents suffer from a similar perspective. Our current culture of parenting causes parents to believe that they should be on twenty-four-hour alert to any empathy demand from their children, including their children's mistreatment of them. As psychologist Diane Ehrensaft writes, " ... it is remarkable to observe that modern middle class parents do not allow themselves to hit their children, but they let their children hit them all the time."

This is true not only for hitting but also for verbal abuse of the parent. Many parents are so worried about stifling their children's emotional lives that they tolerate outbursts and manipulations unheard of in prior generations. This confuses children about what is reasonable to expect from a parent and what they're entitled to receive from others. It causes parents to feel shamed and inadequate when they should feel annoyed and empowered. I'm not suggesting that those emotions are the primary ones to have in your dealings with your children, but if you don't have them comfortably in your repertoire, you're pretty much screwed as a parent.

BURDENED CHILDREN

Another quote from Jung comes to mind: "Nothing affects children more than the unlived lives of their parents." This quote has many layers, but it speaks to the burden children feel about the unhappiness of their parents. Unfortunately, awareness of a parent's unhappiness may bring out the worst behavior in adolescent and adult children. Children may shame or reject a depressed, anxious, or unfulfilled parent as a way to decrease the weight of their feelings of empathy for us—their vulnerability to being weighed down by our sorrows, tied up by our unsuccessful lives, disillusioned by our disappointments in them, in others, or in ourselves. Sometimes children find that the only way they can achieve a healthy distance from our feelings is by rejecting us or moving far, far away.

As more than one of my clients has said, "It's such a drag to talk to my mother because all she ever talks about is how hard her life is. She's such a martyr!" But why are people so burdened by mothers who are martyrs? Why is it so hard for so many of us to listen and be sympathetic, or not get upset when spending time with someone who complains a lot? It's because we're trying to counter the demands imposed by empathy.

As Nathanson observes, other people's feelings, especially family members', have the potential to take us over. An infant's nonstop crying can be infuriating, not only because it feels so demanding, but because they sound so *outraged* at our inability to give them what they want. It's as if they're saying, "What in the hell is your problem? No, I'm not hungry! No, I don't want to hear another one of your inane baby songs! No, I can't tell you any more clearly what the problem is! I'm a baby, for Christ's sake! *Do something!*"

Nathanson suggests that an "empathic wall" is a healthy and necessary part of human development because without it, we'd be vulnerable to picking up the transmissions of every being around us. For example, let's say you're on a playground, a site of frequent displays of children's distress caused either through miscalculating the distance between the monkey bars or through learning that their parents idea of "a long time" playing on the swings differs from theirs. If you're sitting there and have no insulation against the crying of every suffering child, you're in trouble. We need to be able to tune out the suffering of others, in some part, to maintain our sanity.

Today's parents are made to feel as though having an empathic wall is the height of selfishness, rather than an essential to mental health. The paradox here is that the more that you believe you are not harming your child by feeling a little more detached from them, the better able you'll be to manage their shaming or rejection of you.

THE POPEMOBILE

Remember that bullet-proof bubble the Pope used to have that allowed him to greet the masses by car without fear of being shot? I want you to imagine that you have a mental Popemobile that insulates you against the emotional gunshots of your children's and other people's attacks. Please note that while I will sometimes counsel you to be more empathic to your children, here I am counseling the opposite. With empathy, we allow ourselves to be taken over by the feelings and statements of the other. Your kid says, "You're a lousy parent," and you feel shamed and sad and regretful. When you are inside the Popemobile, your kid says, "You're a lousy parent," and you say, "I'm sorry, darling, I didn't hear you. Did you say something? Can't hear you in this danged Popemobile."

The goal is to try to allow the feelings to be largely reflected off of you, and to instead get curious about the statements, rather than deeply feeling what is being said about you. So you might say something like, "Really? In what way?" Let them talk it out and practice remaining curious without taking it in. It's what I call being *affectionately detached*— you're detached enough to prevent every pore of your skin from being open to the acid rain that's about to fall on you, and loving enough to let your children know that you *do* actually care about what he or she has to say. It takes practice, practice, practice, but if you're like most parents, you'll have no shortage of opportunities.

"Shame" Questionnaire

Circle the items that most closely relate to you or your relationship with your child:

- My child tells me that I'm a terrible parent.

- My child behaves in ways that make me feel embarrassed, shamed, or humiliated.

- My child doesn't want to be close to me, and this makes me feel bad about myself. It also causes me to believe that I look like a bad parent in the eyes of others.

- I feel disappointed that my child doesn't do well socially, academically, or professionally, and I believe that it reflects poorly on me.

- _____
- _____
- _____

Changing Your Reactions Questionnaire

The key to changing the dynamic of conflict with your child lies in changing your reactions. You can't necessarily change your child, but you can modify what happens between the two of you.

Circle the items that most clearly describe how you respond to your child when he or she is difficult:

- I give in.

- I become verbally or physically abusive.

- I get quiet and shut down.

- I take it out on my partner.

- I get my other kids to ally with me.

- I get confused about who's right or wrong or what is right or wrong.

- I use drugs, alcohol, or food to numb the feelings.

- I get even.

- _____
- _____
- _____
- _____

LEARN TO STOP RESPONDING OUT OF EMOTION

If you have a child who is shaming, your emotions may lead you to give in more frequently than is good for you. It may be useful for you to err on the side of being more self-interested for a period of time until you clearly know whether you are caving in to a demand or agreeing to a demand because it's genuinely unimportant to you. Keep a journal of these situations. Make note of the date, the situation, how you acted, the emotions evoked, and your automatic thoughts. Write out a positive self-statement and a new behavior that you'll try next time as a way to counter the automatic thought.

Date: Past three months

Situation: Son refuses to take or return my calls

Emotion: Despair, guilt, shame

Automatic thought: I'm a bad parent. I'm a bad person. He's a bad son.

Positive self-statement: I have worked hard to repair the mistakes that I made as a parent. Hopefully, one day we'll have a closer relationship. Until then, all I can do is to keep the door open and not be hard on myself. I am deserving of love, compassion, and forgiveness, even if he is unable to provide those for me.

New behavior: Make sure that I'm getting enough support by talking to other parents who are struggling with similar issues. Do daily affirmations when I'm feeling too self-critical.

HEALING STEPS FOR REDUCING SHAME

Shame is self-perpetuating because the belief in our defectiveness causes us to avoid talking about our pain with others. This avoidance makes the sufferer feel even more isolated, lonely, and burdened with the feelings of shame. Bearing this in mind:

Work to understand the irrational nature of your shame. Did your parents shame you? Did you have other experiences in your life that led you to believe that you're somehow defective, such as being teased or humiliated by peers, siblings, or others?

Shame can make you feel undeserving. Work to accept more love and support from those closest to you. Don't deny yourself pleasure or meaning from other activities because you believe that you let your child down. Commit to doing something nurturing for yourself on a weekly, if not daily, basis.

Get more help determining whether you need to take further steps to address the problems in your child or in your relationship. If you have any doubt, get a consultation with a therapist, drug counselor, learning specialist, or others.

Remind yourself of your child's strengths and assets, and of your strengths and assets as a parent. Many parents become so worried and filled with shame over their children's problems and treatment of them that they fail to see what is valuable in the child and what they're doing right as parents. Make a list and review it on a daily basis.

As these issues are being addressed, remind yourself that you are doing everything possible and therefore shouldn't be punished.

You can't let the thoughts that cause you the most pain rule your roost. Practice being in loving dialogue with yourself where self-compassion, empathy, forgiveness, and self-love are at the core of your experience. Work to actively root out the harsh, critical, and unforgiving voice in your head and replace it with a voice that is kind, nurturing, and understanding.

SEVEN

WHERE DID THIS KID COME FROM?

Mismatches Between Parent and Child

Ronnie played pro ball for two years after he graduated from college. If it weren't for an ankle injury received sliding into home during a pennant game, he would probably be making serious money on a Nike sponsorship like his other friends who went pro. Ronnie came to see me at his wife's request to talk about parenting issues. His wife was concerned because Ronnie had a hard time relating to their fourteen-year-old son, Bruce. Unlike Ronnie, Bruce showed little interest in sports, and failed to improve no matter how many times Ronnie took him out to play. In addition, Bruce was shy and intellectual, the kind of child who is more interested in reading and spending time on the computer than running around with a bunch of rambunctious boys. In fact, his few friends were girls, something else that Ronnie found bewildering—especially since he didn't seem to have an attraction to any of them.

Ronnie had a hard time relating to his son or enjoying him. On more than one occasion he called him a "sissy" or "wimp" when Bruce had cried after falling down, or expressed anxiety about an upcoming school function. Ronnie knew he was wrong to call his son names, but he had a hard time managing his emotions. His wife was concerned because her son seemed increasingly withdrawn from his father, and she worried that they could one day move beyond the point of no return.

Personality and temperamental mismatches between parent and child can be a source of conflict, disappointment, and heartache for both. They can also lead to long-term alienation between parents and their children. In this chapter I'll help you determine if mismatches are an issue for you and your child, and provide guidelines to work around the potential conflicts and misunderstandings that can arise.

SIBLING REALITIES

If you have more than one child, you have probably observed how dissimilar they are from each other, how differently they respond to you as a parent, and maybe even how unlike they are in their memories of your lives together. In part, these separate realities exist because the differences between siblings *exceed* their similarities on almost all characteristics: some 90 percent of siblings differ from each other, not only in physical traits such as hair color, hair texture, and skin complexion, but in personality as well. Personality traits known to have a strong genetic component to them are: openness to new experiences, conscientiousness, extroversion/introversion, antagonism/agreeableness, and neuroticism (you can remember these with the acronym OCEAN). Because of these differences, a parent could have a very close relationship to one of her fraternal twins and be completely mismatched with the other.

The genetic differences in siblings highlight another way that parents aren't as omnipotent as our current culture deems them to be; it's simply not in our best interest as a species to make parents that powerful. But, you may ask, what possible value could *neu-*

roticism, an inherited trait, have to an individual, family, or social group? Well, one of the defining characteristics of neurotics is a tendency to worry or obsess about past failings or future catastrophes. Having a family or clan characterized only by extroverts may have been a good trait for exploring novel and forbidding terrain, but foolhardy in those situations where real caution or reflection was required. Similarly, a conscientious temperament would be useful to bond the group together or to bond that individual to the group, whereas, an antagonistic or even antisocial personality would be useful for situations requiring survival when banished from the tribe.

You could think of the family, a microorganism of the social group, as operating much like a Swiss Army knife. From this perspective, you have a greater chance of survival if each member has some quality that is more useful in some situations than others. For example, in the same way that species develop under pressures to inhabit a new geographical or ecological niche, expressions of personality, biology, and intelligence have varied within humans because these differences mattered enough at some point to help the person survive long enough to pass those traits (genes) on to the next generation. Biological variation in siblings increases the likelihood that a particular family member might survive to pass on the parents' genes when exposed to some environmental danger or nasty microorganism. In fact, vulnerability to disease is one more way that siblings greatly differ from each other.

HOW SIBLINGS AFFECT EACH OTHER

While parents matter, siblings are also active players in the shaping of what our children experience and who they become. Learning how to navigate the relationship with a receptive or unreceptive sibling can teach lessons about how to get along in the rest of the world. As psychologist Daniel Shaw states, "In general, parents serve the same big-picture role as doctors on grand rounds. Siblings are like the nurses on the ward. They're there every day."

Birth order can affect siblings' feelings of well-being. For example, older siblings often complain that the younger one is preferred, and probably with cause. A large percentage of mothers admit to feeling a greater sense of affection for their youngest child in comparison to an older child. Human mothers, as well as other primates, tend to lavish much more attention and care on their younger children. In several studies conducted by Robert Plomin and colleagues, only 12 percent of mothers said that they disciplined their children with equal frequency—in the majority of cases the older child received much more discipline.

Moreover, younger children are formidable adversaries in the war for parental attention. In two studies of preschoolers, researchers found that children as young as fourteen months vigilantly monitored the relationship of an older sibling with the mother, and over time become increasingly adept at moving the conversation and attention in their direction. As researchers Judy Dunn and Robert Plomin write, "By thirty-six months of age, the children managed on a high proportion of occasions to turn the mother and sibling discourse to the topic that they were most interested in, themselves!"

"HOW COME MY BROTHER ALWAYS GETS HIS WAY?"

Charles Dickens wrote in *Great Expectations*, "In the little world in which children have their existence, whosoever brings them up, there is nothing so finely perceived and so finely felt, as injustice." But, what is the nature of this felt injustice? Some parents treat their children similarly, and the siblings *still* experience that treatment very differently. It's not unusual for three siblings to have three different opinions of their parents: one harsh, one sympathetic, and one neutral. An aggressive child, for example, is temperamentally more likely to believe that his parents and siblings treat him more aggressively than they treat others in the family. This is another instance where the temperament of the child may serve as a filter through which he experiences relationships, and where the interaction between genetics and parenting can continue to create painful dynamics for each, with long-lasting effects.

In a recent study, researchers Barbara Shebloski, Katherine Conger, and Keith Widaman found that later-born children suffered in their feelings of self-worth if they perceived, correctly or not, that their earlier-born sibling was being treated preferentially. However, the researchers also found that while 30 percent of mothers and 30 percent of fathers were rated as treating their children equally, earlier-born siblings viewed their parents as treating the later-born siblings in a more preferential manner. As Conger said, "The key thing that the siblings in our study emphasize is that most of them understand that their parents cannot treat them 'equally,' per se, due to differences in age, gender, developmental stage, skills and interests, and sometimes even shared interests between parent and one child; but the siblings are concerned that the parents treat them fairly! A nice balancing act for parents!" Her study highlights that even when parents try to be fair, the place that one occupies in the family can color how equitably that treatment is viewed.

DIFFICULT TEMPERAMENTS

Some children are so resilient that they'll land on their feet no matter how many times they get tossed out of the window (okay, so maybe that's not the best metaphor). In addition, some kids are so easygoing and self-managing that they require little input from their parents in order to thrive; they still need love and attention—they just don't need as much of their parents' involvement in regulating their mood and behavior.

However, not all children come into the world with such a treasure trove of temperamental and organizational giftedness. Some children require a far greater degree of patience and psychological savvy than others. By contemporary standards, they require that the parent behave in a way more often seen in a therapist's office than a living room.

RAISING AGGRESSIVE AND DEFIANT CHILDREN

In child psychiatrist Stanley Greenspan's useful book *The Challenging Child: Understanding, Raising, and Enjoying the Five "Difficult" Types of Children* he gives the following advice for dealing with a young child with an aggressive temperament: "If your child is lining cars up in a row, come in as close as you sense he will let you ... Keep your motions slow and relaxed. Try to remember to use voice tones that he is comfortable with. If he is sensitive to touch, be respectful of that." He goes on to recommend that the parent avoid mussing the child's hair or giving him unwelcome hugs.

This is good advice, especially if you had read it when your kid was two and could practice it for twelve years before he became a teenager. However, what if you, like millions of other parents, weren't aware that there was a way to deal with children with a temperament that even the most patient and insightful parent would find exasperating and burdensome? Or what if you were stretched thin personally as a single parent and didn't have the time to hunt for self-help books, let alone to pony up the funds to see a child psychologist? Or what if your marital stresses or your partner undermined all your attempts to be a more conscientious parent? What if your financial stressors were so overwhelming that you couldn't manage to be a great parent to *any* of your children, much less to one who was so hard to manage or relate to? Or what if your kid's aggressive temperament reminded you of your father's aggressive temperament, and since you decided long ago that you weren't going to let *anyone* ever push you around again, you *damned* sure weren't going to be pushed around by some kid, especially your own!

Did you make a ton of mistakes parenting your defiant or aggressive kid? I bet you did. I bet you had no idea what to do when your kid hit you, yelled at you, drained every last ounce of patience from your exhausted, sleep-deprived body. I bet when he called you names, you didn't have a clue about how to respond to that kind of verbal abuse, and something in the primitive part of your brain made you push back, hard. I bet you didn't know what to say to your sister with the incredibly easy kids when she gave advice about raising your child when you know full well she'd be drowning in the same sea of self-doubt, self-criticism, and shame that you swim in, if she had your children.

FEELING INADEQUATE AS A PARENT

Part of what's gratifying about parenting is feeling effective. Parents who can successfully comfort a distressed child feel more competent as parents and closer to the child because they're not being refused or pushed away. Parents of aggressive/defiant children suffer from a deficit of opportunities for feeling competent, and a surfeit of opportunities for feeling isolated, bewildered, and ineffectual.

This is because aggressive/defiant kids are damned hard to parent. They're especially hard when they're matched with a parent whose character or past makes him or her especially ill-suited to deal with the emotional and behavioral roller coaster common to children with this temperament.

Aggressive/defiant temperaments can be revealed as soon as children begin to learn that communication has a demanding aspect to it, no matter how gently tendered. This can occur as early as the first year and is manifested by the child's resisting or refusing the parent's attempt to comfort him. Children with this disposition are often inconsolable or respond to frustration and pain with aggressive acting out. Unfortunately, this behavior often creates a wedge between the parent and child: the parent, feeling repeatedly rejected, may withdraw in an attempt to feel less rejected. On the other hand, the parent may also reject back, saying or believing that the child's behavior is a manipulative or dangerous form of willfulness that needs to be eradicated.

SHADES OF AGGRESSION

Children differ in the reasons why they behave aggressively. Some children are aggressive because they need a lot of stimulation; that is, they sense the world through physical engagement. They like rough-and-tumble play and contact sports because their brains are organized in such a way that lower levels of sensation just don't reach them. As a result, they enjoy ramming into a parent or another child as a way to create contact and, in their own way, closeness. As adults, they enjoy arguing and have a hard time understanding why their own children feel so criticized, or why their spouses constantly ask why everything has to be an argument.

On the other hand, some children's aggressiveness comes out of a kind of over-sensitivity. They push back strongly because they experience interaction as a form of intrusion. Children who are highly sensitive can show aggressiveness because they constantly feel as if other people's needs and requests, even requests to help or nurture them, are demands that intrude on their individuality or personal boundaries.

AN AUTHORITARIAN PARENT RAISING AN
AGGRESSIVE/DEFIANT CHILD

Sometimes children's aggression is a reaction to the parents' treatment. Authoritarian parents emphasize control in their parenting and are far more likely to use punishment, criticism, guilt, or shame than praise or affection. In addition, they typically demonstrate far less interest in the child's feelings or in understanding the child's behavior. Parents who are overly authoritarian, hypercritical, shaming, or rejecting may cause their children to become more aggressive because they're fighting against the pain caused by the behavior of their parent. In some cultures, an authoritarian approach is considered an important way of training children for adulthood, preparing them for a harsh, unforgiving world. Parents in those cultures believe that the ability to respect and respond to authority is the key to a successful life.

At the mild end of authoritarianism, children may experience parents as remote, controlling, critical, benign, or involved. At the more extreme end, authoritarian parents can be experienced by their children as harsh, rejecting, or destructive to the child's burgeoning sense of self. This is because parents at the extreme are far more likely to use spanking, hitting, or verbal abuse as an ongoing part of their parenting. These are sometimes the parents who, one day, look back on their parenting with regret—especially when faced with a child who has become an out-of-control teenager, has ongoing hostility to the parent, becomes dysfunctional, or doesn't want a relationship as an adult.

Authoritarian parents are especially mismatched with children whose temperaments incline toward antisocial behavior. As David Lykken, a behavioral geneticist at the University of Minnesota, says, "The same temperament that can make for a criminal can also make for a hot test pilot or astronaut. That kind of little boy— aggressive, fearless, impulsive—is hard to handle. It's easy for parents to give up and let him run wild, or turn up the heat and the punishment and thereby alienate him and lose all control."

For example, Liam came from a long line of abusive fathers and continued the tradition with his own children. His son Rory "came out of the womb fighting" according to his mother, and was never one to back down from his father or from anyone else. As a teen, he developed a problem with crystal meth and was in and out of juvenile delinquency institutions, and later jail as a young adult. Even before he left home, he had stopped having a relationship with his father other than shouting matches and trying to avoid Liam's violent rages.

Rory was the last child to leave home, and the empty nest brought the difficulties in his parents' marriage much closer to the surface. Rory's mother, Catherine, had always hated how aggressive Liam was as a father and—with the children out of the home—was faced with her own feelings of regret for not protecting them more.

Rory had cut off contact with both of his parents after he moved out at seventeen—with his father because of his violence and with his mother for her passivity in the face of his father's behavior. While Catherine had tried to reach out to her son after he left home, he refused to take her calls, saying, "Yeah, it's easy to be a mother now that I'm out of the home, isn't it? Where were you when I needed you?" These conversations, short as they were, always buried Catherine in grief and regret.

Fortunately, Rory was forced into a recovery program as part of his probation at twenty-four, and through the twelve steps of AA began to find a way to get his life on track. As part of doing his ninth step, he contacted his mother in an attempt to make amends for the way he had hurt her by refusing contact. Catherine was overjoyed when he called; the door was finally open.

Aggressive-defiant children with an authoritarian parent are at risk for several reasons. These parents often see their central role as getting the child to respect their authority, aggressive-defiant children can produce an escalation in the parent's behavior resulting in a feedback loop where the parent's controlling or aggressive response causes the child to escalate his aggression, which causes the parent to escalate his, and so on.

Moreover, aggressive-defiant children tend to view their behavior as a natural response to others treating them unfairly, harshly, or cruelly. They experience their parents and others this way, even in homes where the parents are mild and democratic. Thus, authoritarian parents are more likely to reinforce a view of the world as severe and unforgiving. This can lead to a decreased concern for the well-being of others' feelings or possessions.

If you or your child has an aggressive temperament:

Strive to avoid:

- Getting into power struggles.

- Letting yourself be ruled by fear. Aggressive children can be very intimidating as they become teenagers and young adults. It may be tempting to give in just to avoid more conflict. This is a mistake because it (a) doesn't help your child learn how to regulate his emotions, and (b) perpetuates alienation between the two of you.

- Adopting a position of right vs. wrong. Assume that there is a kernel of truth or validity in your child's communication, however ineptly put.

Strive to:

- Set clear limits and follow through with them. For example, "I understand that you were mad, but you know the rules about speaking in a disrespectful way. Because of that, you're grounded for Friday night." Or for an adult child: "I'm going to get off of the phone now if you can't speak to me in a more respectful way."

- Schedule time doing activities that are mutually enjoyable and have a low probability of conflict. The behavior of aggressive/defiant children can cause parents to want to avoid spending time with them because they (a) pull to engage through conflict, and (b) can make the parent feel too exhausted, angry, or hurt to want to engage with them. However, if your child is available, try to do activities where you can build a connection.

A SENSITIVE OR LOW SELF-ESTEEM PARENT WITH AN AGGRESSIVE-DEFIANT CHILD

If you begin the role of parenting with low self-esteem, it's unlikely that an aggressive-defiant child is going to do any wonders for your feelings about yourself. As one mother said, "She just makes me feel so bad about myself—like I'm the most clueless person in the world."

If you suffer from low self-esteem it may be harder to find the inner strength to set limits with your aggressive-defiant child. In addition, your sensitivity may have caused you to be overly empathic to your child's protests or exaggerated complaints. If you were reared by authoritarian parents, you may believe that any use of authority is a form of abuse, and that every protest from a child should be taken seriously and discussed in detail. This may also hold for parents who aren't as sensitive, but who believe that a permissive approach is the key to developing good self-esteem.

Part of a parent's job is to help socialize the child about appropriate and inappropriate behavior. Parents who don't set limits can cause their child to escalate aggressive behavior because these children learn that it's an effective way to get what they want. The absence of limits robs them of the opportunity to learn how to regulate the demanding aspects of their temperament by internalizing their parents' management of them. If you're a low self-esteem parent raising an aggressive-defiant child:

Strive to avoid:

- Caving in out of fear

- Shouting down your child as a way to establish control

- Being inconsistent with your rules or limits

- Using excessive guilt

Strive to:

- Get enough support so that you can be stronger with your child.

- Remind yourself that limit-setting is a healthy and important part of parenting. It helps your relationship with your child and helps your child learn self control.

- Get assertiveness training.

AN AUTHORITARIAN PARENT
RAISING A SENSITIVE CHILD

Sensitive children are more vulnerable because they lack the wiring to internally counter the authoritarian parent's sometimes-harsh demands for submission. As a result, these children are more likely to internalize the parents' negativity and conclude that they are inadequate, worthless, or shameful. In addition, sensitive children often require a greater degree of attunement to their experience of the world than the authoritarian parent is able or willing to provide.

However, not all sensitive children are shrinking violets. Even with more sympathetic parents, sensitive children can be tyrants, insisting that the parent provide an exhausting level of attention and reassurance. Overly sensitive children may become especially trying as they're faced with the hormonal onslaughts of puberty, or the complex and often hurtful behavior of their peer group. As one father put it, "Thomas has always needed a lot from us as parents. When he was younger, it was always some physical complaint such as his stomach hurting, or not being able to sleep. I hoped that it would get better as he got older, but now that he's a teenager, it's ten times worse. He seems to blame us for every cut or wound he ever gets in life. I'm not sure how this kid is going to ever grow up and move out on his own."

If you are an authoritarian parent raising a sensitive child:

Strive to avoid:

- Seeing your child's behavior as something that needs to be beaten down by your authority

- Power struggles

Strive to:

- See your child's behavior as a communication of distress rather than a refutation of you

- Talk to your children about their feelings so that they can learn how to express them through means other than acting out

A HIGH-ACHIEVING PARENT
RAISING A LOW-ACHIEVING CHILD

Harriet did something that none of her other women friends from law school had done—she achieved partner by the time she was twenty-nine. Harriet wasn't surprised—she had hit every target she had ever aspired to, from becoming president of her high school class to getting a full scholarship to college; from graduating from law school with honors to marrying her college sweetheart, and then having a child when she was thirty-two.

Raising an academically successful daughter was the first thing that Harriet was unable to achieve. Becky was a sweet though spirited child, and by the second grade it became clear that she had severe learning disabilities in reading, writing, and abstract thinking. Despite tutoring and intensive parental involvement, Becky barely made Cs throughout grade school and high school. She refused to apply to more than one college and was rejected by that school. While this was a great source of concern for Harriet, a greater concern was not being close in the way that she had wished for. She'd hoped to have the intimacy with her daughter that she hadn't had with her own mother. She also longed to be a role model for how to be a strong and successful woman in a competitive world.

Becky provided challenges for Harriet unlike any she had ever encountered. No matter how hard Harriet worked to help Becky and how much money she spent on tutors, educational specialists, and private schools, Becky never succeeded in school. Moreover, Becky's low aspirations brought out the worst in Harriet. Her worry for Becky's future caused her to be obsessed with her school performance and to do little other than ask why she wasn't studying for the test that was coming up, why she wasn't turning in her homework, why she was waiting until it was past due before starting on her history paper.

Harriet's unrestrained worry caused her to be harsh and controlling with Becky. Despite the advice of the learning specialists, Harriet couldn't stop herself from being critical of her daughter or revealing her ongoing feelings of disappointment. Not surprisingly, Becky responded to her mother's negative broadcast by being difficult, argumentative, and, as a teen, acting out with drugs. When I met with the family, the threads of connection between Harriet and her daughter had frayed to a few fragile strands. As Becky approached her eighteenth birthday, these lines of connection were close to being permanently severed if Harriet didn't learn the tools to better manage her feelings of worry, guilt, and disappointment.

Most parents today are terrified that their children won't get into a decent college, find a decent-paying career, and go on to have a generally decent life. These worries result, understandably, from the increasingly narrow path available to become a success-ful adult. However, as Harriet's case illustrates, these worries cause many well-meaning parents to ruin their relationships with their children by over-focusing on their children's achievements or lack thereof. A high-achieving parent with a low-achieving child can be a particularly nettlesome combination, especially when it causes the parent to not value what is positive in the child. This may set the stage for ongoing or later wounding of the parent, as the child responds to the parent's treatment with anger, shame, or rejection.

This dynamic may also continue after the child moves out of the home because parents who feel deeply worried can subtly or overtly communicate a lack of faith or support that creates a host of problematic interactions. For example, a young adult may manage his life even more poorly as a way to demonstrate his in-dependence, much like bright teenagers who get lousy grades as a way of snubbing their grade-obsessed parents. Parental worry, criticism, or advice can also cause a young adult to doubt her own abilities, leading her to feel alienated from her parents or to re-spond by distancing herself from the relationship.

This was true for Dale, a young man I saw in my practice for many years. Throughout the course of his therapy, he would show me the letters from his very successful mother that expressed how worried she was about his not finishing college, how he was going to end up a pauper, and how disappointed she was in him for fail-ing to, in her words, "take advantage of all of the gifts that God gave you."

I had no problems empathizing with Dale's mother. I could read the maternal love and concern between the lines blurred by guilt trips and disappointment. However, she was making the mistake that I see so many parents make with their adult children: giving unwanted advice or expressing unasked-for concern. She was not only hurting him but also her relationship with him.

Here's what I would have said to Dale's mother if he'd wanted me to, and if she would have listened. (In my experience, many parents *don't* want to listen to their adult child's therapist because they assume we're the ones putting funny ideas in their kid's head in the first place.) I would have told her that her worry feels to him like a vote of no confidence. He is a big boy now and unless he explicitly asks for her advice, she should not give it, as wise as it may be. I would also tell her that expressing her disappointment in him is bad for his self-esteem because it makes him feel like his life is hurtful to her. Don't ask him when he's going back to school, don't tell him how severely underemployed he is, and don't tell him that he's wasting his life. I know that these statements are well meant, but he feels undermined by them. The best thing that she can do for him right now is to enjoy him: tell him what she likes, loves, or appreciates in him and remove the part of the communication in which she tries to help him.

Knowing when to stop acting like a parent is not always so obvious or easy. Here's a clue: *if your kid is out of the house and your advice always leads to conflict, it's time to keep your wisdom to yourself.*

If you have a low-achieving teen or adult:

Strive to avoid:

- Making all or most of your interactions about grades, college, or career.

- Expressing a lot of worry or "concern," especially if your child is clearly turned off by it.

- Being a micromanager. Some kids have to fall down a lot more than others before they find their way.

- Criticizing your child's lack of ambition, motivation or follow-through. Once children become teens, your role becomes more consultant than manager. Once they become adults, your best influence is their feeling of trust and affection for you.

Strive to:

- Get consultations from professionals to get reassurance that you're doing everything you can to be a good parent. This will help insulate you from later accusations from yourself or your child that you didn't do enough to help her launch an adult life.

- Enjoy the wonderful qualities in your child that have absolutely nothing to do with colleges or careers.

- Ask your grown child what he or she needs from you before providing it.

A DEPRESSED PARENT RAISING A HIGHLY ACTIVE CHILD

Some children's motors are set to rev at an rpm much faster than other children's. Hyperactive children, or simply children who are active without the "hyper" part, demand a level of parental involvement that can strain the relationship if the parent isn't up to the task.

Studies show that ongoing depression in a parent can cause problems in the children. Children require a certain degree of attunement in order to develop identity and self-esteem. Parents who are burdened, preoccupied, or withdrawn are less able to attune to the child than those who are more energetic and emotionally available. As one mother said, "I just never had enough energy for Carl and I know he took it personally. He used to get so mad at me, maybe because I couldn't give him very much, maybe because he felt sorry for me, I don't know. I spent so much of his childhood in bed with the curtains closed. I couldn't have been much of a mother to him. My daughter was so easy, you could set her in a corner with a book and she'd sit there and read all day. Not Carl, though. When he was young, he was always tugging at me, breaking things by being so clumsy, making noise, I nearly had a nervous breakdown trying to keep him quiet. Once I began taking antidepressants, I felt a lot better, but maybe the damage was done by then. Since he moved out, he always seems to be in a hurry to get off the phone whenever I call."

If you're a parent with active children and you suffer from depression:

Strive to avoid:

- Making your children feel as though they are a burden to you. If you believe that you have communicated that to them in the past, make amends by letting them know that you regret it. Say something like, "I'm sorry I have been so impatient (unavailable, tired, withdrawn, and so on). You were just being a normal kid and I just didn't have the wherewithal to give you what you needed. I was depressed at the time and I'm now getting help for that." Make these statements from a position of self-love, not self-hate. The subtext is, "I'm a good person who wasn't able to do any differently given where I was in my life at that moment," not, "I'm a terrible person and deserving of hatred and contempt for not giving you what you needed."

- Putting your children in the role of caretaker of you.

- Making them feel guilty about being independent or having a better life than you.

- Blaming them for how bad you feel. It's common for depressed parents to experience their emotions as being caused by their children's behavior.

Strive to:

- Get a lot of support. There is now ample research showing that a combination of antidepressant medication and psychotherapy is very effective in the treatment of depression.

- Let your children know that you don't need them to take care of you.

- Communicate that your depression isn't their fault.

- Get a consultation with a pediatrician or psychiatrist for your child's hyperactivity.

OUTSIDE INFLUENCES

There are many social forces that can create a rent in the relationship between parent and child. Financial stress and worry make it more difficult for parents to be as involved or sympathetic to their children's needs. Long work hours, low pay, and insecure working conditions have been found to greatly increase the likelihood that parents will be inconsistent, harsh, or explosive with their children, a tragic fact that may come back to haunt the parent years later.

In such situations, mismatches or normal difficulties in children may become exaggerated as the parent tries to eradicate any behavior that increases their feeling stressed, overwhelmed, or inadequate. Or, as historian Stephanie Coontz writes, they may see their children's resistance " ... as yet another challenge to their authority and self-esteem which are already threatened by economic setbacks which have nothing to do with the kids." In addition, economic insecurity can make children feel less secure, less motivated, and less certain of their future, forces that also increase the tension between parent and child. Financial worries and inconsistent work schedules can create marital conflict and increase the likelihood of divorce. Men often respond to extended marital conflict by withdrawing from their children, particularly from their daughters.

EXTENSIONS OF OURSELVES

We often see our children as extensions of ourselves. This is why we're more vulnerable to feeling shamed by their failures and proud of their successes. It can also cause us to hate in our child what we hate or fear in ourselves. A mother who has repressed her own healthy feelings of aggressiveness may feel very uncomfortable when her daughter is assertive or appropriately angry. A man who was raised to believe that sex is dirty may react harshly to his children's taking pleasure in running around the house naked, or innocently touching themselves. Women who have been molested may feel uncomfortable when they see their infant sons' erections because of the memories it evokes. While some parents may experience pride at watching their children achieving what they never could, others may feel jealous, and respond with criticism or withdrawal.

Each stage of children's development poses a different challenge to a parent. A parent who is overly sensitive may do well when his or her child is young and dependent, and poorly when the child begins to individuate. In the same way, an authoritarian parent may do far better when the child is young and compliant than when he begins to be old enough to defy the parent. Parents who feel burdened by dependency, or afraid of their own, may be far less interested in their children when they're infants and toddlers, yet take great pleasure when they're old enough to engage in a more equal way.

In addition, some children come into the world gifted with the ability to read their parents' expressions. This may affect how rewarding the parenting is, and how successfully the child gets what she needs. For example, a child who can tell when she's close to chewing through mom's last thread of restraint is going to fare better with her and be more liked by her than a child who, willy-nilly, wanders into the bear trap of her exhausted irritability with one more request.

DIFFERENCES BETWEEN PARENTS

Parents often have very different ideas about how to best respond to a difficult child. These differences can create a negative feedback loop in the household that circulates tension and conflict from child to parent, then parent to parent, and then back to the child. It is not uncommon for a mother to err on the side of being empathic, and for the father to tighten the screws on the child's demanding behavior. In addition, a child may be mismatched with one parent's temperament and well matched with the other. These differences are not only trying for the parent/child relationship, but for the parents' relationship as a couple.

Robert and Rhonda was such a couple. They consulted me when their daughter Lori was turning sixteen. Lori was much as I imagined her mother at her age: burdened with anxiety, socially awkward, overly sensitive, and very, very bright. Robert was loud and gregarious, with a harsh and cutting sense of humor. This couple couldn't have been more different, and these differences, were reflected in their attitudes about how to best deal with Lori's social anxiety. Robert was against therapy and medication, thought Lori would outgrow her problems, and believed that her mother spent "too much time thinking and talking about it for anyone's good." Rhonda thought therapy and medication were both useful and necessary for Lori, since she herself was in therapy and had experienced a lessening of her anxiety with medication. Like many couples with very different outlooks, they became caricatures of their positions, unable to see or discuss what was useful or valuable in the other's view. Their disparities created a constant source of tension in the household that increased Lori's anxiety and feelings of worthlessness.

While parents often have different ideas about how to best raise their children, kids with demanding temperaments increase the likelihood of tension in a marriage because they exact so much from the parents. Each person's instincts about what is required to be a good parent is shaped by their own parenting attitudes as authoritarian, permissive, or authoritative. Their instincts are also shaped by their desire to repeat their own parents' philosophies of parenting, or to correct them; their own temperamental inclinations; and their current level of stress.

Dissimilarities in parenting attitudes are sometimes the most damaging in divorce, where disparities can be acted out in the nonstop drama of "Who's the Good Parent?" This was true for Jonathan, a teenager I saw for several years in my practice whose parents were divorced. Jonathan was burdened by his mother's constant belittling of his father's strict approach to parenting, and his father's consistent criticism of his mother as "coddling him" with her sympathy over his low academic achievement and depression. The parents' inability to manage their differences in a cooperative fashion trapped Jonathan in a loyalty battle, unable to use what was valuable in each parent's perspective.

While it's far more complicated in divorce, different ideas about parenting can be addressed with the following guidelines:

Strive to avoid:

- *Power struggles.* The high stakes of raising children can cause debates on this topic to become quickly inflamed. Once inflamed, couples get more concerned about proving their points than dispassionately listening to see if there is something useful about a partner's position.

- *Moralizing.* Conversations about parenting differences can quickly deteriorate into right vs. wrong. "*Everyone* knows that the best way to parent is ..."

- *Character assassination of your spouse.* It's common for couples to use parenting differences as "proof" of the other's defectiveness. "You're so easily intimidated. That's why he feels like he can do whatever he wants! You refuse to set any limits. No wonder people feel like they can walk all over you!" "Oh yeah? You think the solution to everything in life is punishment. No wonder your best friend stopped calling you!"

- *Blaming the child for your marital conflicts.* Difficult children can increase the likelihood of marital tension. However, it's our responsibility as parents to find a successful resolution to these conflicts without blaming our children for them. Getting a difficult child is one of the many possible outcomes when we role the dice to become parents.

Strive to:

- *Assume good intentions on the other parent's part.* In all likelihood, your partner wants what's best for your child in the same way that you do.

- *Find the kernel of truth in your partner's perspective.* There are many paths to being a good parent. Reflect and honor that kernel of truth as both worthwhile and valuable.

- *Speak to that person's values with respect.* For example, "I know and respect your belief that we should spend more time talking with our kids about their behavior before setting a limit. I don't always agree with doing that, but I can see what's valuable in it."

- *Agree to try a parenting method for a set period of time, such as three to six months, and observe what happens.* Then try the other parent's method for three to six months. Make an honest evaluation of what worked and what didn't work in each approach.

"Mismatches" Questionnaire:
How are you and your child different?

Circle all the items that apply.

- He/she is far more aggressive/assertive.

- He/she is far more sensitive/compliant.

- He/she is much less driven.

- He/she is much more driven.

- He/she is much more athletic.

- He/she is much less athletic.

- He/she has a much harder time with academics.

- He/she has a much easier time with academics.

- He/she is far more confident.

- He/she is far less confident.

- _____

- _____

Exercise #1:
Finding the Strengths in Their Behavior

On a separate piece of paper, write out all of the behaviors that you find troublesome, worrisome, or irritating in your child. How do these differences interfere with your relationship? Mismatches often create disapproval and disappointment in parents. If you communicate disapproval, make a list of what you value and appreciate in your child. These may be the same behaviors that you find exasperating. For example, you may dislike your child's aggressiveness, but also admire her fearlessness. You may feel burdened by your child's oversensitivity, but admire the way that this sensitivity reveals insights about the world that you might not have seen. You might dislike your child's seeming lack of ambition, but admire her ability to be relaxed and carefree.

Bearing these concepts in mind, write a few paragraphs about your child's strengths and assets. Commit to communicating your admiration of these on a regular basis. If you're voicing a complaint about your child's behavior, try to lead with what you like about it. This is good parenting, but it will also help you to not feel wounded with guilt and regret.

For example, "I really like that you're able to just enjoy life and have fun. I admire that and believe that it's key to a happy and successful life. I'm wondering if there's some way I can be more helpful around your academic life because it seems like you're starting to fail in school and we don't want that to happen."

Exercise #2:
What Do Your Feelings Reveal about You?

Consider what you can learn from the ways that your child is different from you. For example, what does your impatience, irritability, or contempt reveal about what you need to work on in yourself? How is this conflict a gift that you can use in other parts of your life, such as learning how to be more empathic, compassionate, or forgiving of yourself or others? Spend fifteen minutes writing about the ways that you can grow from this experience. One mother put it in the following way: "The surprising and wonderful gift about learning these skills is that they don't stop with the family. I got to take this new approach of 'owning my part' and taking my more realistic expectations into the workplace and out into the world. I didn't realize it until I started teaching. I now see what's right, beautiful, and potentially fabulous about a student's essay rather than what's wrong or messy. Also, my boundaries about acceptable behavior are clearer. I refuse to allow any abuse of me, or others. And what I used to be angry about is now the basis for my 'funny' stories. The 'work' I did with my own three kids has now blessed me with a new career and sixty wonderful kids."

Feeling mismatched with a child can create endless opportunities for conflict and misunderstanding. Work to be forgiving of yourself for whatever mistakes that you have made with your child, and to forgive your child for the mistakes that were made with you. Try to see the emotions that get stirred up as an opportunity for growth. And speaking of endless opportunities for growth, let's look at teenagers and their effect on how parents feel about themselves.

EIGHT

TAKING IT PERSONALLY

*How Teenagers Take a Pound of Flesh—
and What We Can Do About It*

Joann, a school counselor, had no idea that her fifteen-year-old daughter, Barbara, had been cutting herself until she surprised her one day coming out of the shower. When she saw the dozen horizontal red marks climbing up the underside of Barbara's forearm, she immediately burst into tears. "Honey!" she cried, grabbing her daughter's arm "What is going on? Why have you been doing this?"

"It's nothing. It's not a big deal," her daughter said, staring angrily at the ceiling.

"It's not a big deal? Cutting yourself isn't a big deal?" Her mother sat down against the door, both to keep from fainting and to prevent her daughter from walking out. "I had no idea you were cutting yourself."

"Oh, *big* surprise you didn't know I was doing something," Barbara said. "You never would have found out if you hadn't waited to surprise me coming out of the shower. It's not like you and Dad ever ask about what I'm doing or what I'm going through. I could be getting Fs and you guys wouldn't even know because you never ask."

"We've never had to ask because you've never gotten an F in your life! Have you been failing your classes? Is that what this is about?"

"I cannot believe how lame you are!" Barbara shouted, wresting her wrist out of her mother's grasp and standing naked above her. "No, Mom, don't you worry. You're little straight-A student is still getting the grades, since that's all you and Dad ever care about. Did you ever once think that I have things going on in my life other than making you and dad look good? I can't believe you! I have to go." She pushed her mother aside and ran out of the room.

Joann was too stunned to get up. Her daughter had always been quiet and serious. She never dreamed that she was in such turmoil. "Oh my God," she thought through her tears. "What the hell is going on with my daughter? How could this have happened? What have I done wrong?"

It's no secret that adolescence is a turbulent time. Rapid changes in a child's physical development coupled with behavioral and emotional changes can cause the most confident parent to feel threatened or insecure. A percentage of children who had appeared well adjusted or were suffering from minor problems are suddenly cutting themselves, becoming addicted to substances, failing in school, isolating themselves socially, or showing severe mood instability.

There is evidence that adolescents today may be experiencing a greater amount of stress than prior generations. Depression is now ten times more prevalent than it was in 1960. The age of onset for depression is also drastically younger: just forty years ago, the age when depression commonly made its first appearance was 29.5 years—today it's 14.5.

The average age of puberty for girls is also getting younger and younger. In 1820 girls entered puberty at 16, in 1900 it was 14, and in 1940, 13. Today it's 12. At the same time that the age of entry into puberty gets younger and younger, the sexualized content of the media becomes more and more a part of daily programming.

This chapter is written to help you manage both the stresses caused by the normal and the abnormal behavior of teenagers.

"Parenting Teens" Questionnaire

Circle the statements that most closely mirror your experience parenting a teenager:

- It's been hard on my self-esteem.

- I worry when my teen isn't home.

- My mood swings with my teen's mood swings.

- I overreact to him.

- I say or do things that I later regret.

- I worry that I'm not firm enough, or allow myself to be bullied and manipulated.

- I feel like a failure as a parent.

- I worry my teen won't be able to transition into adulthood.

- I feel like I'm always on my teen's case, and it's ruining my relationship with her.

What are your biggest concerns about adolescence?

- Drugs and/or alcohol

- Sex

- Getting involved with a bad crowd

- Not having friends, dating, or fitting in

- Dealing with my teen's feelings of anger, sadness, fear, or anxiety

- Knowing the best way to set limits

- Poor grades

- My teen's distance from me and/or the other parent

TEEN LIVING

If you think it's hard to live with a teenager, try being one. Okay, you were once—I knew that. But you probably forgot how much stress teenagers experience on a daily basis. Think back on the social aspects of your own adolescence: How many seconds does it take you to come up with an incident where you felt completely shamed or humiliated? How often did you have significant doubts about your attractiveness, appeal, or ability to be liked by others? How frequently did you worry about your intelligence, athleticism, or creativity?

Now consider drugs and alcohol, the topics that strike fear into so many parents' hearts. How many stupid, careless, irresponsible things did you do? None? Consider yourself atypical. Most people who are raising teenagers feel like saying, "Do as I say, not as I did."

You probably tried a lot of different behaviors because adolescence is a period of great experimentation. Why? Because they're trying to figure out who the hell they are. It's part of what makes being a parent of a teenager so scary; they need to experiment with a host of styles, actions, and attitudes in order to find out what they like and what they don't. Knowing who you are is only gained through a process of ongoing trial and error, success and failure, pride and humiliation.

Most teens feel a sense of desperation about being included in their social group, hanging out at parties, and spending time with their friends. The intensity of longing to be seen, validated, in-

cluded, and liked creates a high-stakes, winner-takes-all approach
to their negotiations with their parents. In a low-key adolescent,
these interactions can be trying, though not debilitating. In situations with a high-risk teen or with a teen that is able to intimidate
or manipulate, these dealings can sour the relationship between
the parent and teen, leaving both feeling hurt, misunderstood,
and hopeless.

Many of these troubling dynamics begin as a result of the teen
innocently trying to define his or her own limits. As Mark Twain
said, "Good judgment comes from experience, and experience
comes from bad judgment." Being defiant, breaking rules, and
doing the precise behavior that will cause your parents to get angry
or upset are all potentially useful in learning that you're different
from your parents, that you can tolerate their disapproval and still
survive (well . . .), and that there are consequences to your actions.

THE WOUNDS OF INDIVIDUATION

At the time of this writing, one of my teens has just walked into
the house after being at his friend's house all day. He called upstairs to let us know that he was home and then headed straight
to his room. Frankly, I feel disappointed. I haven't seen him all
day and was hoping he'd come upstairs and want to hang out. Of
course, I could go down to his room, and—depending on his
mood—engage him in some form of interaction with greater or
lesser success, contingent on his energy, his blood sugar level, or
the injunctions of his testosterone. But I confess to feeling a bit
hurt that his first thought upon coming home isn't to come upstairs and want to spend time with me.

Welcome to adolescence. I am no longer the center of my son's
universe, and if things go the way they're supposed to, I will grow
increasingly less like the sun, providing light and sustenance, and
more like the moon, drifting in and out of view—my influence
more tidal than anything else.

Adolescence heralds the beginning of a slow but steady reversal in the balance of desires of who wants to spend time with whom. Misunderstanding or mismanaging this rotation in desire can cause long-term problems in the parent-child relationship. Some parents cope with their subtle or overt feelings of rejection by withdrawing or rejecting back; or they mistake the lessening of their influence to mean that they no longer have *any* influence. Other parents try to support their teenager's independence by backing so far away from the relationship that the teen is left with too much responsibility to fend for himself.

It may be helpful to know that despite an almost aggressive refutation of our ideals, values, and identities, teenagers typically emerge from adolescence with values and ideals much like our own. In other words, just because your teenager acts as if he thinks you and your ideas are "lame," that doesn't mean that he won't one day embrace those lame ideas as his.

SOPHISTICATED COMBATANTS

Many parents feel wounded by their teens because they seem so determined in their efforts to separate and so precise in their attacks. As one mother said, "Everything about me has suddenly become the object of inspection and contempt from my teenager; the way I laugh, how I talk, the way I eat, the way my arms jiggle. I feel like I'm living under a microscope—and a very unsympathetic one at that!"

This is mild compared to what some parents experience. As children enter adolescence, their ability to correctly perceive our many inadequacies becomes more and more refined. So does their ability to pinpoint where we have the greatest anxiety and insecurity. "My sixteen-year-old sat me down the other night," said one dad, "and told me in great detail all of the reasons why it was my fault that his mother left me. Just right down the line, like a surgeon cutting through flesh, except without any anesthesia: 'You're a self-centered person; you always come first no matter what. You put your job above everything, no matter what anyone else needs. You never ask anyone about what's happening in their lives. You never told mom that you loved her, and you never tell me or Hannah (his sister) that you love us.' I was speechless because frankly, he's right. I didn't know whether to smack him or sob."

THE NEED FOR LIMITS

It is neither in the teen's nor the parent's best interest for the parent to give her free rein or run her life like a prison warden. Since limit-setting is often a point of confusion for parents, I'd like to review some of the essentials.

CHOOSING CONSEQUENCES

Many parents get stymied about how to choose a consequence and how long to enforce the limit. There are a variety of consequences from which to choose. They are: money, phone, freedom, computer, car, trust without checking up, and shopping. I'm sure you have your own list of consequences, so by all means use those too.

In psychologist Scott Sells's book, *Parenting Your Out-of-Control Teenager*, Sells discusses ways for parents to regain stability in the home when a teenager has lost control, or when the parents have lost control of the teen. Sells recommends that parents write out a contract, with their teen's input, about the rewards and punishments for breaking the rules. The actions that constitute respectful or disrespectful behavior vary from home to home. My definition of what is respectful behavior is somewhat looser than what my parents considered respectful. What's important is that I know, and my teenagers know, where the line is—and they know what the consequences are of crossing it.

It's important that you and your teen also know exactly where that line is, and what the consequences are for crossing it. If disrespect is an issue in your home, you should write out a contract, with your teen's participation, that says something like the following: "Disrespectful behavior is defined as rolling your eyes, mimicking me or others in the family, rude gestures, swearing, and refusing to do what's asked of you the first time. If you behave in a way that respects other people in the ways that have been clearly defined, you will have access to the car on the weekends, an allowance of $10 a week, and (*fill in your own reward here*). If you break the rule, you will have the following consequence: (choose something that will work, such as *no use of the car for the weekend, no allowance for that week, no cell phone for that week*, or *grounding*. Grounding means no TV, phone, computer, or visitors. Reading is okay.). Each consequence should have contingencies. For example, "If you break the rule again within the week you will also be grounded Saturday day and night. A third incident will ground you for the whole weekend."

LOVE AND LIMITS

The most effective strategies with teenagers combine a mixture of love and limits. One of the ways that you can show love for your teen is to enlist her help in setting up the contracts. Ask for her input about what would be motivating. Also ask how you could be different to make her behave better.

The behavior of your teen is often more about wanting to get something than wanting to injure you. This is often difficult to see in the moment, because their goal is to wear you down, throw you off, or get you so mad that you give up in frustration and exasperation. From their perspective, they have little negotiating power and have to use whatever is at their disposal. As Sells writes, "Any time you say to yourself, 'my child is doing this to me,' you are taking button-pushing as a personal attack. If this happens, you will become hurt and lose control of your emotions. Over time, you may lose the ability to show tenderness because you will feel so wounded and angry that it poisons your entire relationship."

TAKE A TIME-OUT

But how is one supposed to productively respond to a teenager's ambushes, verbal assaults, aggressive humiliations, and flurries of derision?

If you sense that an interaction is teetering on the verge of being unproductive, take a break. Say something like the following: "I really don't like where this is going, so I think we should take a time-out and come back to this when we both feel more calm." If your teen won't exit, then you should exit. This is good role modeling and it shows that you care enough to end an unproductive interaction.

If your teen has broken a limit, such as treating you with disrespect, then you should say, "You just broke the contract on respect, we'll discuss the consequences later," then walk away to prevent escalation. Once you're both calm, you approach your teen and say, "You broke the contract we have about speaking with respect, so, as you know, you won't get the car this weekend." Do not let the conversation go off-track here into a litany of how unfair or cruel you are. Stay calm and stick to your limit.

ALCOHOL AND DRUGS

A teenager's experimentation with alcohol and/or drugs is a source of conflict in many homes. While experimentation is not desirable, it is not unusual and doesn't necessarily indicate the presence of more serious problems. However, use that is more than casual has to be taken seriously. Part of our role as parents is to put safeguards in place so that recreational use doesn't turn into full-blown addiction.

It's a good idea to give your teens the opportunity to talk to you about their drug and alcohol use. In order for this to happen, you should let them know that you'd like to have a conversation about it, and that there won't be any consequences for being honest about anything that has occurred in the past. During this conversation, ask them when was the last time they used or drank (ask "when" not "if." Open-ended questions with teens are much more likely to provide you with more information). If your teenagers tell you about their use, thank them for their honesty. Let them know that there are no consequences whatsoever for anything that has happened in the past, but there will be consequences going forward if you have reason to be concerned.

If you have strong suspicions, or you have reasonable cause to be worried, you should let your teen know that you reserve the right to ask him or her to submit to random drug or alcohol screening. You should say that if he tests negative, you will apologize and trust will be restored and deepened. If he tests dirty, the consequences will be grave. This is especially true if there is any evidence of driving under the influence. You can let him or her know that consequences can be lessened if he or she admits to using before the screening. (Drug tests can be purchased at most local pharmacies and alcohol testing kits can be purchased online.) While these tactics may seem severe, the value of drug or alcohol testing for an at-risk teen is that it gets you out of the role of second-guessing or sneaking around playing detective.

PARENT AS CONSULTANT

Adolescent expert Mike Riera, Ph.D., observes that one of the key tasks in parenting teenagers is to move from a role as manager to one as consultant. Another way to think of this is that parenting is a task of giving more and more of the reins to your child until you actually hand him the reins.

Difficult teenagers or temperamental mismatches between parent and teen can cause parents to either be overly intrusive or overly restrained in their parenting. In the former case, the parent doesn't give the teen enough room to make mistakes and learn from them. For example, Gerry was a seventeen-year-old junior at a public high school in San Francisco. His parents consulted with me because they were concerned about his attending parties and getting involved with drugs and alcohol. As a result, they refused to let him go to any of his friends' parties and maintained a weekend curfew of 10:30 p.m.

In my interview with Gerry, I learned that he was a B+ student, well-liked by his peers, and a moderately serious sax player. He admitted to occasionally drinking with his friends, but said his use was recreational, and not so different from that of his friends. (Of course, teenagers always say that their drug or alcohol use isn't any different from that of their friends because people tend to flock to those with similar habits.)

My job as a psychologist is to make an assessment based on the parents' perceptions of their adolescent, the teen's self-assessment, and the available evidence of the teen's ability to achieve academically, manage a social life, demonstrate adequate social adjustment, and maintain outside interests. Based on all of these, Gerry looked pretty well-adjusted to me.

Because Gerry's mother had an alcoholic father, she was terrified that Gerry was going to develop a drug or alcohol problem, and that it would ruin his life in much the same way that it had ruined her father's. This wasn't a baseless worry, since addictions have a genetic component. However, the limits set by Gerry's mother were inappropriate for a well-functioning seventeen-year-old and were creating a large rift in their relationship that didn't need to be there.

I encouraged the parents to say something like the following: "We know that you're a very responsible kid and that you're doing well in the rest of your life, so we've decided to start giving you more freedom on the weekends and a later curfew. As you know, your grandfather is a serious alcoholic, so we have some worries about your drinking since you may carry the genes that put you more at risk. We know that there are drugs and alcohol at parties and, even if it isn't a problem now, it could still become a problem later on. But you're at an age where you have to start making some of these decisions for yourself, so we hope you'll use good judgment. Obviously, if we have any sense that you're abusing drugs or alcohol, we will have a very different conversation. We reserve the right to do a drug or alcohol test if we have any reason to be concerned that this is becoming a problem. If there is a problem, we will have you get treatment, and we'll have to go back to the more restrictive curfew." Gerry responded very positively to their position, and, as a result, felt closer to and more respected by his parents.

This was a very different situation from another teen I worked with, Mark, also a seventeen-year-old. Mark's school counselor referred him to me after he went from being a straight-A student to a D student over the course of two semesters. According to the school, his problems appeared to develop once he started dating Dionna, a sophomore at a neighboring Catholic girls' school. Dionna was everything that Mark had always wanted to be, but couldn't allow himself: rebellious, outspoken, and adventurous. Dionna had been abused by her parents and was drawn to Mark's quiet kindness and sincerity. When Dionna asked Mark if he wanted to get drunk with her, he was alarmed, having abstained from any drug or alcohol experimentation to that point. Dionna teased him about being a "puritan" and he relented.

Mark found that he loved the confidence and power that he felt when he was drunk, especially with Dionna. However, he quickly became addicted to alcohol and began the downhill slide that eventually brought him to my office. After doing an assessment, I met with his parents and told them, with Mark's permission, that their son had a serious drinking problem, and that they should (a) monitor him more closely, (b) consider a treatment program, and (c) establish consequences for his drinking.

They refused! Both parents had used a lot of drugs and alcohol in their lives, and still smoked pot regularly. They said that I was overreacting to his "experimenting" with alcohol. When I pointed out that his grades were falling and that the school counselor had heard from his friends that he had a problem, they said that schools put too much pressure on kids to succeed, and he probably needed the relaxation that he got from partying. I told the parents that I wouldn't take on their case unless they were going to treat his alcohol use more aggressively. While Mark denied that he had a drinking problem, the quantity, frequency, and related behavior changes made it clear that he was in trouble. Nonetheless, they stopped the therapy.

I cite this case because, years later, I got a call from Mark when he was in his mid-20s. He called to thank me for taking the stand that I did, and said that he had been in recovery for the past several years and was doing well. Because of his parents' passivity, he continued his decline over the next year after I saw him, resulting in his dropping out of his private high school, and then getting a GED. He later went to college and was now employed, and considering law school. He hasn't had much contact with his parents and carries some anger at their failure to protect him more from the self-destructive slide that he was on.

Mark's parents were so worried about alienating him, and so over-identified with his drug use, that they failed to take the kind of stand they needed to in order to protect him from his self-sabotaging behavior. This later caused them to be hurt when he withdrew from them. Mark's case illustrates the wounds that can be incurred as a result of being too inactive and permissive when parenting teens.

FOUR COMMON MISTAKES AROUND SETTING LIMITS

Well-meaning parents exhibit a number of behaviors that allow their teens to persist in acting out. One of these is to make threats and not follow through. This is a big error in judgment: Your teenager is like a running back looking for any hole in the defense. If you don't consistently follow through, you're sending a message that your consequences don't carry any weight.

Another common mistake is to give a limit that is so extreme that it's (a) counter-productive, (b) punishes the parent, or (c) is impossible to enforce. An example is when parents ground a teen for several months at a time.

A third mistake is to constantly give in. This reinforces manipulation and out-of-control behavior.

A fourth mistake is to react differently at different times to the same behavior. An example: when disrespectful behavior is tolerated on one occasion, and severely punished the next.

VIOLENT TEENS

Parents sometimes have a hard time knowing which behavior to address first in a teenager who is defying limits or acting in an out-of-control manner. Behaviors that put you or your teen at risk have to be prioritized over all other behaviors. Therefore, if your child is threatening suicide, threatening you or anyone in the family with violence, setting fires, or is out of control with drug or alcohol use, you must act immediately to protect his or her well-being and the well-being of your family.

A recent study found that teen violence towards parents is on the rise. Currently, more teenagers abuse a household member than rob, deal drugs, or violently assault strangers. This is true despite criminal behavior of teens falling to its lowest level since the 1980s. The government-supported National Family Violence Survey estimated that 900,000 children abuse their parents, and that one in ten hits their parent at some point in their lives. This is believed to occur in roughly 18 percent of two-parent homes and in 30 percent of single-parent homes. While juvenile crime typically appears with greater frequency in urban or poor families, teen violence toward parents occurs in middle- and upper-class homes as well.

How should you respond to your violent teen? There should be absolute and iron-clad rules about hitting, threatening to hit, or the destruction of property. If there has been violence in the past, it is critical for your safety, the safety of the other members of your family, and the well-being of your teen to have a contract that says: "If there is violence or the threat of violence in this household, the police will be called and you will be arrested." Sound extreme? Not as extreme as allowing a teen be abusive to others and teaching him or her that there are no consequences.

WHY IS MY TEEN VIOLENT?

There are a number of reasons why teenagers abuse their parents or threaten them:

- Parental abuse of the teen

- Alcohol or drug addiction of the teen

- Alcohol or drug addiction of the parent

- Overly punitive or restrictive parenting style

- Absence of love in the home

- Difficult divorce/stepfamily problems

If your teen has been out of control for a long time, it's unlikely that you'll feel very motivated to be loving. You may have to first get the house under control before your more tender feelings return. However, there are low-emotional-cost behaviors that you can begin to do right away—behaviors that are crucial to helping your teen and your relationship with him or her.

One of the most powerful pieces of parenting advice I know for children of *all* ages is to *catch your child doing something right*. Many parents give up on this behavior as their children get older, or give up out of exasperation when their children become out-of-control teenagers. If you have given up, that's understandable, but now we have to help you to get back up on the horse.

Here are some easy ways to express love:

- Tell your teen something that you like, love, or value in him or her on a daily basis.

- Leave notes of appreciation for anything he or she did that is remotely in the right direction. Your teen will act like you're crazy, but keep doing it anyway.

- Be sure to continue to leave notes of appreciation or words of praise, even if your child hasn't yet gotten control of his behavior. Why? Because he'll respect your ability to try to be positive in the face of his being negative. It will also make him feel more guilty about defying or mistreating you.

- Use the 5:1 ratio: for every negative exchange, try to have 5 positive exchanges.

PARENTING BY GUILT

Causing your teen to feel guilt is one of the tools in your parenting arsenal. When properly applied, it may help her to develop an awareness of her impact on others and the costs that are incurred by bad behavior. Improperly applied, it can lower self-esteem, increase resentment, and increase acting out. One of the complaints

I hear most often from my adolescent and adult clients has to do with the way their parents make or made them feel guilty. The heavy-handed use of guilt may cause a teen or adult child to reject that parent, or distance themselves in order to make sure that that parent doesn't cause them to feel badly about themselves.

Common Parental Guilt Trips of Teenagers

- You don't care about anyone but yourself.

- You're never going to get anywhere in life because you never apply yourself.

- You don't care about me.

- You're so lazy.

Recommended Substitutions for the Common Parental Guilt Trips of Teens

Instead of saying,

"You don't care about me."

Say,

"I miss spending time with you. Let's find a time when I can take you out to lunch" (or whatever it is that they like to do that you can do together). In all likelihood, your teen misses spending time with you too, especially if you were once close.

Instead of saying,

"You're never going to get anywhere in life because you never apply yourself."

Say,

"I'm concerned that you're not putting in the kind of effort that you need to in order to succeed. I want to spend some time talking with you about that. What are your ideas about why you're not trying harder?" This question isn't just lip service. Many teens will open up to their parents as they learn that they're really going to listen without judgment.

Instead of saying,

"You don't care about anyone but yourself!"

Say,

"When you treat me like that, it makes me not want to do things for you that I actually like doing (or " … that I don't mind doing)."

REPAIR IT WHEN YOU BLOW IT

If you realize that you laid a big guilt trip on your teen, or said something that you know was wrong, go back and repair it. The chance of your saying something really stupid is fairly high if you have a teenager who is constantly trying to wear you down or belittle you. For example, I was about ten minutes into a loud argument with my teenage son that started after he began deriding me over how long it was taking me to learn a Bach prelude on piano. I countered by telling him that it was, perhaps, a bit more challenging than learning "Stairway to Heaven," as he was engaged in on guitar.

Okay, everybody knows that the prelude is harder and that I'm right and he's wrong. However, I got pulled in by his contempt and the tone of his voice. A mature me would have said, "Well, son, I think we may have to disagree on that."

Or, better,

"Do you think 'Stairway to Heaven' is harder? How come? Interesting."

I can be an impatient parent and, as a result, the most mature response isn't always the first out of my mouth—maybe the third or fourth. So, I later apologized for overreacting and told him that any idiot knows that Bach can kick Jimmy Page's ass all around the neighborhood, any day of the week, sunrise to sundown, so give me a friggin' break—when you know as much as I do, then you'll see that I'm right.

I mean,

I said that it really didn't matter who was right or wrong and he was entitled to his opinion without my behaving like I was the same age and level of immaturity as he.

Wait,

I said he may well be right: Led Zeppelin is probably to rock what Bach is to classical.

There. Third time the charm.

NOTE: Parenting is a lot like marriage—conflict is unavoidable, so what happens after a fight is sometimes more important than the fight itself. So, if and when you have said something hurtful, or just plain dumb, take responsibility and apologize. Your teen will respect you for it, it's good role modeling, and it makes for the possibility of a better relationship.

WHAT'S NORMAL TEENAGE BEHAVIOR?

Because adolescence can be characterized by mood swings, behavior changes, and personality changes, it may be difficult to know what is normal and what is worrisome. The following guidelines are provided to help you in this effort.

*You Should Consider Consultation with
a Professional If You See:*

- A sudden decrease in academic performance

- Ongoing social isolation

- Ongoing symptoms of depression or anxiety such as inability to experience pleasure, lack of appetite, disavowal of usual interests

- Significant weight loss or gain

- Changes in sleep patterns

- Marked changes in self-esteem

- Ongoing self-disparaging thoughts

- Consistently pessimistic outlook about the future

- Apathy

You Must Get a Consultation with a Professional If You See:

- Frequent inability to control behavior

- An arrest for driving under the influence

- Incursions with the law

- Expression of suicidal thoughts or suicidal actions

- Cutting or any other kind of self-harming behavior

- Violent or threatening behavior to you or other members of the family

- Malicious destruction of property

TEENAGERS IN DIVORCE

Divorce can make parenting of teens especially challenging. Teens are better able to withhold information from one parent in order to form an alliance with the other parent, or to avoid punishment. They may disclose important details about their lives to one parent and extract a promise that they not reveal it to the other. In addition, teenagers typically have greater legal freedom to choose where they'll live and may move in with the more lenient parent. This arrangement may put the teen at greater risk, and may increase the alienation between the teen and the other parent.

While being a single parent at any age is stressful, single-parenting teenagers is especially challenging. Teenagers are inclined to use whatever behavior they know to get their way, and single parents may be more likely to give up or give in out of frustration and exhaustion without another parent to provide backup, support, or relief. Because of the potential for the relationship between parents and teens to be negatively impacted after divorce, more specific guidance on this topic is provided in the next chapter.

THE EFFECT OF PRIOR STRESSORS ON ADOLESCENT DEVELOPMENT

Adolescence and young adulthood require large advances to be made in one's ability to navigate a more complex social world with less parental support. The stresses created during these developmental leaps may cause earlier traumas to surface. For example, Bea was abused by her psychotic mother throughout much of her childhood. While Bea appeared well adjusted in her earlier childhood, it wasn't until she encountered the social demands of dating and increased academic pressures that she began to deteriorate. As a result of this huge increase in pressure, Bea gained almost fifty pounds in the course of a year, and developed a serious depression.

There may also be a sudden development or worsening of symptoms during adolescence for genetic reasons. Some psychological illnesses such as schizophrenia, major depressive illness, or bipolar disease may not emerge until middle-to-late adolescence, and they can be triggered by ongoing marital problems and stressors outside of the family.

However, some illnesses with a genetic component can emerge in an otherwise-healthy family environment. "Jacob was never the happiest kid in the world, but he wasn't the saddest either," said Ken, the father of a schizophrenic nineteen-year-old. "When he was picked up by the police telling everyone that the CIA were after him, I assumed that he was on LSD or something. But it didn't get better, so we took him to the hospital. That's when they told us he had schizophrenia. It's been really hard on my wife and me because, supposedly, it's a lifelong condition; it's not something you mature out of. We used to feel like he'd outgrow whatever issues he had growing up, but this—this is something else entirely."

Recommendations for Parents of Teens with Addictions, Mental Illness, or Other Diagnoses

- *Join a support group for parents of children with similar diagnoses or problems*: Talking to parents with similar struggles is one of the most therapeutic experiences you can have. Giving support to others can also be profoundly healing.

- *Minimize harm*: Troubled teens invariably provoke responses from parents that exacerbate the situation. Make sure that you have educated yourself on your child's problems so that you know what is within or outside of her control. Get support in communicating productively. Work to gain control over your feelings of disappointment and anger at your teen and at yourself.

- *Grieve and accept*: Many disturbing behaviors of adolescence resolve over time; however, adolescence sometimes presages the arrival of a more permanent change in personality or behavior. Don't be so afraid of a feared outcome that you live in denial.

- *Avoid catastrophic thinking*: While a dose of feeling sorry for yourself can be useful in developing self-compassion, it may also burden your life if insufficiently balanced against the positive aspects of yourself and your life. Be sure to stay involved with people or activities that can increase your feeling cared about and hopeful. Work on the techniques of self-talk discussed throughout this book.

- *Get outside consultation*: When in doubt, see a specialist. Early intervention can sometimes decrease the severity of symptoms or the length of time that a problem exists. Ask your pediatrician or family practitioner for a referral.

- *Consider family therapy*: A troubled teen has the potential to unfairly divert resources from the healthier members of the family, and cause them to resent the parents and the teen.

- *Develop a long-term perspective*: While some problems may be chronic, others will improve over time. Reassure yourself that, either way, you will get better at coping with your feelings of sadness, fear, or disappointment.

If you have areas of vulnerability (and we all do), odds are that your teen will find them. If you take the time to know your soft spots, it will help you be less reactive to your teen's assaults over time. Knowing yourself means taking a full inventory of your relationship with your parents, your siblings, and any other significant people in your past or present. It means appreciating whatever ways that you're blessed or cursed by your inherited temperament; it also means understanding how your view of the world makes you react productively or unproductively to your teen's treatment of you.

The most important thing to work toward is finding the right balance between love and limit-setting with your teen. It won't make for a perfect household, but it will keep open the possibility of a good and loving relationship for the present and for the future.

NINE

DIVORCE WOUNDS

Healing the Parent

Dear Dr. Coleman,

I read your article about being a divorced dad, "When a Family Man Thinks Twice," in the San Francisco Chronicle. I sobbed like a baby. My wife and I split up several years ago and, since then, my daughter refuses to see me. Her mother blames me for the divorce and she buys into everything she says. My question for you is, "What can I do to get my daughter back?" I don't think I can go through the rest of my life like this.

Letter received August 2006

I wish I could say that letters like this are a rarity, but they're not. I regularly receive phone calls or e-mails in response to an article that I published in *The San Francisco Chronicle* on Father's Day, 2000, titled "When a Family Man Thinks Twice" (see appendix). The piece was loosely based on my feelings about being a divorced dad and was written late one night after coming back from hanging out with my friends and their young adult children. As on so many occasions during that era, my daughter had been invited but had refused to come. Sitting at my friend's table with their wine and appetizers, their adult kids laughing at their jokes, disagreeing with their "lame" politics, and bragging about their own stimulating, but grossly underpaying jobs filled me with envy, sorrow, and anger. *Where is my daughter and how come I have to hang out with other people's grown children and not my own?*

So, like any writer, I wrote for the solace of getting it out of me and onto the dispassionate, somewhat comforting two-dimensional world of paper and pen. This book was in many ways inspired by the letters I received in response to that article.

Children's lives sometimes improve after a divorce, especially if the divorce ends an ongoing and severe conflict in the home. In addition, divorce can provide adults with the opportunity to get out of a dysfunctional marriage, and to partner with someone with whom they share a greater sense of meaning.

However, while divorce may change things for the better, it can also change them for the worse. As marital researcher E. Mavis Hetherington writes, "Every divorce is a unique tragedy because every divorce brings an end to a unique civilization—one built on thousands of shared experiences, memories, hopes, and dreams." Divorce often means a fundamental reshaping of alliances and can place parents at risk for greater distance from their children, in part because divorce may unveil troubled dynamics that existed in the marriage but were successfully hidden from the child's experience prior to the divorce. Divorce may introduce new adults into children's lives—adults who can cause the child to feel disloyal to the parent who's not there; adults who may compete for the love, attention, and resources from the parent who is; adults who generally have less investment in the child's well-being than the biological parent.

Divorce also provides the opportunity for history to be rewritten by either of the parents. Children may be induced to believe incomplete or inaccurate narratives of how their mother or father behaved in the past. As one adult child of divorce said, "My mother used to tell me all the time how awful my father was, how he was never there for us kids, and how he didn't care about anyone but himself. I completely bought into it growing up; I just figured, she's my mom; she's not going to lie to me. I have to say, though, the older I get, the more I don't believe her version of things. I feel like she used me for her own selfish desires to get back at him. That's pretty screwed up."

Parents may also seek to justify their decision to divorce by telling their children a version of the marital history that omits important ways they contributed to its failure. One adult child said, "My father used to act like my mother destroyed him since she was the one who left. He always acted like he was the perfect husband and she was the selfish wife. My mother was really good about protecting us from the reasons why she left my father until we were grown. I have come to really respect that she waited until we were old enough to understand before giving us her side of things. I wish my dad had done the same."

Much has been written about the long-term effects of divorce on children, yet very little on helping parents repair the damage to their *own* identity and self-esteem when their day-to-day relationship with their children is profoundly and forever altered. This chapter is written to help those parents.

Divorce Questionnaire

Circle the items that apply to you.

How has your divorce affected your relationship with your child or children?

- I don't see them as much as I used to, and that causes me sorrow.

- They seem mad at me a lot and I have a hard time knowing whether it's the divorce, my ex, or just normal adolescence or adulthood.

- There are far more ups and downs in our relationship.

- I don't have as much control over their behavior as I used to.

- We're more like buddies than parent and child.

- We're closer than ever.

- _____

- _____

- _____

How has the divorce affected your feelings about yourself?

- I'm glad to be divorced, but I worry a lot about my children.

- I didn't want the divorce, and my feelings about that have affected my self-esteem, my parenting, and my relationship with my children.

- I wanted the divorce, but my guilt about how it has affected my children is a constant source of torment.

- I grieve over not being able to be a full-time parent.

- I feel bad that I don't get to be the kind of parent I always wanted to be.

- I think the divorce was a big mistake and wish I'd never gone through with it.

- I feel bad about the ways that the divorce has hurt my children's relationship with the other parent.

- _____
- _____
- _____

*What have you done to try to heal
your relationship with your child?*

- Nothing, and I'm not ready to.

- Nothing, and I don't want to.

- Nothing, and I don't need to because my relationship with my children is good.

- I've talked to my kids, but it never seems to help.

- I've talked to them and it helps, but there's a long way to go.

- I've talked to them a few times but I don't want to keep having that conversation because it's too painful.

*What do you think is your biggest obstacle
to talking with your children?*

- My anger.

- My guilt.

- My worry that it will increase my anxiety or depression.

- My fear of what they'll say.

- My partner wants me to take a more distant approach.

- If I admit to behaviors that I regret, they'll use it to make me feel even worse than I do now.

- My ex will use it against me if he or she hears of it.

- They refuse contact with me.

FATHERS AND DAUGHTERS

Studies show that a father's relationship with his daughter is the most vulnerable to disruption with a divorce. The relationship between mothers and sons is next. Why do the risks line up in this way? Children tend to see themselves as more similar to the parent with the same gender. In an obvious way, boys learn to be men by watching their fathers, and girls learn to be women by watching their mothers. This need creates a kind of gender loyalty that can cause children to ally with the same-sex parent when the family splits up. In other words, children may sense that in the decreased-resource environment of divorce, they had better side with the person who can help them the most with their need to develop an identity as a male or female.

In addition, a girl may unconsciously experience that if it's happening to mom, it's happening to her. In a healthy or low-conflict marriage, these effects may be subtle, or sufficiently in the background that a rigid alliance behind one or the other parent is unnecessary: a mother may take pride and pleasure in the way that her daughter is "daddy's little girl" and a father may enjoy the many ways that his wife ensures the well-being of his sons.

In general, mothers appear to be good at facilitating the closeness between daughters and fathers in a healthy or a low-conflict marriage, and fathers between mothers and sons. This is probably because fathers are more active and successful at reining in the more rowdy behavior that boys can exhibit with their mothers, while mothers may actively bridge the intimacy gap that can exist with daughters and their fathers.

While a maturely handled divorce may decrease the likelihood of a loyalty conflict, the ways that children's lives are divided can greatly increase the pull on children to take sides, especially if one of the parents seems invested in gaining that loyalty, sees himself or herself as the victim, or behaves in a clearly egregious fashion. It can also occur if the child, rightly or wrongly, perceives the parent as needing the child to express allegiance by criticizing or rejecting the other parent.

MOTHERS AT THE GATE

Studies show that one of the predictors of a father's relationship with his children during marriage and after a divorce is the mother's facilitation or obstruction of that relationship. Mothers who feel wronged in the marriage or divorce, who believe that the father is harmful to the children, who believe that mothers are more important than fathers, or who have psychological problems may directly or indirectly interfere with the father's desire to have an ongoing relationship with his children. As one dad put it, "Last year I got remarried to a fantastic woman. Unfortunately, this has made my ex even more resolved to keep me from my children. She has waged custody battles from the beginning and now invents new reasons why my children shouldn't come over when they're supposed to. My daughter completely buys into it and acts like I'm the bad one. She's a teenager now and the court gave her discretion over how much she sees me. Her brother is ten and always wants to see me, but even he has started asking me why I'm so mean to his mother—and I haven't done anything wrong."

Vicky, a divorced mother, talks about her anxiety over letting her children visit their father. "He does nothing to make sure that they've done their homework, eat healthy, or go to bed at a decent time. His place looks like a scene from *Animal House*; it's a pigsty! There's pizza boxes lying all around. He doesn't supervise them so they end up in front of the PlayStation all weekend. They come home to me on Monday and it takes me practically a week to get them back onto some kind of schedule before they go back there and the whole thing starts up again. I know that the kids love him, but what kind of role model is that? Lately they've been talking about not going over there as much, and I'm thinking, 'Yes!'"

MOTHERS AND SONS

Because boys can feel a greater sense of allegiance to their fathers after divorce, they may be more likely to act out on their mothers. Studies show that women's feelings of anger last longer after fighting with their sons than after fighting with their daughters. Mothers are also more likely to feel depressed when raising sons alone. This can result from feeling less temperamentally suited to handle the unruly and aggressive behavior more common to boys, and from the ways that sons might manage feeling rejected by their fathers by taking it out on their mothers. Only 25 percent of fathers see their children more than once a week after divorce, and 25 percent never see them again within a year afterward.

"My son, Bobby, blames me for the divorce, and it *was* my idea to end it. But it isn't my fault that his dad moved out of state and hardly makes any effort to see him. I feel like I get the worst of both worlds: not having another parent to share the responsibility with, and having a son who blames me for his father abandoning him."

ENTER THE STEPMOTHER

A stepmother's life is hard. Her own maternal instincts or empathic urges may be completely rebuffed by a child who experiences her as trying to replace her mother or take away her father. She may have her own powerful ideas about how children should be raised, ideas that may be in direct conflict with those of her husband or the children's mother.

A stepmother may also experience her new husband's tender relationship with his children as a threat to her relationship with him. If a stepmother and father have children together, she may feel a strong desire to give more time and money to those with whom she shares a biological tie. This preferential treatment can trigger hostility, decreased visits, or outright rejection of the father by his children. As one dad complained, "My daughter recently told me that that my wife and my stepchildren are her enemies and, therefore, I'm her enemy too, since I live with them."

For other women, parenting a stepchild may be her one opportunity to be a mom if she is unable to conceive, or if her husband doesn't want more children. In such instances, she may be highly vulnerable to her stepchildren rebuffing her overtures. Moreover, a man who believes that his new wife should embrace the maternal role may misjudge how disinterested or uncooperative his children may be in that effort.

WOUNDED STEPPARENTS

I have heard many stepparents (mostly women) talk about feeling wounded by their stepchildren. The rejecting behavior of the child, brewed from the volatile feelings of disloyalty, loss, and anger resulting from divorce, can put stepparents at the center of the conflict in ways that they have neither the experience nor the stomach for. These dynamics may explain why a very small percentage of adult daughters of divorce say that they have a close relationship with their stepmothers. As one stepmother said, "I have never been treated with such hatred and loathing by anyone before in my life. But I'm just supposed to smile through it all and act like, 'Oh well, no big deal, I can take it.'"

ENTER THE STEPFATHER

Stepfathers often have a much easier go than stepmothers. While stepmothers may be burdened by their partner's and their own expectations of maternal involvement, stepfathers generally have lower expectations of themselves—and everyone else in the family seems to share those lower expectations.

This isn't to say that stepfathers are immune to conflicts. While boys may see them as allies, girls sometimes experience them as rivals for their mother's attention. This is why divorce can be more difficult for sons, while remarriage can be more upsetting to daughters.

In remarriage, both mothers and fathers feel caught between their desire to spend time with their children and time with their partners. Some stepparents, male or female, make it difficult for the biological parent to maintain a healthy relationship with the kids. A stepparent who feels threatened by his wife's need to spend time and money on her children may take out his feelings of frustration or disappointment on his stepchildren. A stepparent who assumes the mantle of authority too quickly or who reacts too aggressively to his stepchildren's low level of interest in him can cause tension to skyrocket in an otherwise peaceful household. As one teenager told me, "My mom's a nice person, but I have stopped wanting to go over to her house because her husband is such a dick! He makes it really clear that he can't stand us, and can't wait for us to leave. I'd go over there a lot more if he wasn't there."

A stepparent who criticizes the parent who isn't in the home or who acts in a competitive way with the parent may endanger the relationship between the parent and child. As Hetherington writes, "Stepfamilies, like machines, are subject to the complexity principle: the more working parts, the greater the risk of a break-down." Perhaps this is why 60 percent of remarriages fail and at least half of the divorces that occur from remarriages are those with stepchildren.

PROBLEM STEPCHILDREN

Not all of the problems exhibited by stepchildren are due to mis-management on the part of the parent or the stepparent. In the same way that children's wiring affects how they get along with their parents, troubled stepchildren can have a big influence on family dynamics. Children who are aggressive, defiant, hyperactive, or who have problems with addictions or mental illness can thwart the best efforts of a dedicated stepparent. Difficult stepchildren can damage a new and fragile marriage because both parent and stepparent may have unrealistically high expectations about what can be achieved by the other's behavior. The biological parent may believe that more love, tolerance, and acceptance will carry the day, while the stepparent may argue that more limit-setting and less indulgence are required.

THE OTHER HOME

While children have to learn how to accommodate the sometimes-confusing maze created by two families, parents sometimes have to contend with their children being exposed to new people or influences that they would never choose for their child. As one father told me, "I can't believe the person my ex-wife married. The kids are always complaining about his temper. I hate that I can't do more to protect them."

Having a psychologically healthy parent in the home can do a lot to mitigate the other parent's pathology through role modeling and through conversations about the other parent's behavior. Some parents delay divorcing or never divorce because they fear what would happen to their child if they weren't there to supervise.

However, unless the healthy parent is also the primary custodial parent, divorce exposes children to the unhealthier parent's problems much more directly, with fewer opportunities for role modeling, nurturing, and explanation. Of course, it is also true that divorce may *increase* the resources of a parent if the marriage made the parent more depressed or dysfunctional.

UNHOLY ALLIANCES

Divorce makes it tempting for everyone concerned to divide the world into good and evil, victim and aggressor, villain and martyr. Grandparents, aunts, uncles, cousins, and others may all line up in hostile allegiance beside their family member. Unfortunately, these relatives fail to take into account that this battle is being waged at huge cost to the child who *does* have a relationship with the "enemy."

I not infrequently hear about grandparents who begin to voice the critical feelings that they always had about a child's parent after a divorce. Doing so increases the wounding of their grandchild. "My grandparents talk about my father as if he and I aren't even related," said Ariel, a sixteen-year-old child of divorce. "It's like I'm only from *their* side of the family. I feel really disloyal to my father, but the things that they say about him make me not respect him as much, and that makes me feel guilty, too."

Grandparents may also increase the alienation between parent and child by funding aggressive custody battles and legal campaigns against the other parent. As one mother said, "In hindsight, it would have worked better for everyone if my parents hadn't gotten involved in my divorce. The fact that they gave me an unlimited bank account to go after my ex-husband probably soured any chance that we'd have a productive relationship around our children. It was almost like they were more mad at him than I was, and I was too confused at the time to think about it from a long-term perspective."

On the other hand, grandparents can also be casualties of divorce. "I've learned not to ask the children's mother if I can spend time with them on her custody weekends: the answer is always no," writes Rachel Pollack in a newspaper article titled "Grandparents Struggle to Hang On After Divorce." "On my son's weekends, when one of my grandchildren asks to spend the night, my answer is always, 'Yes, but let's ask Dad first.' It rarely works out the way the children and I want it to." This is a sad reality for many grandparents with divorced children.

GAINING CLARITY

Below are the scenarios common to divorced parents. Part of your healing will come from accepting whatever ways you contributed to the conflict between you and your child, or, yes, you and your ex. If you're like most divorced parents, you have made more than one of the mistakes that I'll discuss, and these examples may make you feel guilty. Read on. One of our central goals is to help you clean your emotional house from the past. Looking fearlessly at your own behavior will lay a healthy foundation for your growth and for your potential relationship with your child.

Check the sentences that apply to you:

☐ *"I didn't protect my child enough from my feelings about the other parent."*

☐ *"I consciously or unconsciously attempted to get my child to side with me against the other parent."*

☐ *"I may have caused my child to feel guilty for loving, admiring, or feeling close to the other parent or stepparent."*

☐ *"My guilt about the divorce, or my role in it, has made it hard for me to let my children talk about their feelings of anger, sadness, worry, or loss."*

☐ *"I made my child a lower priority than my new partner."*

☐ *"I had my child keep secrets from my ex, and that placed an unfair burden on him."*

☐ *"I regret whatever ways I was unsympathetic to my children feeling displaced by my new partner."*

☐ *"I regret not being able to do a better job protecting my children from my partner's problems or my ex's problems."*

Let's look at these in more detail:

"I didn't protect my child enough from my feelings about the other parent."

Divorce creates endless opportunities to feel hurt, disappointed, and angry. It's not unusual for there to be differences around alimony, child support, custody arrangements, pain about your children's blame or rejection, jealousy over your ex's new partner, and worries that the children will love your ex's new partner more than they love you.

It's also common for one of the parties to feel deeply rejected or disappointed that the marriage didn't work out. If you initiated the divorce, you may still be feeling hurt or angry over the dynamics that caused you to leave. Some parents do a better job than others in protecting their children from these emotions. Those who don't may find that their children are hurt or alienated by the experience, leading to wounds in their relationship with them.

Confiding your feelings or opinions to your children about the divorce or the other parent can create problems in your relationship with them because it:

- Makes your child feel burdened with worry or responsibility for you or the other parent

- Places your child in a loyalty bind

- Causes your child to lose respect for you if you're too revealing about your inner conflicts

Strive to avoid:

- Confiding your feelings about the other parent to your child.

- Confiding your feelings about the divorce to your child.

- Defending your decision to divorce by providing details about your ex's behavior.

- Discussing details such as alimony or child support.

- Defending yourself against wrongful accusations of your ex except to say, "That's not correct, but that's between your mother/father and me." Or, "I understand that is your mother's/father's perspective, but that's not the whole story."

*

Strive to:

- Confide your feelings to your friends, therapist, or others who can offer heartfelt support.

- Consider telling your child your perspective when he is in his mid-20s or later, but generally not before. If you feel you must talk about your feelings, do it in a family therapy session where you can get support about how to communicate these feelings.

- Make amends to your child if you believe that your confiding was burdensome.

"I consciously or unconsciously attempted to get my child to side with me against the other parent."

It's not unusual for a parent to want the child to side with him or her in a divorce. Even those parents who remain respectful toward the other parent will experience *some* pleasure at hearing their children complain about the other parent. Unfortunately, most children figure this out and may seek to reassure or please their parent with statements like, "I can see why you left Dad. He's really impossible to get along with." Or, "Mom's such a bitch. I don't know how you lived with her as long as you did."

Your children may also learn how to use this awareness in their negotiations with you, complaining about the other parent as a way to soften you up before some request: "Dad's so cheap, he never buys me any clothes or anything. Could you take me shopping?" Conversely, they may try to increase their influence by talking about how superior the other parent is in their provision of money, time, or decreased supervision. While this may engender anger or guilt in you, it may also make you too pliant in your negotiations with your child.

Strive to avoid:

- Intensifying the differences between you and the other parent by joining in on discussions about the other parent's relative inferiority.

- Using the other parent's weaknesses as a way to improve your position with your child.

Strive to:

- Listen impassively to complaints about the other parent or stepparent without joining in with agreement or excessive validation. Make the interaction about your child, not you. "I'm sorry that Daddy was late picking you up. Sounds like you were upset," Not, "That's so typical. He did that kind of crap to me all of the time!"

- Represent what is reasonable in the other parent's behavior, wherever possible. If that's not possible, strive to be supportive without revealing your own feelings. Even if your child can sense your emotions, she will appreciate your restraint.

"I may have caused my child to feel guilty for loving, admiring, or feeling close to the other parent or stepparent."

Parents are sometimes very direct in their desire to get their child's allegiance. One adult child of divorce put it like this: "I couldn't do anything that reminded my father of my mother. If I laughed a certain way, he'd say, 'You sound just like your mother!' in a really hostile way. Or if I disagreed with his politics, he'd say, 'That sounds like something your mother would say. You're becoming just like her!' I pretty much learned that I wasn't supposed to be like her in any way if I wanted to get along with him."

Even when the parent tries hard to mask his or her feelings, divorced children may decode how their parent really feels. "My dad tries really hard to hide how jealous he is over whatever is happening in my mom's house," said Carla, a thirteen-year-old child of divorce. "Whenever I tell him something nice that my mom or stepdad does, he'll say something like, 'That's good, honey,' but I can see the wave of sadness fall over him. I think I'm just going to not tell him what's happening there, or maybe make it so it doesn't sound so good."

Fear about being displaced by your ex's new partner is a common source of wounding for parents. "The first time I saw my four-year-old daughter holding hands with my ex-husband's new wife, I went nuts inside," said Tanya, a divorced mother. "Frankly, I wanted to kill her. Fortunately, because I was in therapy at the time, I didn't say anything to her or my daughter, but I wanted to—I *really* wanted to."

Strive to avoid:

- Criticizing your ex or the ex's new partner

- Discussing with your children feelings of jealousy, insecurity, or any other way that you feel displaced by your ex's new partner

Strive to:

- Let your child know that you want him or her to love the other parent.

- Over time, show some pleasure or approval in your child's recounting of pleasurable events with your ex and/or your ex's new partner. It's okay to fake it.

- Over time, let your child know that you are comfortable with his love or enjoyment of your ex's partner. It's okay to fake it.

- When possible, praise the other parent.

- When possible, praise the ex's new partner.

- Make amends to your child if you criticized the other parent. Say something like, "I'm sorry I said that about your mother. I know it puts you in the middle and that isn't fair. I was upset but it wasn't an appropriate way to handle my feelings."

"My guilt about the divorce, or my role in it, has made it hard for me to let my children talk about their feelings of anger, sadness, worry, or loss."

If you or your children hold you accountable for the divorce, or for the problems in their lives following it, you may be reluctant or unwilling to hear your child's complaints. This may cause you to criticize or reject your children, express inappropriate anger at the other parent, or shut down any conversation that heads in that direction. "I felt like talking about the divorce was taboo with both of my parents," said Kim. "I asked my dad one time when I was little when he and my mom were going to get back together and he glared at me and said, 'We're never getting back together, okay? Never! And don't ask me that again. Do you think I really want to go back to that?' I wasn't sure what 'that' meant but I wasn't about to ask. Talking about missing the other parent was definitely off limits with both of them."

Strive to avoid:

- Shutting down their attempts to talk about the divorce

- Blaming the other parent when your children talk about the divorce

Strive to:

- Allow your child to complain about the divorce.

- Give voice to what you suspect are his or her feelings about it: "I know it's hard on you to go back and forth," or, "I know it's confusing having two sets of rules to remember," or "I know you sometimes feel like you have to choose sides," or

- "I know it's really hard on you that we don't all still live to-gether."

- Allow your child to complain about your role in the failure of the marriage. (You will likely need a lot of outside sup-port to get this one right.)

"I made my child a lower priority than my new partner."
One of the more difficult adjustments for a child comes when the parent starts dating. As one adult woman of divorce said, "I wasn't happy that my mom got divorced, but I did like all of the time that we got to spend together, afterwards. We did *everything* together—she let me sleep in her bed sometimes and I really liked that. It was like we had become best friends. That all changed when she started dating my stepdad. I felt like I just got dropped!"

Chip, a father, said he was so desperate for comfort when he was going through his divorce that he spent every available minute he had with his new girlfriend. "My girlfriend, Sherrie, really got me through that first year and I'm really indebted to her for that. I was a mess. But I don't think my kids got very much from me and they were going through their own hell at the time. I'd do it all different if I could do it over again."

Strive to avoid:

- Bringing a new boyfriend or girlfriend into your children's lives until you are very serious about that person.

Strive to:

- Keep your visitation or custody arrangement as consistent as possible so that there is minimal disruption to them.

"I had my child keep secrets from my ex, and that placed an unfair burden on him."

There are many reasons why divorced or divorcing parents, indirectly or directly, make their children keep secrets. For example, parents sometimes tell their children to not tell the other parent about a recent purchase or vacation for fear that it will strengthen the other's argument for a change in child support or alimony. "My mom was always saying things like, 'And don't go and tell your dad about our new couch or car or whatever,' said Darlene, an adult child of divorce, 'because he's just going to use it to give me less money!'"

Children may also be asked to provide information about the other parent's behavior that causes them to feel as though they're betraying the other parent. Gerry, a seventeen-year-old child of divorce, put it the following way: "My dad says to me the other night, 'So, has your mother started seeing anyone?' I was really on the spot because they're going through this nasty divorce and I don't know what's supposed to be secret and what isn't. I know that she's had a boyfriend since he moved out, but I just shrugged my shoulders. He pushed it, though, saying, 'Come on, I have a *right* to know!' as if that's my responsibility. I felt like saying, 'Ask her yourself if you're so damn curious.'"

Perhaps the biggest secret that children are forced to keep are affairs that happened during the marriage. "I remember my mother telling me in this schoolgirl way when I was seventeen all about how she was cheating on my dad and how much fun she was having. My dad and I were never very close, so maybe she thought I'd say something like, "Oh, Mom, gee, that's so wonderful. I'm just so happy to hear that you're betraying my father!" And the really weird thing is that I *did* feel kinda good that she trusted me with her secret, but it also really made me lose respect for her. Some things you really don't want to know about your parents. Now that they're divorced, I'm wondering, 'Am I supposed to tell my dad about her affair or what?'"

Strive to avoid:

- Making your child keep secrets from the other parent

- Placing your child in the position where she is asked to provide information about the other parent or the other parent's partner

Strive to:

- Make amends to your child if there were times when you required him or her to keep a secret.

- Make amends to your child if there were times that you used him or her to reveal information about the other parent or parent's partner. Say something like, "I know I put you in a terrible position by asking you to do that, and I'm really sorry. That wasn't fair."

"I regret whatever ways I was unsympathetic to my children feeling displaced by my new partner."

All divorced parents want their children to love their new partner, but many fail to see the impossible loyalty bind that they're placing their children in by bringing a new person into their lives. Parents who expect their children to be affectionate, inclusive, or overly respectful toward the new partner set themselves up for being wounded.

"My father made it clear very early on that he and his new wife were a package deal," said one adult child of divorce. "If we didn't send her a birthday card or get her a Christmas present, he'd be furious at us. I felt like, 'Hey, I don't even like her and now I'm supposed to get her a birthday card?' He actually told us that if we didn't fully embrace her, he didn't want to see us. My sister caved in, but I just stopped calling him because I got tired of feeling blackmailed."

The issue of treating the new partner with respect is often a point of confusion for many parents. "My kids don't have to like him but they do have to be respectful," said Marie in regards to Timothy, her new husband. "When they come in the room, it's always, 'Hi Mom,' but they act like he's not even there. If he walks in the room, one of my sons will actually get up and walk out without saying anything. I feel caught in the middle because, on the one hand, I feel like they didn't choose him, so they don't have to like him; on the other hand, my husband's putting all of this pressure on me to make them be more respectful. I've said to my kids, 'You know, give him a chance, he's a decent guy. Just show him the same respect you would anyone.' But that just seems to make them even madder, so I just don't know what I'm supposed to do."

Strive to avoid:

- Obligating your children to like your new partner.

- Criticizing your children for not wanting to spend time with your partner. This doesn't mean, however, that you have to cancel plans with your new partner if your children show up, unannounced.

Strive to:

- Use the same rules about treating your partner with respect that you have for treating other members of the family with respect. However, don't put your partner in the role of disciplinarian. That's your job.

- Let your children know that they are not required to like your partner.

- Be understanding of their having negative or mixed feelings about your relationship.

- Be empathic to your partner about how thankless and rejecting it can be to be a stepparent. Get counseling if it feels too confusing or it is causing too much conflict.

"I regret not being able to do a better job protecting my children from my partner's problems or my ex's problems."

Parents often feel extremely guilty and sorrowful if they didn't protect their children from the other parent's or the stepparent's problems. As Nick, an adult child of divorce, said, "I can forgive my mother for divorcing my dad—he was really mean to her. But bringing my stepdad into our lives, that's something that I have a really hard time letting go of. She allowed this man into our home who used to beat me, *and* he molested my sister. Whenever I've tried to talk to my mother about it, she always says, 'I'm sorry, but

I did the best I could.' Yeah, Mom, well, sometimes your best isn't good enough."

Eventually Nick's mother came to therapy at his request. His mother was a small, frail woman who looked at up at me like I was an executioner when I entered the waiting room to greet her for the first time. "I'm sure you must think I'm a terrible person," she said, almost before she sat down on the couch. She looked on the verge of tears.

"I *don't* think you're a terrible person," I said.

"I know Nicky's mad at me about all of the things that his step-dad did to him and his sister. Jim wasn't a good stepfather to my kids and I feel awful about that. I just wasn't in any position to do any better by them. I was dirt poor after their dad left, and I don't know how we all would've survived if I had made Jim move out. I don't even know if I *could've* made him move out, even if I tried to. You know, maybe since I grew up with a dad who used to beat us, I felt like, 'Well, that's what happens you know? That's life.' That part about him molesting my Suzie, I didn't hear about that until after she moved out. I guess by then, it was too late. Damage done." She stared out the window at the trees moving in the wind. "She won't return my calls or anything—I haven't seen my little Suzie in about fifteen years."

I met with Nick and his mother in family therapy over the next few months. With my help, his mother was able to make amends to Nick for the ways that she hadn't protected him. Her guilt and sorrow made it hard for her to find the words, but she was brave enough to let Nick talk about the many ways that he felt hurt and betrayed, and as a result, he was eventually able to understand and forgive her.

Strive to avoid:

- Telling them that you did the best you could. That's what you say to yourself, not to them.

- Not talking about your past behavior because it's too painful.

Strive to:

- Make amends for not being as protective as you wished you had been.

- Work on building self-forgiveness and self-compassion using the techniques discussed below.

HEALING EXERCISES

Writing a Letter

Write a letter to your child regarding any of the themes that you related to in this chapter. This isn't something you have to send or otherwise act upon. The purpose is to help you identify and clarify your feelings so that they don't weigh on you so heavily. The letter could be a letter of anger, disappointment, regret, or love.

Making Amends

When you're ready, consider talking with your child about whatever regrets you have about the past. Be prepared: your child may be appreciative, but may be just as likely to be critical or rejecting, especially if he or she feels wronged or is overly allied with the other parent.

Part of your healing comes from being willing to let your self-punishment end. If you believe that you've wronged your children, then you may believe that you're supposed to suffer for the rest of your life. It doesn't help anyone for you to live in pain. You have the most to give to others through embracing and forgiving yourself.

Stress Reduction Exercise

Sit in a quiet place where you can be undisturbed for five minutes. Focus only on your breath going in and out. Count your inhalations and exhalations up to ten and then back down again to one (inhale 1, exhale 2, inhale 3, etc.). When you get back down to one, begin again. If you get distracted, calmly redirect your attention to counting your breaths. This will take a little practice, so don't get mad at yourself if you find your mind constantly wandering.

Do this twice a day for a week. At the end of each week, add another five minutes to the length of sitting time until you reach twenty minutes. This is a meditation exercise that has been shown to reduce stress, anxiety and depression. Why? Ongoing feelings of worry, guilt, anxiety, and depression trigger the stress hormones that mediate fight-or-flight reactions. While those adrenaline-based responses are key to survival, we are not meant to have them locked into the "on" position 24/7. Meditative techniques are useful because we tend to feel what we think. It is harder to think troubling thoughts if you are focusing on your breath. Focusing on your breath and clearing your mind allows the fight-or-flight reaction to move into the background and a calmer, more focused experience to move into the foreground.

Once you have gotten into a more relaxed frame of mind, review the HEAL steps discussed in chapter 4. To recap, these are:

Hope: What were your original hopes as a parent?

Educate: Educate yourself about what is or was outside of your control.

Affirm: Affirm your core values and strengths as a parent and as an individual.

Long-Term Commitment: Make a long-term commitment to change whatever you need to change in order to be more forgiving of yourself and others, to make amends, and to put your life on a healthier course.

Part of step three, *affirm*, is to remind yourself of what you have done right as a parent. Review the exercise in chapter 4 titled *My Value as a Parent Healing Exercise on What I've Done Right*.

Practice Gratitude

Take a few moments and remind yourself of five things to be grateful for. Some possibilities are:

- Your health

- Being alive

- Your relationships with your friends, spouse, partner, or your other children

- Your talents or achievements

- Your home

- Your faith

- _____

- _____

- _____

- _____

Divorced parents are vulnerable to becoming estranged from their children. For this reason, you may have to work particularly hard to develop or maintain a connection with your child. Try to take a long-term perspective and not get too discouraged too early on. As I'll discuss in later chapters, continuing to reach out and keeping the door open is one of the best strategies to create a closer re-

lationship down the road. While divorce can create alienation
between parents and children, so can a bad marriage. In the following chapter, we'll look at the reasons why bad marriages can
cause problems between parents and their children, and suggest
solutions for when this occurs.

~~~~~~~~~~

TEN

PROBLEM MARRIAGES AND TROUBLED SPOUSES

*Healing the Relationship Between
Parents and Children*

Georgia's husband has a temper problem. A serious temper problem. Most of our sessions are spent strategizing how to protect her children's self-esteem and her own feelings of well-being from his frequent verbal assaults. "I think about divorcing Evan all of the time," she admitted to me early in the therapy, "but there's no way I'm going to put my children or myself through a divorce. The kids and I would go straight to the poorhouse and I wouldn't trust him with any type of custody arrangement because he's rich and smart enough to fool a judge into granting him half-time custody."

While Georgia has decided that staying married is the better of two evils, she is unable to provide her children with the kind of emotional security and comfort that she wants for them. She feels inadequate in her capacity to protect them, frightened by her dependence on an unstable man, and worried about what kind of model she serves for her kids.

• • •

An individual's desire to be a good parent is sometimes thwarted by his spouse. Adults who are or were married to partners with addictive disorders, mental illness, impulsivity, depression, or abusive behavior may be constantly challenged to find new ways to insulate themselves or their children from their partner's behavior. Even conflict among "normal" spouses, if it is ongoing and severe, can hurt your capacity to parent and interfere with your ability to have a good relationship with your children.

This chapter will look at the many ways that people's relationships with their children can be affected by their marriages.

THE EFFECTS OF A BAD MARRIAGE

In my first book, *The Marriage Makeover: Finding Happiness in Imperfect Harmony*, I provided guidance for people who wanted to consider staying in a marriage with children, despite low marital satisfaction. I wrote the book for those who may never have a great marriage even if they get a lot of psychotherapy and read every self-help book on the topic; for those who remain married because they believe that a divorce will cause lasting sorrow for their children or themselves; for those whose partner is a great parent even if a lousy spouse; for those who fear the downward mobility that could arise with divorce; for those who don't trust their ex's ability to parent without their supervision; for those who worry that their ex will drop out as a parent (as do some 25 percent of men); and for those whose culture or religion forbids divorce.

While not for everyone, these are all legitimate reasons to remain married. I highlight this because our current culture makes people feel as though they are existential cowards if they remain in marriages that aren't romantically fulfilling. While there are valid reasons to stay married other than romance, deciding to stay for your or your children's sake requires doing it in a way that doesn't harm you, your children, or your relationship to them. In other words, you're not doing you or them any favors if you're staying together, presumably for their sake, and acting in a victimized way around them. You're also not doing you or them any favors if you're engaging in ongoing verbal or physical abuse—the so-called "high-conflict" marriage. In fact, most of the time, children appear to do better when high-conflict marriages end, at least when divorce brings about a cessation of hostilities.

Even without yelling and shoving, a bad marriage is not generally a great thing for children. It provides a poor role model of relationships and diverts the positive energies that tend to flow in children's direction when there is goodwill between the parents. However, the syllogism popular among therapists and the general public—"If you're unhappy in your marriage then your children must be too: therefore you should get divorced"—is a little too simplistic and self-serving; it depends on how that marital unhappiness is managed. It isn't always better for children when marriages end, even with an angry or mentally ill spouse. In many cases, children benefit from having a healthy parent to be with them in the home full-time, and a divorce may significantly reduce the quantity or quality of time children get with the healthier parent.

In addition, some parents do a much better job of being great parents than great romantic partners, and children benefit from that full-time parenting even if they don't get the role modeling of a romantic marriage.

However, while it can make sense to stay married in an attempt to protect oneself and one's children, you have to be careful to do it in a way that provides a good model, or you can harm your children and become a wounded parent in the process.

"Difficult Spouse" Questionnaire:

Circle the items that apply to you.

*How has your spouse's or ex-spouse's behavior
interfered with your parenting?*

- He constantly undermines my authority.

- She behaves in ways that are harmful to my child.

- He is a poor role model.

- She puts the kids in the middle of our conflict.

- He poisons the children against me and it weakens my relationship with them.

- She constantly criticizes my parenting to me or to the children.

*What are your biggest complaints about your
spouse in relation to the children?*

- His mental illness, addiction, or difficult personality cause him to act in destructive or bizarre ways toward me and/or the children.

- Her spending habits result in our never having enough money.

- His rages have caused everyone in the house to feel unsafe.

- She acts like she's married to the children and I'm always on the outs.

- The way he treats me makes me do or say things to the children that I later regret.

Let's return to Georgia, because she's not so unusual. Georgia is a good mother. She is dedicated, conscientious, and hardworking. But she is married to someone who limits her ability to provide the kind of security and safety that she wants for her children. This has had several outcomes:

- Her teenage son is angry at her because she can't or won't make his father be nicer to him.

- She feels guilty that she can't protect her children from his flare-ups or rejection of them.

- She feels mad at and sorry for herself that she didn't choose a better partner for herself and father for her children.

TAKING RESPONSIBILITY

There were a number of questions that I asked Georgia to consider as a way of working on her situation. These are the same questions you should be considering if your hurt stems from your marriage:

Is my view of my spouse fair?

Are there ways that I passively or unconsciously participate in provoking the negative behaviors in my spouse?

Do I subtly or overtly undermine his relationship with the children because of my anger or disappointment about my marriage?

Am I doing everything possible to protect my children from my spouse's negative or destructive behavior?

Let's look at these more closely:

Is my view of my spouse fair?

A fair view of your spouse means that you have a realistic perspective on what is genuinely hurtful to children. In our current culture of the fragile child, parents can view any raised voice as an act of violence. If you came from a home where there was abuse, you may be especially concerned that expressions of anger on your part or the part of your spouse will be destructive to your children.

I not infrequently hear spouses accusing each other of verbal abuse for behavior that I would simply call obnoxious or sometimes just loud. While I don't think children *like* being scolded or having their parents raise their voices at them, a raised voice doesn't necessarily constitute abuse. If a mother yells loudly at her teenagers for leaving their stuff all over the living room floor, that's not abuse. If she says, "You're a worthless piece of shit; I wish you had never been born," that's abuse. If a parent yells, "What in the hell were you doing driving drunk? Are you out of your mind??!!" that's not necessarily abuse. If he says, "I wish you had gotten maimed or killed!" that's abuse.

There are many, many dedicated, committed, and loving parents who also yell from time to time. The effect of your partner's volume has to be balanced against the ongoing quality of your marriage and how he or she behaves the rest of the time as a parent. For example:

- Is he affectionate?

- Does she make time for the children?

- Does he show an awareness of his children's needs and inner lives?

- Does she have the capacity to apologize if she hurts their feelings?

- Is he receptive to your feedback about his behavior?

- Does she spend time with you or the children talking about the children's future?

- Is the amount of time spent yelling balanced with quality time?

Marital researcher John Gottman found that in successful marriages, there are five positive interactions for every negative one. He also found that the happiest couples are those who have loud fights, periodically. In other words, it isn't the absence of conflict that predicts marital well-being, it's the ratio of positive to negative. While parenting isn't conducted on the same equal playing field as marriage, I suspect that there is a similar ratio for child well-being. In other words, children can tolerate a certain amount of parental volume, irritability, and anger if it occurs in an otherwise dedicated and loving environment.

Are there ways that I passively or unconsciously participate in provoking the negative behaviors in my spouse?

It's very difficult to see the subtle ways that we may keep a situation inflamed with our own behavior. As Georgia and I worked together, it became apparent that her husband felt rejected by her. Georgia grew up in a very constrained and conservative household where the expression of emotions was strictly forbidden. When she met her husband, Evan, she was drawn to his passion and freedom with his feelings. While he occasionally lost his temper, this was largely balanced by his love of life and his ability to deeply experience the world around him, something that Georgia had great difficulty in doing.

However, when Georgia and Evan became parents, she began to experience his emotionality as a threat to the children. She felt obliged to police his behavior and express fury at him for any scolding or sign of irritability expressed to their kids. Over time, she retreated from him emotionally and put all of her energies into being a mother. Tragically, Evan responded to his feeling rejected by rejecting their children, a response common to men. This precipitated a dynamic where Georgia became even more distant and angry with Evan and more protective of the children against his mistreatment of them.

By the time Georgia showed up in my office, a lot of harm had been done to the children and the marriage. Fortunately, Georgia was able to take responsibility for her behavior toward Evan and make amends to him for her part of the dynamic. She also made a conscious effort to voice what she still loved, admired, and appreciated about him. Fortunately, Evan was able to respond to Georgia's reaching out to him by reinvesting himself in being a parent and by making amends to his children for the many ways that he had hurt them by his withdrawal and criticism. He also made amends to Georgia for how his behavior had been hurtful to her.

I say *fortunately* because sometimes so much fouled water passes beneath a marital bridge that a relationship can get beyond resuscitation. In those situations, one or both partners lose the energy or desire to do the work needed to repair it.

> *Do I subtly or overtly undermine his relationship with the children because of my anger or disappointment about my marriage?*

Because Georgia was unable to see how her rejection of Evan fed his withdrawal, she grew to be increasingly hurt, angry, and shut down. When the children complained about their father, she acted overly empathic to them and morally outraged to Evan. This behavior fueled his alienation from them and the children's identification of him as being an ogre. While some degree of empathy about their complaints was reasonable, even appropriate, Georgia unconsciously used her children to vent her anger and elevate herself as a more innocent player in the family dynamic.

Do I do that?

If you are unsure about your role in marital conflict, ask yourself the following questions:

- Do I like it when my children are mad at the other parent because it makes me feel validated in my complaints?

- Do I side with them against the other parent because I like having them as allies?

- Do I complain to them about my disappointment in the other parent as a partner?

- Do I empathize with them by providing my own examples of how the other parent mistreats me?

If you answer *yes* to one or more of these questions, you are contributing to a negative dynamic in your household. This is wrong for your children, and it sets you up for their feeling angry at you when they're older for your having used them. Researchers Alan Booth and Paul Amato found that marital unhappiness and instability "appear to weaken relationships between children and parents later in life, even if it does not result in divorce. But if a divorce occurs, it is followed by a further deterioration in child-parent relationships." They also found that relationships with fathers are more negatively affected in both the cases of divorce and in low-quality marriages. Bearing these cautions in mind, the following guidelines are provided:

Even if you like it when your children are mad at the other parent, keep your reactions to yourself. Unless they're in physical or emotional danger, your children don't benefit from knowing that you enjoy their dissatisfaction with the other parent, whom they also love. If he's really an ogre, they can come to that conclusion on

their own. While there may be times where it's appropriate to intervene if your partner is behaving in a way that you find objec-
tionable, it is generally not a good idea to side with your children
against the other parent.

*Even if you agree with your children's complaints about your part-
ner's behavior, you should voice that privately to your partner when
your children are out of earshot.* If the situation at home is too volatile, drag her into a parenting consultation. If she refuses, go by
yourself so you can learn the best way to protect your children.

Don't tell your children your complaints about the other parent. You
may think they'll feel validated but they won't—they'll feel burdened and guilty. And it may come back to haunt you later on.

*Am I doing everything possible to protect the children from
my spouse's negative or destructive behavior?*

Adults living with a verbally or physically abusive spouse are
faced with many dilemmas. Much like Tevye in *Fiddler on the Roof*,
you have to reconcile very difficult choices:

On the one hand, you want to protect your children from your
spouse's destructive behavior by stepping in and making him
stop.

On the other hand, doing so escalates the behavior because he
feels invalidated, ganged up on, or shamed.

On the one hand, you want your spouse to feel a sense of part-
nership to you around parenting, so you are reluctant to intervene.

On the other hand, you worry that your children will experience
you as being insufficiently protective if you don't intervene. You
worry that your lack of intervention will harm your children, and
sow the seeds of hurt and resentment about your seeming unwillingness to protect them.

On the one hand, you want to be able to talk about your parenting concerns to your spouse and problem-solve the dynamics.

On the other hand, doing so risks your spouse's feeling criticized and reacting in a way that leaves everyone feeling blamed and guilty.

WHAT'S A DEDICATED PARENT TO DO?

This was Aaron's dilemma: His wife, Paula, had very little patience as a parent and was given to outbursts of uncontrolled anger for relatively trivial misdemeanors. Whenever he tried to calmly talk with her about her parenting, she blew up at him and accused him of siding with the children against her. She often told him that the reason the children didn't respect her was because Aaron didn't treat her with respect.

I went through the same series of questions with Aaron that I did with Georgia to establish whether his view of her was fair, whether he passively or unconsciously participated in provoking the negative behaviors in her, and whether he subtly or overtly undermined her relationship with the children because of his anger or disappointment about the marriage.

I concluded from my work with Aaron that he was married to a very fragile person who carried profound feelings of self-hatred; she experienced even the most trivial show of independence by her husband or children as a refutation of her worth as a human being. Given this, my first recommendation was *that he stop yelling back at his wife*, even if she was behaving terribly. It took a lot of practice, but over time he got good at remaining calm, or walking out of the room if he couldn't. Did this end her outbursts? Hardly. But it served two purposes: it modeled for his children that there are a variety of ways to respond to hostility other than meeting it head-on, and reduced the frequency and intensity of her eruptions.

NOTE: The only thing more upsetting to children than one out-of-control parent is *two* out-of-control parents! Children are reassured to see that at least one of their parents is holding down the fort, even if the person that's setting fire to it is the other parent.

SHE CRITICIZES MY PARENTING

Parents are sometimes wounded by the other parent's constant critiques of their parenting. Aaron's wife frequently told him how bad he was as a father. "It's all of the time, every day. She's always saying how I'm spoiling them and how they can manipulate me. Of course, if anything goes wrong, like they don't have a perfect report card, she takes that as more proof of why my parenting is such a failure. I know I'm not supposed to care because obviously, I'm not dealing with a stable person here. But it still makes me feel bad and doubt myself. I end up feeling like, 'Well, maybe she's right. Maybe I'm not a good dad.'"

For most of us, being a good parent sits at our core feelings of self-worth. Criticism from a spouse may be especially hard to resist, since they often spend more time than anyone witnessing your parenting and can allege to know you better. In addition, they can claim squatter's rights on criticizing you since your parenting affects their children as well.

CRITICIZING YOU TO THE CHILDREN

"Whenever my husband gets mad at me, he tells the children, 'You have a mean mother. Your mother is *mean*,' which puts me in the very awkward position of having to explain to my teenagers why I'm not being mean if I have a view that's different from their father's. But what really worries me is that they're going to grow up thinking that I must be mean since they love their father and he's the one who's telling them that."

There are times when it makes sense to set limits on the other parent's criticism of you in front of the children and there are times when you shouldn't. If you have tried ignoring it or changing the topic and it keeps escalating, you should tell your partner to knock it off. Say something like the following, clearly and firmly, "Okay, that's enough! You can't call me names. If you have a complaint, you can tell me without putting me down." Stay with that in response to any other criticism. If he keeps escalating, then say, "This isn't feeling productive, so I'm going to leave the room now. I'll be happy to hear what you have to say to me when you want to talk about this in a calm and productive way."

GUIDELINES FOR COMMUNICATING WITH AN ANGRY SPOUSE

When you are both calm, and ideally feeling close, tell him that you'd like to brainstorm some parenting questions. Follow this structure:

#1 Don't escalate:

It's very tempting to respond to provocative behavior by becoming critical, rejecting, or furious. You should refrain from doing this because your children are harmed by your participating in the escalation of a fight. They need you to remain grounded enough to respond in a calm way.

#2 Start a conversation about parenting with a compliment and a self-disclosure of your own struggles as a parent:

In Aaron's case, I recommended he say, "I think you're a dedicated mom and our son really benefits from the ways that you do *x* or *y*." (If you start with an appreciation, it lets your partner know that you're not going for blood; that you want a collaborative communication. In Aaron's case, he wasn't telling his wife she was perfect, he was telling her that there are some things she does well.)

"I know that I can feel overwhelmed by him sometimes and I don't always like my responses to his behavior." (Self-discloses and admits fallibility. Again, this shows that he's not a saint and doesn't expect saintliness from her. This also signals to someone who is vulnerable that he doesn't want to shame her by calling attention to behavior that she, in all likelihood, knows is wrong.)

"I'm wondering if you feel like you get enough support from me around parenting because I know that our son can be tough. For example, I know you were really upset this morning and I wasn't sure about the best way to support you." (Here, he acknowledges there may be a rational reason for her irrational behavior despite all evidence to the contrary. This is the ideal way to approach your partner about parenting or, for that matter, any marital hotspot.) With a reasonable spouse, this approach should generally be productive. However, here's the way it went with Paula:

Aaron: "I'm wondering if you feel like you get enough support from me around parenting because I know that our son can be tough. For example, I know you were really upset this morning and I wasn't sure about the best way to support you."

Paula: "You can support me by backing me up. When Elliot is saying that he wants apple juice and I want him to have tomato juice, don't take his side, take mine. That pisses me off and makes you look like the good guy and I'm the evil witch."

Aaron: "Yeah, I think I was confused about why you cared what kind of juice he had. I didn't mean to undermine you." (Explains his behavior in an attempt at clarification.)

Paula: (loudly) "It *matters* because apple juice is full of sugar and has absolutely no nutrition in it and we wouldn't even have it in the house if you didn't keep buying it whenever it's your turn to shop."

Aaron: (trying to ignore the escalation in her tone) "Do you feel like Elliot's nutrition is bad? Seems like he's a good eater." (Here, he is trying to show that there may be a good reason for her strong reaction that he doesn't yet fully understand.) "I buy it because I like it and I don't like tomato juice." (Shows that his motivation isn't to belittle or invalidate her.)

Paula: (louder) "You just don't get it, do you, Aaron? You have a hard time seeing it any way but your own. I don't want you contradicting me in front of them, all right? (escalating further) Is that so freaking hard for you to understand? I don't care whether it's about apple juice or the way that they talk to me. I'm tired of looking like the bad guy all of the time and you getting to act like Mr. Sympathetic Father of the Year. Forget you!" (At that, she stormed out of the bedroom.)

I present this conversation to illustrate that you should:

(a) Try hard for a long time to have productive conversations with your partner, and

(b) Know that sometimes—and with some partners—your conversations may easily derail. If you're married to someone with untreated mental illness, alcohol or drug addiction, or simply someone with a really difficult personality, you may be only so successful at involving them in useful negotiations and interactions.

This is where Aaron found himself with Paula. While his staying calm and not matching her intensity was good for Elliot, it didn't solve the problem that she continued to be verbally aggressive and hurtful to him. He rightly worried he was being harmed by her, and that he could experience Aaron's restraint as weakness or passivity.

#3: Reduce conflict by allying with the out-of-control parent:

I encouraged Aaron to experiment by calmly siding with his wife when she complained about their son if there was a grain of truth to it. Thus, if she screamed about his leaving a dish in the sink, support her by calmly telling his son to—as his mother requested—put the dish in the washer. This change in Aaron's behavior also went part way in reducing the conflict.

#4 Intervene sometimes:

In a healthy marriage, parents are often able to correct the other's parenting without too much upset. Thus, if one parent's tone is too harsh, he or she doesn't strongly object if the other parent takes over or tells the hothead parent to chill out. They both trust that the correction is in the service of the children's well-being, not to look superior to or inflict pain on the partner.

Aaron's wife was threatened and destabilized by his intervening, but it was important to Aaron to feel as though he was being protective of his son when his wife was being harsh or saying cruel things to him. Given this, I encouraged him to periodically say, "That's enough. Don't call him names. You can say what you have to say without putting him down."

Or,

"That's unfair. You can tell him that in a more productive way."

Or,

"Okay, Stop! Enough. I'm taking over now."

Paula typically reacted by feeling betrayed and by escalating the argument, so Aaron couldn't step in every time. But intervening in a more protective way helped send a message to his son that Aaron wasn't being complicit in his mother's verbal abuse.

#5: Debriefing:

Parents should strive to avoid talking about the other parent's behavior when that parent isn't there. Talking about the other parent
has the potential to make children feel guilty for ganging up on
him or her. It can also cause a greater escalation if the excluded
parent learns of it.

However, troubled spouses call for unconventional approaches.
In Aaron's case, I recommended that he occasionally debrief his
son about his mother's behavior by saying something like the following:

> "I love your mother and she's trying hard. I don't think that
> she means the hurtful things that she says to you. They cer-
> tainly aren't true. Her parents were mean to her when she
> was a child and that's where she learned how to communi-
> cate. Mom doesn't always know how to communicate pro-
> ductively or understand how it makes you feel. I know
> you're mad at her. I'm talking with you about this because I
> think it's understandable and even appropriate that you
> would be mad at times; you don't deserve to be talked to
> that way by Mom or me or anyone else. You're a great kid
> and I think in her heart she knows that."

FEELING REJECTED AND DISPLACED

It's not uncommon for one member of the marriage to feel rejected
by how much time and attention is lavished on the children by the
other parent. "I pretty much feel like Vic wishes he had married
someone like my daughter since he has everything in common
with her and apparently nothing with me. They're both really adventurous, super athletic, love being outside, love being loud and
rowdy, and I'm basically a homebody who hates the outdoors or
anything physical. I mean, a lot of moms would kill to have such a

dedicated and involved father, and on the one hand, I'm grateful; it's just that I don't feel like I get any of his love or attention and she gets *all* of it. I'm embarrassed to admit it because you're not supposed to be jealous of your own daughter, but it's really hurtful to me!"

Many fathers feel displaced by the children when their wives become new mothers. This creates a wound that can derail a marriage and prevent it from getting back on track. "I was happy to become a father," said Micky, a fifty-year-old father of twin fifteen-year-old boys, "but, Jesus, did our marriage ever go to crap after that. She used to be this super fun girl, loved sex, really outgoing—and ever since she became a mom, game over, party over, time to devote every single waking moment to our kids. I can't remember the last time we went out just the two of us. We've never even had a babysitter! I really understand why some people start having affairs."

If you feel rejected by your spouse because of her involvement with the children, consider the following recommendations:

- Approach your partner when you're both feeling close.

- Tell her what you like about her and her parenting.

- Use a loving tone of voice.

- Make a request. For example, say, "I sometimes find myself feeling jealous of how close you are to our sons and I end up feeling a little hurt and left out. I'm wondering if there's a way that we could spend more quality time together so that we can feel more close and connected."

- Get her to agree to a change in behavior that you can both track, such as going on romantic dates two to three times a month, increases in affection, or increased statements of appreciation.

- Keep the discussion on the table. Don't get discouraged if there isn't immediate change.

SPOUSES WHO ALIENATE THE ADULT CHILD

Alison's son Abe moved out when he was eighteen and has refused to visit since then. Part of the reason is that Alison's husband won't make amends for how he treated their son when he was under their roof. While their son remains fond of his mother, he says that being at their house reminds him of how much he hates his father.

Alison is furious at her husband for not only being an insensitive and critical father, but for refusing to acknowledge that her son's unwillingness to visit them has anything to do with his behavior. She feels jealous of her friends who have close relationships with their adult children. She feels sad to know that she has far less time with her son than she would have if her husband were mature enough to reach out to him and make amends.

Guidelines for Raising an Important Topic

- Approach your partner when you're calm or feeling close.

- Start the conversation by telling him that you have an important topic to discuss, and you'd like his undivided attention.

- Empathize with whatever part of his perspective you can find. For example, "I know that you and Abe never had a close relationship and that he bears some responsibility for that. Sometimes parents and kids have bad chemistry in the same way that anyone else can."

- Make a request: "But I would like you to be the bigger person here. Abe doesn't come over because he feels hurt by you, even if you think he has no cause. I see your perspective, but as his mother, I also see his. I would like you, as a favor to me, to reach out to him and make amends to him."

- Use leverage: if this is something that causes you constant heartache and you've been stonewalled in your attempts for years to find a solution, then you may have to bring out the big guns, such as threatening separation or divorce.

THREATEN DIVORCE

If you think about divorce all of the time, it may be time to let your partner in on it. A large study found that one-fourth of men were completely surprised when their wives served them with divorce papers. Moral of the story: your spouse may have no idea how unhappy you are with his or her behavior. In my practice, I have found that there can be nothing so motivating to better behavior than witnessing the sincerity of a spouse who says she's really ready to file the divorce papers. At that point, a husband may become suddenly willing to do many of the things that he was unwilling to do before, such as get a medication consult, go to individual or couple's therapy, attend an anger management class, or attend a parenting workshop. Threatening or pursuing divorce should be a last-ditch option, but if you've tried everything else and you're at the end of your rope, you might have to play that card.

Three precautions:

1. *If you're going to threaten it, do it while you still have some gas in the tank.* Don't wait until you have absolutely no desire to keep your marriage if your spouse changes.

2. *Don't make it an idle warning.* This means that after you have threatened divorce, you should wait no longer than three to

six months to see if your partner is willing to do any of the behaviors that you've requested, such as get into couple's therapy. If he refuses, then you should go forward with a separation.

3. *Don't let the separation play out for years.* I have worked with too many individuals who took too much faith in their partner's saying they didn't want a divorce while refusing to do what was necessary, such as break up with the girlfriend, get into recovery, attend the anger management class, or move back into the house. They wasted months and sometimes years extending deadlines on the highly unreasonable request for more time without any clear evidence of change or commitment to change.

In this chapter we've discussed the many ways that marriage or your spouse's behavior can hurt your relationship with your children. The following are some additional suggestions that many find helpful:

Get into Individual Therapy

Being in a family can be confusing. It can be very easy to lose yourself and lose sense of what is wrong and what is right. Having your own therapist can be useful in helping you develop your own view and find the best ways to protect yourself and your children.

Get into Couple's Therapy

Your spouse might accept someone else's interventions when she won't accept yours. The couple's therapist may also be able to make referrals to a psychiatrist for medication, or for individual therapy for your spouse. Do it sooner than later. Most people wait way too long before they get into couple's therapy.

Take an Assertiveness Training Class

Living with a difficult spouse is no place for the unassertive. Difficult spouses are constantly breaking boundaries, saying or doing hurtful things to you or the children, spending money or overly restricting yours—the list is endless. If you lack assertiveness, enroll in an assertiveness training course at a community college. The techniques are easy to learn and straightforward. Properly practiced, they can make the difference between a reasonable life and one where you feel completely under your partner's thumb.

Make an Appointment for a Medication Consultation

If you are worried about your partner's behavior, tell him that you'd like him to get an evaluation to see if medication could be helpful. If you feel plagued by feelings of depression, anxiety, or anger, medication may also be helpful to you.

You may not be able to change your partner but you can work to increase your serenity, decrease your anger, increase your support, stop saying the harsh things that you say to yourself, and change how you contribute to the dynamic in the household. This will make for a happier life and will increase the chance of a healthier relationship with your child.

ELEVEN

FAILURE TO LAUNCH

When Teenage and Adult Children Aren't Thriving

Thomas and Ginny are seventy-five years old and have four grown children, ages forty, forty-two, forty-four, and fifty. They came to me for consultation on their eldest child, Mona. Thomas and Ginny struck me as parents almost from another culture. Unlike the vast majority of people who sit down in my office and break into descriptions of their lives and challenges, Thomas and Ginny sat quietly with their hands folded, their faces lined and somber as if waiting for a translator to arrive before they began to speak. For a San Francisco couple, they were dressed in a way that I was more likely to see in the Midwest of my childhood, an almost intentional neglect of effort to coordinate plaids with plains.

"How can I help you?" I said, my usual question for those who need me to get the ball rolling.

"It's about our daughter," Thomas began in a slow, questioning way. "We don't know what to do with her." He then sat back as though I would know what do with her now that he had gotten me that far.

"What are your worries about her?" I asked.

"Well," he said, sitting forward again, "we think she's depressed." He then looked at his wife, who hadn't stopped looking at me since they sat down. She nodded without looking away.

"Why do you think that?" I asked.

"She's always been that way." Ginny finally spoke in a tender, resigned way, her eyes quickly welling with tears. She, like her husband, fell back into silence.

"Has she tried suicide?" I asked. "Or is there some other reason that makes you seek help right now?"

"No," Thomas replied, looking over at his wife to make sure he was right. "I don't think she ever did try to suicide?" Ginny shook her head, no.

"She's just always been that way," Ginny said, making a white pretzel of the Kleenex in her hands, tears falling down her lightly rouged cheeks. "I just finally said to Thomas, '*Somebody's* going to have to do something for this poor girl. She needs help. She never had any friends in grade school—well, maybe one. Never popular, always kept to herself. She's had a weight problem most of her life and that never helps anything."

"Sounds like she's had a really hard life," I said, meaning it. "She lives with you two?"

"She did for a while, but she doesn't anymore," Thomas said, and looked at Ginny with an expression that seemed to say, "I told you this wouldn't go anywhere."

"She lives in an apartment in the Mission. It's in an awful place," Ginny said. "I hate to go over there. There's always police on every corner, drunks hanging out on the street. She just doesn't do anything with herself. She's always changing jobs. First it was Target, then it was Blockbuster, then it was Krispy Kreme or one of those doughnut houses, I can't remember which."

"Krispy Kreme," Thomas confirmed. "We just don't know what to do for her," he continued. "All our other kids are doing pretty good. They're married—well two of them are, the other is divorced. But they all have careers, kids. Mona doesn't have anything. Never did. Probably never will."

"I mean, she's a grown woman," Ginny said in a pleading way, her blue eyes wide and wet like a young child's. "She should have a husband, a baby, a house, right? Something? She doesn't have anything and I'm just sick about it. It's a terrible thing to have your baby have such a hard life," and she fell into sobs. Thomas reached over and grabbed her hand and looked at me with a soft, sad smile. "It's hard on Ginny," he said to me quietly. "It's hard on me, too, don't get me wrong. But it's really hard on her. Can you tell us what to do for our girl?"

These are painful cases. Realistically, if someone hasn't developed a career or a long-term relationship by the time that they're fifty, the chance of my successfully jumping in and waving a magic wand over their problems is low. It happens. It just doesn't happen very often. More often, my role is to help the parents gain some peace that they've done everything possible to help their adult child, and to move toward a position of acceptance and serenity. This chapter is written with those goals in mind.

WHY DO SOME KIDS NEVER GET OFF THE GROUND?

There are many, many reasons why children don't successfully launch adult lives:

- They may suffer from alcoholism or drug dependency.

- They may have a subtle or overt form of mental illness.

- They may be damaged from how their parents treated them.

- The mismatch between the parents and the child may have prevented them from developing the skills or resources needed to create an adult life.

- The parents may have been so possessive that the children concluded it was hurtful to the parents for them to grow up.

- Their parents may have been so overprotective that the children were never able to develop an ability to cope with adult challenges.

- The negative effects of peer-group or other traumas outside of the family may have damaged the children's capacity to navigate the stresses of adulthood.

Almost all of us wish to see our children succeed, partly out of simple love and partly for the reassurance that we have done our job as parents, and have not failed our children. In generations prior to the twentieth century, the inability of adult children to develop a successful life was seen more as a character flaw in the child than a result of inadequate child-rearing practices. Today's change in the vector of responsibility makes parents suffer under the weight of two burdens: the burden of sorrow for their child, and the burden of guilt and shame for their inadequacy as parents.

MENTAL ILLNESS

Paul, age thirty-eight, lives with two roommates in East Oakland. Paul had been an angry and defiant child, given to severe mood swings throughout his childhood. While Paul was reasonably smart, he was never able to succeed in school long enough to pull together a decent GPA. During adolescence, his mood swings were worsened by his entry into drug and alcohol use. His parents were very eager for him to move out of the home when he entered adulthood because his angry outbursts were a source of tension in the house for everyone. At eighteen, Paul had a psychotic break and was hospitalized with a diagnosis of bipolar disease (manic-depressive illness).

Paul's family met a good psychiatrist during his hospitalization who recommended that he be treated with Depakote, a drug commonly given to people with mood disorders. In addition, he recommended that Paul be seen in psychotherapy twice weekly.

It was a sound and reasonable plan, the kind that if consistently followed, could make all the difference between a successful life and an unsuccessful one. Unfortunately, Paul wouldn't comply. He refused to take his medication because he liked the energy and vitality he felt from his manic phases, even though the highs often resulted in his having drug or alcohol binges and going through whatever money he had in his bank account. He also consistently refused psychotherapy, claiming that therapists just wanted to take his parents' money, and that they weren't going to be able to tell him anything about himself he didn't already know.

While his parents financially supported him for many years after he moved out, they eventually stopped doing so. They were advised by the psychiatrist that Paul would need to fall off of the horse enough times in order to learn how to take hold of the reins of his life.

But Paul didn't take hold of the reins. When his parents sought consultation from me, Paul was thirty-eight and had been living one step away from homelessness for many years. Because of his mental illness, he was able to collect Social Security disability from the government, and this at least provided him with food stamps and a place to stay, however unglamorous the dwelling.

In my consultation with Paul's parents, I learned that he had tried psychotherapy sporadically over the past twenty years, but had never stayed in treatment for more than a few sessions. To be thorough, I suggested that the parents offer to provide limited and temporary financial assistance if he agreed to see a therapist on a weekly basis and to stay on his meds. He declined in a not very polite way.

A PARENT'S DILEMMA

What's a parent to do for their child when they've offered help, frequently way past the point of utility, and nothing has changed? Often, precious little. They can continue to have him over for dinner (assuming he won't steal the silverware), call him regularly, and extend other offers of help that don't reinforce his dependency. They can maintain an offer to pay for therapists and psychiatrists, or other adjuncts to his independence and mental health, if they can afford the bill. If they have a *lot* of money, they can send him to a residential treatment center for several months or longer in the hope that he'll get enough intensive therapy and recovery to commit to a different life course. But they can't make him. He'd have to agree to go.

What else is there? They can't lead his life for him. They can't give him money if he won't use it to launch an adult life. They can't pay his bills if it's going to further infantilize him. They have to grieve that he, in all likelihood, will never have the kind of life that they would wish for him.

While it's tempting in such situations to gloss over the pain by offering words of hope and inspiration, I don't find that kind of happy talk very useful to parents who have already tried everything. It's more likely to leave them feeling shamed, since it implies that they haven't tried hard enough. While I am an eternal optimist, we have to accept that sometimes hope is a bad idea, especially if it is based on the notion that we still have significant power to influence our adult children's lives. At some point we have to accept that they are on their own and, despite our worst mistakes and best efforts, now have to find their own way. We will always be their parents, but our ability to parent, at least in a significant way, eventually ends. At that point, we have to separate the verb from the noun.

However, there *is* reason to be hopeful about having a life where you don't feel so filled with worry, sorrow, or guilt. Gaining serenity comes in accepting what can't be changed, forgiving your child and yourself, and experiencing gratitude for what is good with or without your child.

DRUG AND ALCOHOL DEPENDENCE

Zoe was a "most likely to succeed" type of teenager. She had a fresh and innocent quality that made everyone want to be in her presence. To no one's surprise, Zoe got a scholarship to a prestigious liberal arts college in the East to study music. It was there that she met Howard, a fellow musician who introduced her to heroin. Like many of her peers, she was cautious about trying it, but her curiosity won out. By her third year of college, Zoe had developed a full-blown addiction and found herself unable to study, and disinterested to boot. She dropped out of college during the second semester of her junior year and moved into an apartment with several other addict friends. She didn't tell her parents that she dropped out because she wanted to continue to cash their checks to help support her habit. They didn't discover the truth until they opened a late tuition notice that she was supposed to have paid with the money they had sent her.

While Zoe's parents had the financial resources to get her into good treatment centers, her periods of recovery never lasted long, and her drug addiction followed her well into middle age. By then, the hard life of being an addict had worn away much of the beauty, brightness, and vitality that had been such a visible part of her. At forty-five, she got into Narcotics Anonymous and found her salvation there. But everyone who knew her recognized that she had lost something wonderful that was once hers.

Were there signs when she was young? Nothing obvious. Many relatives on her father's side were alcoholics, so there was certainly a genetic vulnerability. In addition, her relationship with her father wasn't especially close, so it's possible that she carried a deeper sense of rejection than either parent knew, though certainly nothing so dramatic that would predict her one day falling into a riptide that would carry her so far out into such destructive waters.

In my discussion with Zoe's parents, they expressed gratitude that she was still alive and in recovery. However, they also carried a profound sadness that this girl with so much promise had lived so much of her life in so much pain. They grieved a little every day—and some days a lot—that their baby would, in all likelihood, never reap the bounty promised by her brilliance and her beauty, the winning lottery tickets to a successful life. The vulnerability of her innocence, once the warm light that drew so many to her, had also drawn influences that she was too weak to resist. Their best efforts to save her from the destructive forces in life had proved fruitless. Throughout my meeting with them I heard the sad ostinato of so many wounded parents, *I failed her I failed her I failed her*, a rhythm so constant they scarcely heard the ragged sound of its refrain.

LEAVING THE PAST

In many ways, Zoe's parents were out of synch with their daughter. It's understandable that they would feel sadness or regret, yet they were stuck in those feelings, unable to let go of the past and move into the future. The guilty feelings they carried for letting her down prevented them from moving ahead with their lives and taking pleasure in what was still good in her life and in their own lives.

Over the next few months, I worked with Zoe's parents using the essential principles summarized in chapter 2. Here's what it looked like with Zoe's parents:

*Fearlessly take responsibility for whatever ways that you have
contributed to the problems in your relationship
with your child or your children.*

I directed Zoe's parents to write a list of the ways that they believed they let their daughter down. I then had them provide the evidence for each item. Many of the items didn't hold up when closely examined, and this offered some relief. However, they *had* continued to support her financially well past the time when they discovered her heroin addiction, and this prolonged the length of time it took before she hit bottom. In addition, her father acknowledged that his constant travel and preoccupation with work made Zoe feel rejected by him.

Make amends for the ways that you were wrong.

Zoe's parents met with her and expressed their regret for the ways that they had contributed to her problems. Fortunately for them, Zoe's recovery program emphasized forgiveness and her taking responsibility for her own behavior. This allowed her to accept their amends, and to make amends with them for the many ways that she had caused *them* pain.

*Move toward forgiving your child for how he or she hurt you
in the past or in the present (this doesn't mean condoning or
excusing bad behavior, or minimizing your hurt).*

While Zoe's parents were guilt-ridden, they were also angry at their daughter for lying to them, wasting their money, and causing them endless worry and suffering. Using the HEAL method, they were able to move toward forgiveness. A short version of their HEAL looked like this:

Hope: "To be able to watch our daughter take advantage of all of her gifts. To be able to have a close and loving relationship with her."

Educate: "We don't always know who is going to become an addict. Zoe's addiction is a disease that caused her to behave in ways that she is not proud of and is working to change. It wasn't her intention to hurt us or cause us pain."

Affirm: "We can still have a close relationship with our daughter and be the kind of parents that we want to be."

Long-Term Commitment: "We commit ourselves to attending Al Anon meetings so we can deepen our understanding of the disease. We will continue to work toward forgiving her for the ways that she hurt us and forgiving ourselves for the ways that we have hurt her. We also remain open to any future discussions of our wrongdoing going forward."

Move toward forgiving yourself for your mistakes as a parent.

I had Zoe's parents use the HEAL method for self-forgiveness as well. It looked like this:

Hope: "To be able to watch our daughter take advantage of all of her gifts. To be able to have a close and loving relationship with her."

Educate: "While we made mistakes, we did the best that we could at the time, given how scared and upset we were. Very few parents get this one right. We also did a lot to help her and remained dedicated throughout." Her father added, "I didn't realize that my preoccupation with work was hurtful to her. If I had known, I would have changed everything."

Affirm: "We can still have a close relationship with Zoe and be the kind of parents that we want to be. We remain dedicated and involved in her life and committed to her happiness."

Long-Term Commitment: "We commit ourselves to focusing on what is still wonderful in our daughter and what is still good in our relationship with her. We also commit ourselves to being grateful for what is good and valuable in her life and in our lives."

Some of the essential principles will follow naturally from practicing other principles. For example, if you work on forgiving your child and forgiving yourself, you'll find that compassion flows naturally out of this experience. In addition, if you practice feeling compassion for yourself and for your child, you will find that forgiveness of yourself and of your child will occur.

Move anger, guilt, shame, and regret into the background of your life and move hope, gratitude, and optimism into the foreground.

The primary burden of Zoe's parents was regret and shame. These feelings stemmed from their "unenforceable rules" about not seeing the clues of their daughter's risk for addiction and from their inability to influence their daughter in a healthier direction once she became an addict. As they were better able to challenge their irrational expectations about themselves as parents, they could reduce their feelings of shame and regret. In addition, they were able to reduce their feelings of shame and regret through the practice of gratitude.

Develop an identity and life story based on your strengths and achievements as a parent and individual, instead of a story about your suffering or failures.

They were many, many things that Zoe's parents did right as parents. They were dedicated, committed, and loving. They made sacrifices of time and money so she could attend good schools and treatment programs. Writing out and reviewing the many ways that they were committed as parents helped them to feel far less victimized by feelings of shame or regret, and instead allowed them to feel supported by feelings of strength and pride.

Get and maintain support from friends, family, or your faith.

Because of their shame, Zoe's parents hadn't confided their struggles in their friends. Through my encouragement, they joined Al Anon and received the support and wisdom of many other parents with similar struggles.

Give something back to society.

As a result of the support that they received from Al Anon, Zoe's parents started a group at their church for parents who were having struggles with their adolescent and adult children. That group continues to this day.

PARENTAL DAMAGE

Children can suffer long-term damage when raised by parents who are severely neglectful or abusive. Current studies in neurology demonstrate that children who live in these households often undergo changes in the brain's limbic system, a collection of interconnected nuclei involved in regulating emotions and memories. In particular, there is evidence that ongoing abuse leads to problems in the development of the hippocampus, which is important in retrieving verbal and emotional memories, and in the amygdala, which creates the emotions involved in fear or aggression.

In the same way that having a severe childhood illness may increase one's vulnerability to disease as an adult, severe abuse or neglect can make children more deficient in the internal resources needed to navigate the social and economic challenges of life. As children, they are more likely to have school failure, truancy, problems with drugs and alcohol, aggressive acting out (especially in boys), promiscuity, anxiety disorders, and depressive disorders. These changes in brain structure place those children far more at risk to develop lifelong struggles with depression, anxiety, aggression, or problems with intimacy. The effects of psychological abuse typically follow children into adulthood where the traumas are sometimes acted out on their own offspring— what psychologists refer to as the intergenerational transmission of pathology.

"My father was a big 6-foot–5 Irishman who wasn't afraid of anybody or anything," said Mike, a fifty-five-year-old. "He used to beat us for everything. One time I got beat just for sitting on the front steps. When I asked, 'What did I do?' he said, 'You didn't do nothing. You just looked like you needed a good reminder.' He was like that—always wanted to let you know who was boss. When I had kids, I was just as big of a sonofabitch as he was. I didn't hit my daughter, but I beat my son, William, probably as much as my dad beat on me. I've heard people say that they would never do to their kids what their parents did to them, but to tell the truth, I never thought like that. Now that he's grown, my son has had all kinds of problems; alcoholism, can't hold down a job. My wife blames me for how his life turned out. I used to say, 'Hey, I did all right with my life and I was raised the same way. You don't hear me whining about what my dad did to me!' But maybe she's right. I didn't have anything to do with my old man when I left home, and it looks like my son's carrying on the tradition."

SEXUAL ABUSE

Psychologist Alice Miller refers to incest and child molestation as "soul murder." Rightly so. Children who have been molested have their innocent trust in humanity stolen from them. It is not unusual for incest survivors to feel chronically endangered many years after the event, often for the rest of their lives.

Incest survivors are vulnerable to developing addictions and self-destructive behavior that prevents them from gaining any traction in adulthood. Their distrust in others often makes it hard for them to find or maintain the kind of relationships necessary to have meaningful work and achievement. Their difficulty in distinguishing good people from bad makes them vulnerable to getting involved in abusive relationships, and unable to end them.

"It took me well into my thirties to just wake up," said one incest survivor. "Wake up to what had happened to me, wake up to all of the drugs I took to hide the pain, wake up to all of the people I pushed away who wanted to help me. One day you realize you have to make a whole new house from the pieces of shattered wood that are lying all around you."

In my work with incest survivors and their parents, I have learned the lesson that I repeat throughout this book: if there is a chance that you can win your child back, it will only come from complete dedication on your part to doing everything imaginable to atone for what was done. Some incest survivors forgive; many don't. But they are more likely to do so if the parent shows *a deep and ongoing commitment, often for many, many years, to repair the traumas that they caused to their child.*

Holly is a thirty-three-year-old single woman whose alcoholic father molested her on several occasions during her adolescence. Her father, Frank, had also been molested when he was a child by an uncle who stayed with the children when his parents were out of town. When Holly began therapy at the age of twenty-one, she started to remember her father's molestations and told her mother. Frank was sent to jail for several years and was required to get psychological treatment.

As a result of his therapy, Frank faced his alcoholism and the ongoing nightmare he had perpetrated on his child. While his daughter had deep feelings of betrayal and rage at her father, she eventually went to family therapy with him when he got out of jail, and over the course of several years was able to move toward forgiveness. She was able to do so, in part, because Frank wrote a series of letters like the following:

Dear Holly,

I am so sorry for everything that I put you through. I recognize that I made your life a nightmare in many, many ways. You have every reason to be furious with me and to never want to see me again. While this would break my heart, I also accept that it might be too painful or confusing given my behavior in the past. I have worked hard to heal the troubled parts of me that caused me to act with you in the terrible ways that I did, and am now able to be a better father to you if you will let me. I understand that you might feel too betrayed and angry to want that.

Love,
Dad

Holly responded in the following way:

Dad,

I can't believe that you think I would even consider talking to you again. Do you know how much I have suffered as a result of you treating me like I was your girlfriend rather than your daughter? Do you have any idea how hard it is for me to just get up in the morning, go to my piece of shit job, go home, lock the door, and then pray to God that I don't have nightmares about my father coming into my room in the middle of the night? I don't think that you can begin to appreciate how hard it is for me to do the basic facts of living that so many people, you included, get to take for granted, such as brushing your teeth, paying bills, or going to the DMV. Did you know that I was addicted to speed throughout high school because I was too afraid to go to sleep at night for fear that you'd come into my room? And that I dropped out of college after the second year because I was too much of a nervous wreck to even begin to think about studying or going to a class? So, would I consider having a relationship with you? Not in a million years.

Holly

Holly's letters buried Frank in grief, guilt, and self-hatred. But with support from his therapist, he wrote her the following letter:

Dear Holly,

   I completely understand and you have every right to feel exactly how you do. I'm sure if either of my parents put me through what I put you through, I would feel exactly the same way. I didn't know that you were addicted to speed during high school, and feel awful hearing it was because of me. Obviously, there is a mountain of suffering that you've experienced either directly or indirectly because of me and are continuing to experience. I can never give you back your childhood or the innocence that you deserved. I want you to know that even if you don't want to see me again, I am more than willing to pay for your therapy, or your college if you decide to go back to school. If it genuinely makes you worse when I write or call, I won't keep doing it. Otherwise, I'd like to keep reaching out to you.

Love,
Dad

Frank continued to reach out to Holly with little return for more than two years. Eventually, she consented to have him attend several sessions with her and me. It has taken many years, and many therapy sessions, but Holly ultimately was able to let her father back into her life.

Why did Frank succeed where others fail? He did a number of things right:

- He took full responsibility for how his behavior had traumatized his daughter and damaged his relationship with her.

- He continued to reach out to her, despite getting nothing in return but more hurt and anger.

- He continued to reach out to her, despite the powerful feelings of guilt and self-loathing that her responses generated in him.

- He got adequate support from his therapist and AA sponsor so that he could work toward a feeling of self-compassion. As he was able to see the connection between his being molested and his molesting his daughter, he was able to contain his feelings of self-hatred so that he could continue to reach out to his daughter.

Many people have a hard time with the idea that someone who commits an act as horrible as incest should ever be supported in working toward self-forgiveness or self-compassion. While I understand this sentiment, I disagree with it. Self-compassion and self-forgiveness are at the heart of ending the cycles of violence that get handed down generation to generation. It was only because Frank got support from his therapist, his sponsor, and his church that he was able to be resilient enough to pursue his daughter's forgiveness and begin healing the damage that he had done. He was not only restored by his daughter's capacity to forgive; his capacity to feel compassion for himself gave him the strength to do the work that made her *consider* forgiving him.

RISK, ANXIETY, AND BECOMING AN ADULT

Becoming a full-functioning adult requires the ability to risk feeling disappointment, shame, and failure. It also requires being able to let your guard down. People who have been abused or neglected are often robbed of this capacity because they have a hard time believing that they should put their faith in *anyone*.

Children whose parents don't make amends, or who deny the abuse or the seriousness of it, rob their children of one of their most precious resources: their ability to test reality and trust their perceptions.

"My mother blamed me when I told her that my father molested me," said Colleen, a twenty-eight-year-old woman. "I know that it happened, but some days I find myself thinking, 'Well, did it? Did it really happen? Maybe I made it up, just like my dad says.'" Survivors of abuse sometimes can't get a clear picture of people's intentions at work or in social situations. They lack the resources to easily distinguish friend from foe, safety from threat, opportunity from cost.

TOO SCARED TO TRY

Some adult children come from homes where the parents were fairly reasonable, but the child's wiring makes him too afraid to take the risks that would lead to a healthy adulthood. For example, children who are fearful, socially avoidant, extremely shy or anxious, or highly sensitive to rejection may lack the makeup that would allow them to take on the challenges of romance, job interviews, or career advancement.

You have to be able to endure quite a few knocks to become a full-fledged adult, and some people are just too scared to stay in the ring. That's the wisdom in Woody Allen's often-quoted statement, "Eighty percent of life is just showing up." People who are traumatized or who carry a biological vulnerability feel too defective, shameful, small, ugly, unlovable, or insignificant to keep showing up. They feel so convinced of the dangerous world out there and of their insufficiency to meet its challenges that they vigorously avoid situations where those feelings might be disconfirmed. They feel too insecure to go for the job interview, call up the girl, challenge the boyfriend, ask for the promotion, apply to the college, or confront the friend. Among other emotions, fear of failure is often at the heart of these adults.

STAYING IN THE NEST

Staying longer in the nest isn't always a sign that something is wrong with the parent, the child, or the relationship between the two. The research of William Aquilino at the University of Wisconsin, for example, has shown that parents who have a positive relationship with all of their children are the most likely to have an adult child still living at home, as are parents who have never divorced.

On the other hand, the current culture of overprotective parenting may make it harder for some teens to enter adulthood. Children whose lives have been so carefully managed, and whose stresses have been so studiously curtailed, are sometimes robbed of the opportunity to develop the resources necessary to gain footing on the rocky slopes of adulthood.

In addition, some parents make it clear that they will feel too hurt, lonely, or rejected if their child becomes an adult. They make their children believe that growing up is a selfish and cruel act; that moving away is abandoning the parent; that independence is a form of patricide.

Nina and Bob came to counseling with their thirty-two-year-old son, Earle, who still lived at home. Earle had briefly moved out of the house for a year when he attended a local college, but moved back in with his parents after he dropped out. While I listened to the parents complain about Earle in tag-team fashion, two things became clear: (1) they had a lousy marriage, and (2) despite their nonstop complaints about Earle's dependence, the last thing they wanted was for him to move away because they would then be left alone in the house with each other—and they clearly didn't want that!

Like many of the "failure to launch" adults that I see in my practice, there was something poignant about Earle. He reminded me of Quentin Crisp's claim: "My father threatened me with the world and my mother sheltered me from it." Earle was caught between his own desires to escape from the toxic pull of his parents' dependence on him and being fully persuaded that he lacked the resources to go out on his own. As a result of this motivational seesaw, he moved between indignation at their lack of faith in him and pessimism about his ability to defy their predictions of his failure.

It is not unusual for one or both parents to cope with the defects in their marriage by becoming deeply invested in raising their children. While kids can sometimes benefit from this extra dollop of attention, it does more harm than good if the parents can't stop parenting when they should. For example, a teenager may unconsciously create personal problems that give mom and/or dad something to do if he senses that their self-esteem revolves around rescuing and solving the conflicts in his life. In addition, a teen may become very confused about how much to invest in her own needs vs. those of her needy parents if she has been made to provide the kind of attention, love, flattery, and reassurance that were more appropriately the responsibility of the spouse. She may develop beliefs that she's abandoning her parent to a lonely life by growing up, moving out, or moving on.

Questionnaire on Leaving the Nest

Circle the items that apply to you:

- I'm worried about how lonely I'll be when my teenager moves out.

- I'm worried about how lonely I've been since she moved out and worry that I make her feel guilty about moving away.

- I sometimes go to or went to my children for emotional needs that I should probably get from my spouse.

- I sometimes give my child mixed messages about whether I want him to grow up and be on his own.

- I don't know who I am or who'll I'll be if I'm not parenting.

- I have put a lot of energy into my children that should have gone to my marriage.

If you circled more than one of the above items, you may need more support in letting your child move out or move on. As a way of working on this, write a few paragraphs about why you might have made the choices that you made. This is an exercise in self-awareness and self-compassion, not self-flagellation. Here's what one parent wrote:

In hindsight, I put a lot of my energy into my children that should have gone to my marriage—that might have gone to my marriage if I had married a better partner. My youngest has hard a hard time leaving the nest and I can see that it's because she's worried about me being alone with her father. I didn't realize that was the reason she kept moving back home. I was happy whenever she'd move back in because I felt like, "Thank God, somebody to talk to," other than her father who won't say boo to you all day long. Because of therapy I see that she needs a little more reassurance that I'm fine without her. I've been really trying to act like that. But I do regret how much she's had to worry about me, though I'm trying to not be so hard on myself about that.

OVERLY WORRIED PARENTS

Many parents are justifiably worried about the subtle or overt ways their children are less confident, popular, smart, or driven than the seemingly countless other happy, successful children riding in cars, walking in malls, and strolling across tree-lined campuses. Unfortunately, parental worry can erode children's feelings of confidence and well-being. It can cause parents to be excessively critical and angry, blinding them to the wonderful aspects of their child that have nothing to do with getting into a good college or establishing a career.

Adolescence can create dynamics that bring out the worst in both parent and child—dynamics that may interfere with the teen developing enough confidence and self-esteem to become a full-functioning adult. Parents may become especially thrown off balance by potential drug and alcohol use, children's inability to be social—or social with the right kind of peers—their school failure, and by the confusing roller-coaster ride of their hyper-emotionality.

For example, Larry is a seventeen-year-old attending a private high school in San Jose that specializes in learning disabled children. Despite a very genial and pleasant demeanor, Larry is sufficiently different from other teens that he defies placement even among the kids who defy placement. As a result, he constantly feels on the outs with his peers.

Larry has another, and perhaps, more serious problem, and that is his parents' terror—and I mean *terror*—about his poor academic performance and inability to find a peer group. In my initial consultation with Larry's parents, his mother cried and his father shook his head. "We just think he's going to end up in a ditch somewhere if he doesn't get his shit together," his father said. "He doesn't try. Every time I go into his room he's playing one of those damned computer games. I got so mad at him last month that I tore the keyboard out of his hands and tossed his computer in the trash. I mean, that's how mad the kid makes me. We're paying all of this money so that he can go to a good high school and this is the thanks we get. He doesn't do what the learning specialist says, doesn't do what the school counselor says, doesn't do what we say. He just does whatever he feels like doing. I don't see how this kid is ever going to make it in the world."

"It's not just that," his mother joined in. "He doesn't have any friends. His school counselor says he always eats lunch by himself. I'm always saying to him, 'Honey, you have to make the effort. People aren't going to come to you in life, you have to come to them.' But he just says that none of the kids like him there, and that breaks my heart. He had the same problem in grade school. Everyone said it would be better in high school, but it's only gotten worse. I shudder to think about college, if he can even get into one, which at this rate ..."

Larry would have a hard time of it no matter who his parents were. It's awful to be the kid who doesn't have any friends, and even harder if you're burdened with a severe learning disability. But Larry's well-meaning, though terrified parents make things worse because their worry makes them blame him for things that are largely out of his control. Most of their time with him is spent criticizing his approach to his schoolwork or social life. Since those are in constant disarray, the conversations result in making him feel more defective and discouraged.

I told Larry's parents that they should take the long-term perspective on their son and try to be less focused on whether he gets into a great college or starts dating within the next year. Many teenagers go on to have successful adulthoods despite a very unpopular adolescence and a less-than-remarkable high school record. Some people don't figure out how to study, how to date, or even who they are until much later in life. Adolescence isn't the last chance, even if it is some version of a last chance for the parents to exert some influence.

Obviously the jury is out on Larry; he's only seventeen and he may find his way regardless of how his parents behave. But he would benefit from a lot more support and a lot less criticism. Entry into adulthood is easier if you're not waging a war on two fronts: one with your insecurities, and the other with your parents.

Worry Questionnaire

Circle the statements that best fit your situation:

- I spend a lot of my time worrying about my child's ability to develop a successful life.

- My worry causes me to communicate in ways that probably make my child feel criticized, shamed, or controlled.

- My worry over my child makes it hard for me to value or think about other positive aspects of who she is.

- Worry about my child has had a negative affect on my marriage and/or my other relationships.

- Worry about my child causes me to neglect other aspects of my life that need attention.

Healing Exercise:
How to Reduce Your Worrying

Worry is often based on irrational beliefs or catastrophizing. The following are common worries of wounded parents. They are followed by positive counter-statements for you to practice:

Belief: My child will never have a good life.
Positive counter-statement: Sometimes people develop better lives as they get older. However, even if he doesn't, my worrying is counterproductive for my child and for me.

Belief: My child's lack of a social life is heartbreaking.
Positive counter-statement: My worrying about it all of the time feels like a vote of no-confidence to her. I may be able to help her solve this problem, but only if she wants my help.

Belief: Worrying shows that I care. If I stopped worrying, it would be equivalent to neglect.

Positive counter-statement: Worry is only useful if I'm truly in danger of missing something. If I'm spending more than five minutes a day worrying, that's too much.

Healing Exercise:
Reducing Worry Through Action

If you find yourself obsessed with worrying, you will need to practice behaviors that reduce your worrying and increase your serenity. Here are some worry-busters:

Make an agreement with yourself that you'll spend no more than five minutes a day worrying about your child. After that you will do one or more of the following:

- Call a friend but don't talk about your kids unless it makes you feel better. If you're going to call a friend, make sure that friend knows how to make you feel supported rather than guilty or misunderstood.

- Put on some loud music that you like.

- Work out.

- Read something that's captivating.

- Go for a walk, a hike, or have some other communal experience with nature.

- Meditate.

- Do yoga.

CATASTROPHIZING ABOUT CHILDREN'S FAILURES

Fear of what will become of their children is a source of torment for many parents. This is especially true for parents whose children are doing poorly academically or socially, or are having trouble launching an adult life or relating affectionately to the parent. I have found in my life and practice that knowing what you have control over and what you don't is a good thing to know. So here's a checklist of some things you can do:

- Get yourself into therapy.

- Get your teen into therapy.

- With an adult child, try to get him or her to go to family therapy with you. If not, consult with a therapist about the best way to proceed.

- If drugs or alcohol are an issue for your teen, tie privileges to their getting into a recovery program.

- Consider an "intervention" if your adult child has an alcohol or drug problem.

- Work on your communication skills.

- Take care of your health with exercise, adequate sleep, and a healthy diet.

- Get adequate support from friends and family.

- Get support from your faith.

- Make sure your life has meaning apart from your role as a parent.

MANAGING PARENTAL DESPAIR

Despair is usually based on catastrophic thinking about yourself or negative forecasting about your child's future or your relationship with him or her. When people feel despairing about their children, it often results from mentally circulating one or more of the following dysfunctional beliefs:

- He'll never get it together.

- Her behavior and our relationship mean I'm a failure.

- I'll feel too lonely or inadequate if things don't improve.

- My life is over.

- I'll feel too empty.

- I'll feel too bitter.

- I'll never be happy.

Let's use a few of these to practice fighting feelings of despair by making positive self-statements:

Automatic Thought: *"He'll never get it together."*
Positive Self-Statement: For teen: "Perhaps he won't. But as long as he's under my roof, I'll do everything in my power to help him. If I'm currently doing that, then I will work hard to feel more self-accepting and self-forgiving using the strategies in this book."
For adult child: "Perhaps he won't. But my ruining my life with worry and regret doesn't do anything except make me miserable. It isn't selfish to enjoy my life."

Automatic Thought: *"Her behavior and our relationship mean I'm a failure."*

Positive Self-Statement: "Every parent wishes they could have done better. If I made mistakes, I'll continue to work hard to heal them in my child. However, I'm committed to look at other areas of my life for gratitude, pleasure, and pride other than or in addition to my parenting."

Automatic Thought: *"I'll never be happy without a close relationship to my child."*
Positive Self-Statement: "I deserve a happy life regardless of what has occurred in the past or what is occurring in the present. Happiness is part of my birthright. While I want my child back in my life, there are many ways for me to have a good life."

Healing Exercise:
Managing Disappointment

Managing feelings of disappointment requires letting go of what you hoped would be. At one end, it may require relinquishing the wish that your child would be as successful academically, socially, romantically, or financially as you'd hoped; at the other, it may mean facing that you and your child may never have the kind of closeness that you wished you'd have. Managing your feelings of disappointment is key to your ongoing serenity and mental health. As one parent put it, "I found it essential to recognize and let go of my 'fantasy' children. I was living vicariously (and unknowingly) through my daughter's modest success as a child actress and my hope that my son would become a successful animator or a pilot (he's thirty now, unemployed and likely still an addict). Once I recognized I was forcing my kids into my own fantasies, I realized my kids could never measure up. My husband, being a college professor, had his own expectations. I had to learn how to be proud of little things: their day-to-day achievements (the C in math instead of an A) instead of being continually disappointed that they didn't measure up to my ideas of success. Today I have a good connection with all four adult kids, regardless of their material and educational success."

Worry about children creates ongoing anxiety and depression in your life. It can severely burden your marriage, if not ruin it. It can cause you to ignore your other children, family members, or friends who also want and need your love and attention—people who have love and attention to give to you. Worry is a monumental waste of your precious time.

TWELVE

ALL GROWN UP
AND WANTS NOTHING
TO DO WITH ME

Parenting Adult Children

"How sharper than a serpent's tooth it is
to have a thankless child."

SHAKESPEARE, KING LEAR

It is every parent's worst nightmare. The child whom you put everything into moves away, won't return your calls, ignores your e-mails, and rejects your attempts to be close. He has his reasons, of course— your lousy parenting, your treatment of the other parent, your selfishness, your inattention, your cruelty, the divorce—whatever; he has decided to execute the nuclear option, which is to completely cut off contact.

It's common, though rarely talked about, even with friends. It's too painful and too humiliating. And it invites *The Questions*:

"Have you tried calling him?"

"Yes."

"Confronting him?"

"Yes."

"Trying to get him into therapy?"

"Yes."

"Setting limits?"

"Yes."

"Apologizing?"

"Yes."

"Telling him your perspective?"

"Yes."

"Explaining what was going on for you at the time?"

"Yes."

"Giving him a taste of his own medicine?"

"Yes." "Yes." "Yes."

It's hard for most people to accept the tragic reality that sometimes there's nothing that can be done to save a relationship between a parent and a grown child. Then again, sometimes there is. This chapter is written to provide guidance, and to help you find peace—whether it will be with or without your child in your life.

FAMILY WOUNDS

There are many reasons why an adult child might temporarily or permanently cut off a parent. Some common ones are:

- Mental illness or alcohol/drug dependency of the adult child

- Anger or hurt over treatment by the parent

- Anger or hurt at how the parent treated the other parent

- Allying with the parent of the same gender

- Allying with the parent who has made it clear that he or she needs that child's alliance, such as in a divorce or in a high-conflict marriage

- Reaction against the parent's rejection of the child's sexuality, politics, religion, living situation, or choice of romantic partner

- Reaction against the revelation of the parent's sexuality

MENTAL ILLNESS AND ALCOHOL/DRUG DEPENDENCY

Adults who suffer from schizophrenia, anti-social personality, borderline personality, or even extreme social avoidance may have little to do with a parent once they leave home because people with these diagnoses may have a harder time forming lasting attachments. In addition, children at risk for developing problems such as anti-social personality or other personality disorders may make it especially challenging for parents to behave in ways that prevent the possibility of long-term alienation. "I don't think a day goes by that I don't remember some stupid thing that I said to Robbie," said Howard, a father of a thirty-two-year-old. "He was such a wild kid. We were always getting into it over something—his grades, stealing the car, taking money, whatever. I never thought I'd ever hit any of my kids, but I hit him on more than one occasion. We had our share of shoving matches, too, especially once he was older. Did I make my share of mistakes? Hell yes, I did. And I'm paying the price every single day, 'cause I haven't seen him since about a year after he moved out."

Studies show that having a child who has a long-standing mental illness is one of the strongest predictors of depression in mothers. Mothers of children who aren't on schedule to become independent adults experience a personal sense of failure. This was certainly true of Helene, the mother of a forty-year-old, Jolene: "Jolene had her first nervous breakdown when she was eighteen and that was awful. Over the next ten years, she was in and out of mental institutions and continued to live with us. She'd never stay on her medications, though, and that was a problem because once she was off of them, she just couldn't function; talking about the government planting things in the garden to spy on her and the like. She decided to move out when she was about twenty-eight. Frank and I were relieved, to tell you the truth. We didn't think she could function on her own, but her living with us made it impossible to have a normal life, never knowing when she was going to have another one of her breakdowns, finding her cowering in a corner sometimes looking just terrified. But I should've never let her move out because I haven't heard from her for years. She's got a cousin she stays a little in touch with and the last time she heard from her, she was moving to some commune or something. It's worse than having a child die, not knowing where they are or how they're doing. I never stop worrying about her. They're always your baby."

Alcoholism and drug dependency can cause adult children to cut off contact with their parents for any of the following reasons:

- Long-standing addiction that began in adolescence may have severely strained the relationship between the parent and child; for example, in those cases where the addiction caused the child to steal from the parents, be verbally or physically abusive, or defy the parents' authority.

- The shame of the addict/alcoholic may cause him or her to cut off all significant others, parents included.

- The addictive behavior may be in response to severe parental mistreatment, such as when a teen seeks to medicate the anger, hurt, anxiety, or fear resulting from parents who are verbally, physically, or sexually abusive.

- The addictive behavior may have started as an attempt to contain a mental illness generally unrelated to the parenting, such as a biologically-based anxiety disorder or major depression.

DIVORCE

As discussed in chapter 9, divorce creates myriad opportunities for long-term alienation between children and their parents for a variety of reasons: Facts about the parent's behavior before or after the divorce, such as infidelity, not paying child support, and so on may cause the child to feel hurt, angry, or betrayed by the parent; for example, when a parent says, "Your mother never really wanted you," or "Your father never spent any time with you when you were little. I had to do everything." Divorce may also increase the possibility that a child feels obligated to support the parent perceived to be victimized by the divorce, or the parent who is less psychologically healthy.

A child may reject a parent out of feelings of loyalty or duty to the parent of the same gender. In addition, the parent's behavior after the divorce may create a rift; for example, if the parent spent less time with the child, chronically complained about the other parent, or married someone the child strongly dislikes.

I have worked with families where the adult child reduced or cut off contact with a parent after learning that the marriage ended because his father revealed himself as gay, or his mother as lesbian. In those situations, the parent is faced, not only with the loss of the child's love, but with the weight of dealing with the feelings of hurt or anger evoked by their child's rejection of his or her sexuality. As one gay father said, "My sixteen-year-old son, whom I had raised to be a tolerant person, was really mean to me when I came out a year after I divorced his mother. I was worried about how my parents would respond, but never my own son. While my parents were great about it, he refused to see me for almost two years. That was easily the most painful thing I have ever gone through in my whole life."

DYSFUNCTIONAL MARRIAGES

Studies show that children are far more likely to choose sides in marriages where there is a lot of conflict. In addition, mothers are less likely to stay involved with their daughters in these marriages, while fathers often withdraw from both daughters and sons. This deterioration in closeness sometimes follows them into adulthood. "My parents probably should have gotten a divorce," said Roberta, a twenty-five-year-old woman. "They hated each other and made no secret about it. They're still together but I have no desire to spend any time with either one of them. Why would I want to? I've built my own family with my own children and husband instead."

Parents in high-conflict marriages manage their emotions through shaming, shouting, blaming, and sometimes physical abuse of each other and their children. As a result, children who grow up in those homes often have a harder time knowing how to productively communicate their feelings. This can create enduring conflict, since neither parent nor child has the tools to begin building a bridge to the other.

PARENTAL MISTAKES

Parents who were verbally, physically, or sexually abusive, drug or alcohol addicted, neglectful, or overly critical may have left emotional scars on the child, making that child reluctant or unwilling to give the parent another chance.

Sometimes, the simple fact of the child becoming an adult sets the stage for a rift, *even* when the young adult doesn't feel negatively about the parent. As one college sophomore said, "My parents had a really hard time with me just growing up and moving out of the house. They put all of this pressure on me to go to a local college even though I got a full scholarship to a good school in the East. My first semester away, they would freak out if I didn't call them every night. I just felt like, "Hey, c'mon, let go. I mean, I know you love me and all, but it's time to cut the cord.' They'd just lay these huge guilt trips on me that really made me not want to call them at all."

A child's transition into adulthood also creates the opportunity for the parent to express criticism of how their child is managing adult life. Decisions around choice of romantic partners (or the lack thereof), religion, finances, child rearing, place of residence, sexuality, and religion are common triggers for conflict between parents and their adult children.

"My mother never liked any of my girlfriends and she can't stand my wife," said Marty, a thirty-year-old attorney. "Yes, my wife is kind of a pushy New Yorker, but she's also a great gal. I finally got so sick and tired of my mother complaining about her that I said, 'Look, Ma, I really don't want to hear another word of complaint about Irene. You want to see me and the kids, you need to keep your mouth shut about her.' She kept it up though, until finally we just stopped going over there."

If you dislike or disapprove of your adolescent or adult child's choice of romantic partner:

Strive to avoid:

- Criticizing their choice. If you want to spend time with your adult child, you need to accept his or her partner, even if you would never choose that person for your child. If your child asks for your advice about how to deal with a partner, give it in a few sentences, but in a mild, uncritical way.

- Giving parenting advice that hasn't been requested. Yes, you have much more knowledge, but that doesn't mean that your child will welcome your provision of this hard-won experience. This also extends to giving advice about money, housework, careers, religious observance, and use of leisure time.

- Placing your adult child in a loyalty bind between you and his or her partner in any way.

Strive to:

- Demonstrate and verbalize acceptance of your adult child's choice of partner. Let him or her know what you like or approve of in him or her. This is one of those areas where the "If you can't say anything nice, don't say anything at all," maxim holds true. If you have some concerns, you can voice them on rare occasions, with a positive. For example, "Robert is really funny. I can see why you like him. It seems like he drinks a lot. Has that been a problem for him?" If your child clearly indicates that he or she wants your help in leaving the relationship, you can shift into much more of an advocacy role. For example, "Robert clearly has a drinking problem and I can see why he'd be really hard to live with. You've been talking about wanting to leave him. Do you know what's making that hard to do?" As you can see, these are very different positions tendered from the same observation of Robert's drinking problem. Obviously, if Robert is also the father of your grandchildren, you'll want to help your child develop a much more graded series of steps before divorce, assuming she'll let you help him or her.

- Catch them doing something right. If you disapprove of your child's parenting, or the parenting of your child's partner, compliment what you approve of in their parenting.

If your child's spouse or partner is abusive, then you would need to be more direct in your concerns. However, even here, you have to accept that your child is an adult and will have to find his or her own way. While it's always painful to see adult children making terrible choices in their romantic partners, we may drive them further into the other's arms by making them feel criticized, shamed, or controlled by our reactions.

THE BEGINNINGS OF ADULTHOOD

Adulthood starts a lot later than it used to, and this creates all kinds of potential havoc between parents and the children who no longer live with them. Here are some reasons why:

- Parents sometimes have a harder time understanding why their children aren't able to do what they did at a similar age, and respond in ways that are hurtful to their children.

- Young adults may feel shamed by their difficulty in gaining meaningful employment, or in becoming financially independent. As a result, they may have to reject the parent as a way to establish their own identity.

- The more intensive relationship that is now common between parents and children means that children's emotional dependence on parents is extended, and therefore the need to "prove" independence from parents may last longer.

STRINGS ATTACHED

These days, a lot more adult children are receiving support from their parents than in prior generations. A study by the Institute of Social Research at the University of Michigan found that 34 percent of young adults between the ages of 18 and 34 receive money on a regular basis from their parents. According to government statistics gathered in 2005, middle-income parents can expect to spend $190,980 on each child through the age of 17. However, these days, parents can anticipate spending an additional 25 percent of that amount again over the next 17 years.

These expenditures are not only financial: today's parents spend an additional nine weeks of their time yearly on helping adult children aged 18 to 34 with babysitting, transportation, and doing laundry. While all of this help can provide rich opportunities for closeness between parents and their adult children, it can create opportunities for more conflict.

Many parents get confused about what they're entitled to receive from their children in exchange for time or financial support, even when that support is partial. "My parents helped me to move out of the house and get me set up with my own apartment," said, Sam, a twenty-five-year-old. "On the one hand, that was really nice of them and everything, on the other hand, I just feel like they used it to keep me tied to them. It was like because they helped me a little, they were entitled to my coming over and spending time with them whenever they wanted me to—and if I didn't, they'd say shit like, 'After all we've done for you, you can't come over once in a while and spend time with us? If it wasn't for us, you'd probably be sleeping in a gutter somewhere.' I felt like saying, 'Just because you help me out now and then doesn't mean that you can still tell me what to do. I'm not twelve.' Finally, I just thought, 'Screw that, how about if I don't come over at all?'"

I also find that many adult children are confused about what they're entitled to receive from their parents by way of time and money. Because it's now more common for adult children to get help from their parents, young adults feel freer to express resentment toward the parents who fails to provide it. This is one more way that today's parents are held to a standard of involvement and care that was less common in prior generations. As one father said, "By his age, I had a job, a mortgage, a wife, and a baby. He doesn't have any of those things and he's still got his hand out. He's twenty-three now and if I don't meet every financial request, I'm treated like I'm some neglectful, abusive parent. Give me a break."

Strive to avoid:

- Giving mixed messages around your gifts of time or money. If your child asks you for money, and you feel deprived of time together, be direct. Say something like, "I'm happy to loan (or give) you the money, but I want to spend some time with you. When can we do that?"

- Acting victimized or overly burdened. It may be that the only occasion you hear from your child is when he needs something. If I had a penny for every time I heard that complaint from a parent, well, I'd have an awful lot of pennies. Don't get too caught up in that. You can say *no* if you want to, but don't get into a big, victimized, self-righteous stance. On the other hand, you can occasionally use it to extract (as in *pulling teeth*) some time with them. You can say, "Sure, let's have lunch next week and I can give it (money) to you then."

She says, "I can't."

You say, "No problem. Why don't you suggest a good time to have lunch or dinner."

She says, "There isn't any good time. I just want to know if you can loan me the money."

You say, "You know, I am willing to, but it has to be more in the context of a real relationship, or it doesn't end up feeling that good to me. I enjoy helping you from time to time, but not if that's the only relationship that I have with you." *Note*: this should not be said every time. Your young adult child may need a lot of independence from you and therefore it's counterproductive to make a demand for every request— and there may be a lot of requests. But, over time, if it's true that the only occasion that you see your child is to fulfill a demand to provide money, then you may want to occasionally make it contingent on a real interaction with you.

- Avoid guilt trips, such as, "When I was your age, I had a house, a car, a job, and two kids. What's your problem?" Or, "What's with you always coming to me with your hand out? I'm sick of it."

Strive to:

- Say yes or no in a clear way. If you want to tell him no, say something like, "I'd love to help you, but I'm not in a position to right now." Or, if that's dishonest, say something like, "No, I'm sorry. I just lent you money last month and would rather you pay that back first." Or, "No, I think I'd rather you find a way to get by without my helping you in that way this time. Hope that feels okay." Even if it doesn't feel okay, you have to do it if you believe it's the right thing to do. Remember: *It's always better to say no, respectfully than yes, contemptuously.*

- Give time or money without demanding anything in return. Giving our children the gift of time or money doesn't entitle us to give them advice about how to best use it. You are under no obligation to give more than you want, and you are completely free to say no if you want. But if you're going to say yes, be careful not to tie up the good feelings generated by your generosity with excessive strings.

SEPARATION GUILT AND SEPARATION ANXIETY IN THE YOUNG ADULT

The late teens and early twenties can be a tumultuous period for today's parents and their children. Both are worried: parents of college-bound children are concerned about whether their kids will go to college, get into a decent college, and function adequately once they get there. Both are rightly worried about the dwindling number of jobs available once they're out of high school or college.

Then there's the psychological task of entering adulthood following a history of intense closeness between parents and their children. In the same way that couples may have to vilify each other as a way of not missing the other person when they break up, some adult children demonize their parents as a way to remind themselves that they don't need them to survive in the world. "I was completely caught off-guard," said Elena, mother of a nineteen-year-old college student. "I felt like I went from best friend to worst enemy in two semesters! Suddenly I started hearing about how selfish I've always been, how she doesn't want to be like me, how I never listened to her. It's really hurtful and disorienting!"

Elena's daughter was struggling to gain independence from her mother by rejecting her. It's never pleasant for the person on the receiving end, but it's a very effective tool for the one who's doing it. Why would this be the case? Because, from the child's vantage point, it's a way of saying to yourself, "How can I miss her when she has so little to offer? Why should I need her when I won't get anything from her?"

Understandably, many parents misread this phenomenon. It's natural for parents to want to counter rejection by rejecting back, especially in our culture where revenge and counter-attacks are pro forma. However, keep in mind that nothing could be more wrong than to return fire when a young adult begins to withdraw or separate from you by being critical of you. Since her developmental goal is to establish independence, your counter-blame or counter-rejection will just feel like a confusing form of possessiveness.

This doesn't mean that you should just smile and nod no matter how you feel. Instead, try to think about why she's saying what she's saying, and proceed in step-wise fashion from there. Here are some actions to take when you're feeling attacked:

1. Take a deep breath and soothe yourself so that you can think
   clearly. Don't say anything until you're relatively calm. John
   Gottman has shown that when your pulse rate rises ten
   beats per minute above its average, your ability to think
   clearly is greatly reduced. If you can't calm yourself down,
   then say something like, "I'm interested in what you have to
   say and want this to be a productive conversation. I'd like to
   sit with this a bit and call you back later."

2. Listen for the kernel of truth. In almost every complaint,
   there's some small aspect that is true. Try to acknowledge it,
   even if you think it's highly exaggerated. "Yeah, I could see
   how you might have felt like that." You're not copping to
   being a terrible person or parent, you're just keeping the
   lines of communication open and reducing the defensive-
   ness in your child.

3. Ask what your child would like in response: More time
   apart? More patience, acceptance, restraint? Don't assume
   that he knows, because these interactions are sometimes
   more about the music than the lyrics. It's less about your
   saying exactly the right thing than showing that you can tolerate your child becoming his own person, with his own
   ideas. Unfortunately for you, criticizing who you are or how
   you raised him sometimes achieves the biggest gains for
   your child. This is one of those times when you just have to
   deal with it and not get too agitated.

4. Approach the topic again in a few weeks. "I was checking in
   to see if you had further thoughts about what we talked
   about. The door is always open." Your goal in doing this is
   to let your child know that you can take the hit; that you're
   not too fragile for her to be separate from you or to have a
   harsh perception of you; and that you think enough of her
   in her new adult skin to want to listen to her opinions.

5. You don't have to tolerate abuse. Tolerating criticism and complaints are not the same as letting yourself be abused or walked on. If you find yourself feeling too upset or defensive, go back to Step 1.

CONTINUE TO REACH OUT

Most parents give up too soon on their grown children who cut them off or greatly reduce contact. This is understandable. It hurts to keep trying to be close to someone who constantly slams the door in your face. However, I recommend that my clients continue to reach out because things often change over time. A child may encounter life situations that require her needing to reach out to you, and she is more likely to do so if the door is open than if it's shut. A child may get a new partner or spouse who is able to help him see that you're not so terrible after all. A child may have children and learn that being a perfect parent isn't so easy. A child of divorce may mature enough to view you as human, not as an ogre.

Parents who *don't* continue to reach out may be inadvertently sending the message that the child has no right to complain and should get over it, already. As one client of mine said, "My mother acts like the fact that she told me she was sorry once or twice that my stepfather molested me means that she's off the hook; end of story—never have to go back there again. Right. It just makes me feel like she doesn't care about me, and it's all about her. Like I'm not supposed to burden her with the pain of my life and act like she didn't have some responsibility to protect me."

Continuing to reach out is a parental act. It's a demonstration of concern and dedication. It keeps the door open. It humanizes you. It shows that you love your child enough to fight for him even when you're getting back—literally—nothing but grief.

Here's a guideline: It's extremely tempting to cut off or withhold support from a child by whom you feel betrayed or hurt.

Don't. Whatever kind of generosity you would extend to one of your children, extend to all of your children. Even if it's through gritted teeth, if you would pay for college, weddings, or child care for the children who are close and loving, you should pay for college, weddings, or child care for the child who is rejecting and hurtful. Why? Because, presumably, you're reading this book for help in finding a way back to your child or into finding a way to feel more at peace. Therefore, you want to keep the door open for the future. Many children in their twenties, and sometimes older, behave in a way that would make anyone conclude that a reuniting with the parents is simply not in the cards. But often things change. In addition, it's simply too hurtful to children when their parents are more giving to their siblings than they are to them.

Here's another guideline: Continue to extend invitations, even if you know they'll refuse. "We're going to go to Wyoming for a vacation this summer and wanted to know if you wanted to come." They may decline, but at least the invitation is on the books. If you really don't want them there because they're too troubled, then that may require more limit-setting than open invitations. "Because of my son's alcoholism, he was really difficult to spend time around," said Jacob, the father of a twenty-three-year-old. "You never knew when he was going to get into some big drama, or just go off about some trivial thing when he was drinking. I finally had to say to him, 'We'd love to have you over to the house this Sunday for dinner, but not if you're drinking. Your personality really changes and I don't think you're very aware of it. So, unless you can commit to remaining sober, I'd rather you not come.' So, we didn't see him for a while and I had to make peace with that, which wasn't easy. I still called him and tried to maintain the relationship, though. Eventually he got into recovery, and things have been a lot better since then."

For children from eighteen to thirty years of age, I recommend that you reach out about one time a week. It could be an e-mail, a phone call, or a card. It can be short, sweet, and to the point. "Hi, honey. Just checking in with you to see how you're doing. Would love to hear what you're up to. Take care."

You may hear from your child one month, and then not again for another few months. You may feel like the relationship is on the mend only to have the Pandora's box of the past blown open again. "I feel like I'm on a merry-go-round with my daughter," said one divorced father. "When I feel the past is behind us, I'll make some comment or she'll hear something from her mother and we're back to square one where I'm the terrible dad all over again. It's pretty damned exhausting. I really don't feel like we'll ever have a normal relationship."

What do you do if your child tells you not to contact him again? At this age, you ignore him. You say, "I can't do that. You're my child and I can't *not* call you." I emphasize this because you're his parent, not his peer. You needn't call him every day, but checking in once a week or so is reasonable; so is sending cards or presents on birthdays and holidays. Even if he deletes the message without listening, throws away the card, or doesn't open the present, it's the symbolic value of the act that counts. In other words, just keep the door open, show you're strong enough to keep fighting for the relationship, and show that you're willing to have a dialogue about the past.

Some adult children will feel guilty if you reach out too often. If you feel certain that they'll experience it as harassment and not love, it may be better to err on the side of more distance rather than less. This would be especially true for children who have demonstrated that they can reach out to you from time to time.

CONVERSATIONS ABOUT THE PAST

As your children get older, it becomes more reasonable to fill in the gaps about their perceptions of you. You should first ask if they want to hear your version of the story. You could say, "The experts say that it's not helpful, so I haven't. Not sure if you're ready, but I'll defer to what feels right to you." One mother I worked with handled it in the following way: "I waited until my son was twenty-four before I told him any of the details about why I left his dad. My ex and I did what our marriage counselor told us to do, which was to act like the divorce was a mutual decision so the kids didn't feel obligated to take sides. It was so hard because my son carried a lot of blame and anger toward me about it all, and I had to bite my lip a lot to not blame his dad in the ways that I wanted to. But I figured by the time he hit twenty-four, it was time to tell him more of my feelings about it. He asked. He said it was helpful to hear my perspective and it allowed him to feel more forgiving towards me. We've actually been a lot closer since then, so I'm glad."

HOW AND WHEN TO DEFEND YOURSELF

I have talked a lot about the importance of taking responsibility for past mistakes. However, most parents feel consumed by guilt when their children blame them, *even* when that blame is way off base. Acting enormously guilty for crimes you didn't commit may be confusing to your child. While contrition is helpful when there are serious mistakes, being repentant for a very distorted rendition of the past doesn't do anyone any favors. As children get older and more mature, it's appropriate to push back harder against wrongful accusations—not in a hostile, defensive way—but from a position of strength. So, for example:

Child says, "You only cared about yourself throughout my whole childhood."

You say, "You've said that to me before, and it isn't true. I certainly wasn't a perfect parent, but I was very, very devoted to you." Note: Avoid a guilt trip. Don't say, "After everything I've done for you, how can you treat me like this?" Just keep it fact-based.

Child says, "You were so mean to Mom after the divorce. You didn't give her enough money for us or for her."

You say, "I know it wasn't enough money for your mom. The money didn't stretch as far as we *both* would have liked. Just so you know, I actually did pay everything that the court stipulated that I was supposed to pay in the settlement." In other words, acknowledge the reality of the other parent: "I know it wasn't enough money for your mom," while showing what your reality was at the time. Your child might have experienced a huge decrease in his standard of living after the divorce, and that may have been shameful or humiliating, so you should validate that, as well.

These conversations are rarely simple. Your child may then respond with something like, "Yeah, but you have a nice, big house and mom's still renting. She's *still* struggling and you're not struggling at all!"

You say, "I know, but most of that money I earned after the divorce" (or, "I had that money before the marriage," if that's the case). "I know that your mom is really angry that my standard of living has gone up since we split up, but I actually don't owe her more than I've given. I can see how it doesn't seem fair." Remember: Don't get into all of the particulars of the past, or about your perspective, in one sitting. Just respond to the specifics that your child raises. These are high-stakes conversations and they have to be handled correctly. You'll probably get more than one chance, but your next chance may not occur for months or, sometimes, years.

Here's another common scenario:

Child says, "You cheated on Dad and I can never forgive that."

You say, "I understand, and I'm not asking you to. But, at that time, your father was extremely critical and rejecting of me, and had been for years. I felt very alone. However, I'm certainly not proud of having an affair."

Child says, "Yeah, well, I still think it's pretty screwed up on your part."

You say, "I understand that. I might feel the same way if I knew that my mother cheated on my father. But it is a lot more complicated than you know. I couldn't let myself think about getting out of the marriage at that time. I didn't want to put you or your brother through a divorce, and I didn't have the adult tools to end the marriage by having a healthy divorce instead of having an affair. Looking back, if I had been able to face those feelings, I would have made much better choices and would feel better about myself today."

It's preferable that adult children be protected from the details of their parents' lives, but, if their opinion of you is being poisoned by other people, especially an influential person like the other parent, then it can be helpful to them for you to set the record straight. Be careful not to overdo it and not to use these discussions, inappropriately, as opportunities to hit back at the other parent. In addition, this is a conversation to have with children in their mid-twenties or older, *not* mid-teens or younger.

Many parents make the mistake of telling their younger children bad things about the other parent with the following excuses or justifications:

- "I just thought they had a right to know."

- "I didn't want them to think it was my fault that the marriage ended."

- "I didn't want them to think it was my fault that we have a bad marriage or a bad divorce."

Fair enough. But don't tell them until they're well into adulthood, and not until they appear to have a need or a readiness to hear it. Why? Because children, even grown children, see themselves as being like their parents. Expressing hatred or contempt for the other parent is like expressing hatred and contempt for *them*. They have too great a need to see their mother or father as fundamentally good, and they're entitled to that, no matter how upset you are.

DEALING WITH OLDER ADULT CHILDREN

The strategies for dealing with children older than thirty are a little different from those used for eighteen- to thirty-year-olds. Although you should give children a long time before you begin to assume that the relationship you have is as good as it may ever get, at a certain point, you may have to move into a position of accepting their decision to not have a relationship with you. By the time they reach the age of thirty, you'll probably have an idea of whether contacting them feels like harassment to them, or is in some way accepted or welcome—however un-reciprocated. While I counsel weekly or semi-weekly contact for children aged eighteen to thirty, after thirty, you should consider backing it off to birthdays and holidays for children who don't reciprocate.

Either way, be careful to avoid triggering guilt in children who need to keep a safe distance from you. Children who cut off contact with their parents are typically in a great deal of pain, even if that isn't obvious. Your blaming them, however justified in your mind, will only increase their desire to have even less contact with you. I have heard more than one parent respond to this advice from me with the following: "I don't care at this point. I have nothing to lose, so I might as well let him know how screwed up I think it is how he treats me." And I always say, "If you truly don't care about what follows, that's one thing. However, if you do care and you're just striking back, then don't do it. There's not enough to be gained and you're hurting your chances for a relationship in the future."

In fact, I recommend that parents take a proactive approach when their children cut them off by saying something like the following: "I'd love to spend time with you, but I want you to be happy, first and foremost. So, even though I don't fully understand why you don't want to see me, I don't want you to feel guilty if you need to not get together." *Remember*: They're doing it *mostly* because they feel like it's in their best interest, not to punish you.

Paradoxically, the children who want the least contact are typically the ones who need the most help from us in managing their guilt. Why work so hard for a child whose thanklessness, in Shakespeare's words, is sharper than a serpent's tooth? Because being a parent means giving when you're getting nothing back in the short term, and may get nothing back in the long -term. It's not pretty, but it's what we sign up for when we have children, so we don't get to feel that sorry for ourselves. Okay, we do get to feel sorry for ourselves—a child's rejection is incredibly painful. But we still have to do the grunt work of parenting, even when we get little back.

So, even if you're moving toward accepting that your child doesn't want a relationship, you should pave the ground for potential contact in the future by writing him or her a letter that goes something like this:

Dear_____,
You are my child and I love you dearly. I know that I made terrible mistakes with you when you were growing up.

Or:

I know that you must be in a lot of pain to want to cut off contact with me.

Or:

I know that how I treated your mother/father when we were married (or after the divorce) was deeply upsetting to you.

Or

Your own introductory line:

    "_____"

The letter would go on to say something like:

As you know, I carry regret about that. I have tried hard to make amends to you and am willing to continue talking about whatever is important to you about the past if it can move us closer together. I do want to hear what you feel and would always be open to a letter, a phone call, or a meeting with a family therapist if that would be helpful.

I really want you to be happy, and I am coming to accept that you don't want to have a relationship with me. It's heartbreaking, as your parent, to not be able to see you. At the same time, if you believe it's in your best interest, then I don't want you to feel guilty. You must have good reasons [note: even if you think they don't], and I can accept your decision if that's what you have to do. I want you to know that the door will be open for the rest of your life if you change your mind.

All my love,

HEALING THE PAIN

There are many wounds that occur in the course of parenting, but being cut off from your child may be the worst. While it requires ongoing effort and practice, there are simple actions that will lead to a greater serenity. Below are some recommendations:

Strive to avoid:

- *Blaming yourself.* You might have made some very serious mistakes as a parent. Looking back, you might be correct in concluding that your child has a right to be mad at you. However, you still deserve forgiveness, if not from your child, then from other people. Ask yourself right now, "How long do I have to spend in purgatory before I'm allowed to live again? How much suffering is enough before I get to have a life? How much penance is enough penance before I get to say, 'Okay, I am now putting this behind me. I have tried hard to make amends and my child has refused me. I'm going forward in my life with or without him even if I still hope someday he will want to be close to me, again.'"

- *Holding onto anger and blame.* Being cut off by one's own child evokes intense feelings of rage. Being angry with your child for a while is healthy: your child probably has treated you in ways that you don't deserve, even if your mistakes were serious. But at some point you have to let it go. Walking around feeling angry all of the time is poisonous to your life. It keeps you mired in a negative state that makes it harder for others to give to you—and for you to give to others. It prevents you from seeing the good things about you, your life, your friends, your family, and the world. As Fred Luskin says, "While anger and hurt are appropriate, they, unlike wine, do not improve with age." One mother put it like this:, "I've met so many parents who are stuck, stuck, stuck in a time warp trying to figure out what they've done wrong with their kids. I'm fortunate that I've moved beyond that (the majority of the time). In fact, today I bought my daughter a Mother's Day card ... very generic and inexpensive. I enclosed a small check and mentioned what a superb mother she is/has been and left it at that. Would I like to do more, say more? You bet, but it is what it is, and I can't spend my days and nights crying over it. Life happens, and I don't want to miss the days I've been given by bemoaning what I'm not able to have today."

There is so much wisdom in Al Anon's saying: "I first detached in anger, then in indifference, then in love." Anger is a useful step to begin grieving. But it's an early step, not a final one. Healing requires a willingness to eventually let go of your anger and move toward forgiveness, both of yourself, and of your child.

HOW TO DETACH FROM ANGER

A first step in letting go of anger is seeing yourself as separate from it. University of Wisconsin neuroscientist Richard Davidson argues that meditation strengthens the brain's executive control center by strengthening and stabilizing neural networks in the medial prefrontal cortex. As writer Katherine Ellison says about meditation: "It changes your relationship to your emotions more than the emotions themselves. It allows you to see mood fluctuations moment to moment so that you can navigate around them."

Ellison cites an exercise by Matthieu Ricard, ".... a Buddhist monk, scientist, and French interpreter for the Dalai Lama," for relief from feelings of anger, obsessive desire, or envy:

1. Bring to mind a situation in which you felt very angry.

2. Recollect this experience piece by piece.

3. When anger arises, focus attention on the anger itself instead of on its object. Don't succumb to the anger but consider it separate from yourself.

4. As you continue to observe the anger, it will gradually evaporate under your gaze.

Practice These Thoughts

- "I am deserving of forgiveness for my mistakes as a parent. While my child is not obligated to forgive me, I can seek forgiveness from my friends, family, or my faith."

- "I accept that my child is still angry at me. I don't have to defend myself by being angry in return."

- "Feeling chronically angry prevents me from having the life I deserve."

- "Punishing myself keeps me mired in unhappiness."

- "Punishing my child keeps me mired in unhappiness."

It's very tempting to shut yourself off from people as a way to avoid talking about your painful relationship with your child; this may be carried out for reasons of shame, self-punishment, or depression. Don't. You deserve the love and support of other people. Make a commitment to increase your involvement with your friends, your family, or your religious community. Healing comes from allowing yourself to be loved and valued. It also comes from giving to others who are in need of your care. Many find that giving to others who are suffering is one of the most powerful actions that contribute to their own healing. As the Dalai Lama says, "A person meditating on compassion for others becomes the first beneficiary."

Loving someone who doesn't reciprocate that love is part of a spiritual path. It requires a courage and openness that will radiate into other parts of your life. The wisdom gained from people who have dealt with severe loss shows that it is not only, possible, but valuable.

THIRTEEN

ADDRESSING THE LONG REACH OF THE PAST

Your Personal History

Colette has few positive memories from her childhood. "I pretty much felt like my parents hated me. It was like I was some character in a Dickens novel where I'd get screamed at if I asked for something to eat. It was pretty freaking grim."

While Colette's childhood left her feeling insecure and anxious, she didn't lack confidence in her mothering. Like many parents, she was able to heal many of the ways that she felt hurt and misunderstood as a child by being the kind of mother to Erica that her mother had never been to her. That was, until Erica turned thirteen and was transformed from a sweet pre-teen into a terrorizing Goth. As Colette said, "It seemed like it happened overnight. I suddenly went from being the source of all of her comfort to the source of all of her anguish. Everything was all about how terrible a parent I was and how I've never listened to her, and how I've always thought only about myself. I know it's irrational, because I do everything for her, but she talks to me like she's been taking lessons from my parents and I have no immunity to it whatsoever. Suddenly, I feel like *she's* the one with all of the power and I'm reduced to this quaking child. I don't show her that, of course. On the outside I'm all, 'You can't talk to me that way, young lady,' but inside I'm shaking in my boots!"

English psychoanalyst and pediatrician Donald Winnicott wrote, "A man sups on his childhood for the rest of his days." Even though our childhoods aren't as directly formative as once thought, our experiences with our parents, siblings, and other caregivers have long-term effects on who we become, who we choose as partners, and the decisions we make as parents.

This chapter is written with three aims: (1) to help you understand how your experiences in childhood affect or affected your parenting, (2) to help you understand how your childhood affects your reactions to your child's treatment or mistreatment of you, and (3) to help you gain a greater sense of self-forgiveness and self-compassion for whatever mistakes you have made as a parent.

"Understanding the Past" Questionnaire

People are often surprised by the subtle ways they are still influenced by the past. The following questions are posed as a way to help you understand how your childhood may have affected you:

What were the sources of conflict between
you and your parent(s)?

Circle those items that apply:

- They were overly-controlling and possessive.

- They were neglectful.

- They were abusive.

- I didn't like how one of my parents treated the other.
- They didn't help me.
- They didn't believe in me.
- They were self-centered.
- They were perfectionists.
- They didn't have any time for me.
- _____
- _____

In what ways did you please them?

- I was a good student.
- I was a good athlete.
- I parented them.
- I made them look good.
- I was well-behaved.
- I stayed out of their way.
- _____
- _____

In what ways were you a disappointment?

- I wasn't a good student.
- They didn't like my friends.
- They never liked anyone that I dated.

- I acted out with drugs and/or alcohol.

- I wasn't neat.

- I talked back to them.

- Nothing I ever did was good enough.

- _____

- _____

In what ways do you or did you treat your children in the same ways that your parents treated you?

- I'm critical.

- I'm impatient.

- I'm nice.

- I'm dedicated.

- I'm a perfectionist.

- I guilt-trip.

- I'm abusive.

- I'm controlling.

- I'm self-centered.

- I mistreat their mother.

- I mistreat their father.

- I'm loud.

- I'm passive.

- _____

How are you different from them as a parent?

- I'm loving.
- I'm dedicated.
- I care.
- I spend a lot more time and/or money on my child.
- I spend a lot less time and/or money on my child.
- I'm patient.
- I'm impatient.
- _____
- _____

*Based on your parents' treatment, what might you have
concluded about what you do or don't deserve in life?*

- I deserve respect.
- I don't deserve respect.
- I'll be rejected if I'm not careful.
- I don't have any authority in the world.
- Everyone else is more important than I am.
- If you give someone an inch, they'll take a mile.
- Children are meant to be seen and not heard.
- Children come first no matter what.
- I'm supposed to give until it hurts.
- I'm supposed to give, and expect nothing in return.

- _____
- _____

How might experiences in your childhood cause you to make mistakes as a parent?

- I can easily feel easily guilt-tripped.
- I'm too reactive to criticism.
- My self-esteem is always on the line.
- I'm too worried about getting rejected or feeling abandoned.
- I'm overly involved in every aspect of my child's life.
- I'm not sufficiently involved.
- I'm too controlling.
- I don't set appropriate limits.
- I have unrealistically high expectations.
- I have really low expectations.
- I have given up.

- _____
- _____

How is your "difficult" child different from how you were as a child?

- She's more confident.
- She's less confident.

- He's more defiant.

- He's less defiant.

- She's a better student.

- She's a worse student.

- He's easier-going.

- He's harder-going.

- She has an easier time socially.

- She has a harder time socially.

- He's less ambitious.

- He's more ambitious.

- She's more independent.

- She's more dependent.

- _____

- _____

My years of practice as a psychologist have taught me that people with terrible childhoods can still grow up to be great parents. However, many who have suffered as children carry those vulnerabilities into their own families, and those vulnerabilities affect how they treat their children, and how they respond to their children's treatment of them.

The effects of our childhoods may be subtle in how they play out in our parenting: In the same way that today's couples have unrealistically high expectations of how much they're entitled to receive from their partners, many of today's parents expect a level of intimacy that is at odds with what their child can or should be reasonably expected to provide in return. An adult may not only hope to be the kind of parent he never had, he may also expect his relationship with his child to repair the many ways he felt let down by his own childhood.

This isn't a big problem if your children turn out to be everything you hoped for, or if your child is difficult in areas where you are secure in your feelings about yourself. However, the pain carried from our childhoods often creates loose ends that snag on the rough edges of our children's needs or temperaments. For example, if you carry fundamental questions about your worth, your own child assailing you is not going to make you feel any better. If you had a domineering father, you may be less able to marshal a productive response to a domineering teenage son. If you felt rejected and unloved by your parent, you may have a much harder time staying centered when your children start lobbing hand grenades crafted by their temperament, their needs for separation, or their healthy reactions to your imperfections. If your adult child cuts off contact, you may experience it as a powerful confirmation of all of the worst things that your parents said about you, things you have worked your whole life to prove untrue.

In the next section we'll look at the common ways that you may have been negatively affected by your childhood, and how those experiences may have affected your parenting. It includes families with:

- Perfectionist parents

- Chronically depressed parents

- Overly possessive parents

- Neglectful parents

- Critical, rejecting, or abusive parents

Perfectionist Parents

Ken came to see me for help parenting his sixteen-year-old son, Marcus. Marcus was an enigma to his school and his parents because he was one of the smartest kids in the school, yet had one of the lowest GPAs in his sophomore class. As I listened to Ken, it became clear that he was a man with very high expectations. For example, while he told me about the success of his other child, he criticized her not doing more.

"Marcus's sister, Sheila, got a full scholarship to Stanford," he said, "but she's been goofing off ever since she got there."

"She's having academic problems, too?" I asked.

"Sheila? Never. It just comes too easy to her. She could get a 4.0 and skip all of her classes. That's the problem with her, she doesn't know the value of hard work."

I looked for the pride underneath the complaint but saw that it was all complaint.

"What's your relationship like with her?" I asked.

"Oh, it's okay. She's been telling her mother she thinks I don't like her, but that's bullshit. She just does that because my wife is a softy who will say, 'Oh, yes, you poor thing. Your life is so hard.' Yes, so hard: Went to the best prep schools, grew up in the best neighborhoods. Full scholarship to Stanford. Give me a break. They both bitch at the other about what a hardass they think I am."

While Ken's daughter was doing well academically, his son, Marcus, wasn't walking that path. He was walking the path where you shoot yourself in the foot so that you can remind everyone that it's your foot to shoot. His school failure was a way of saying to his father, "You may be able to say that I don't measure up, but I get to remind you and me that it's my life, not yours. So I'm going to do exactly what you hate the most, and that is to be a slacker."

I asked Ken about his own upbringing because I sensed a critical parent in his past. "Nobody got my father's approval," he said. "No matter what me or my brothers did, it was never enough. He always pushed us. But, guess what? It made me who I am today so I can't complain."

I asked Ken how close he is to his own father. "Not that close. He's kind of a jerk to my mother and that gets a little tiring to be around."

"Hmm, sounds a little like how your wife talks to your daughter about you."

"Ha!" he looked surprised and a little irritated. "I hadn't really thought about it that way. I'm not my dad and I wouldn't want to be."

"Well, I don't know you or your family, yet," I said, "but you sound like you've done a good job providing a nice home and life for them, and that's something to be proud of. However, when a dad comes into my office and tells me that his daughter thinks he doesn't like her and his gifted son is flunking out of school, I have to wonder what's going on inside the father. I think a parent needs to take it very, very seriously when his daughter says that she thinks he doesn't like her. Kids don't make those things up to get attention—or if they do, it's because they don't know a better way to get the attention they really need. I work with too many adult children who eventually write a parent off because their interactions with that parent leave them feeling bad about themselves. So, we have to start by changing what's obvious, and I'm going to guess that your high standards are one of those things."

Over the next few months, Ken was able to take my recommendations to shift out of being a CEO with his children, into simply being supportive. He needed a lot of coaching, but he was willing to do the work, and, fortunately for him, his children responded positively to his efforts. As he was able to be more appreciative and less critical, his son felt less of a need to define himself in opposition to his father. As a result, he began to do well in school. Ken hadn't realized how powerfully his own father's perfectionism had influenced his own tendencies in that direction. He was able to use that insight to relax his standards more in other parts of his life in order to enjoy it more.

A lot of dads get confused about when to back off from pushing their kids. They have mixed feelings, though. Sometimes they have positive memories of coaches or friends or fathers aggressively pushing them to work harder and run faster—where the reward was a brief nod or a single, short pat on the back—or the withholding of anything negative. They feel skeptical of the idea that parenting has to always occur in a mutually tender environment.

This attitude is different from perfectionism. While perfectionist parents may teach their children that hard work gets results, they don't teach them that life is supposed to be enjoyed. They rear children who can be more at risk for anxiety and depression because these children constantly hold themselves to a standard where the bar is constantly being raised. Children need a sense that they can please their parents to feel secure and happy, and those raised in perfectionist homes are often denied that opportunity.

Perfectionists sometimes have problems working on their relationship with their children because they are unable to see the ways that their high standards may have wounded the child. They may also have problems healing the relationship because their children's criticisms or complaints cause them to feel so self-critical that they become rejecting in response.

Perfectionism Questionnaire

*If you're a perfectionist or were raised by perfectionist parents,
then some of the following may be true for you.*

Circle the sentences that most aptly describe you:

- I can't tolerate my child being second best.

- I make my children feel like nothing they do is quite good
  enough.

- I take it personally if my children don't do well, or if they
  don't look good.

- My children constantly complain about how much I push
  them to achieve or behave.

- I spend way too much time worrying about whether my
  children are good enough or whether they're doing enough
  to get ahead.

- My spouse and friends have told me that I need to back off
  on my kids.

- Because I hold myself to such a high standard, I feel terrible
  if my child criticizes some aspect of my parenting.

- Because I hold myself to such a high standard, I feel terrible
  if my spouse criticizes some aspect of my parenting.

- I constantly feel as though I should be doing something
  better as a parent.

Healing Exercise:
Reducing Perfectionism

- On a separate piece of paper, list the areas where your standards may be causing problems for you and/or your child.

- List the advantages and disadvantages of continuing on this path.

- Describe how your parents' perfectionist expectations were helpful to you.

- Describe how they were hurtful.

Healing Exercise:
Reducing Perfectionism

Consider how your relationship with your child and with yourself will improve if you can relax your standards.

Circle those items that relate to you:

- I could enjoy my life more.

- I could enjoy my children more.

- My children would feel more appreciated by me and less criticized.

- I would feel less guilty about all of the ways I make my children feel unappreciated or controlled.

- I could feel less anxious about whether or not they are measuring up.

- I would feel less vulnerable to their complaints about me.

CHRONICALLY DEPRESSED PARENTS

Brenda grew up in a large family where her mother suffered from chronic depression. "I didn't really think of my mother as depressed when I was little," Brenda said to me in one of our first sessions. "I don't think any kid does. I just felt like she wasn't that interested in me, and couldn't be bothered. She wasn't mean. More like apathetic; more like I didn't exist."

Studies show that children are more at risk for depression, anxiety, and a host of other psychological problems when raised by mothers with chronic depression. This is partly because depressed parents are unable to provide their children with the kind of day-to-day reflection and attunement necessary to develop a sense of self.

*If you grew up with a depressed parent, or have suffered
from chronic depression, then some of the
following may be true for you:*

- I had to take on a lot of responsibility for my siblings, my parents, and myself. While that may have made me a stronger person, it also makes it hard for me to not be in charge, or to believe that others will or can take care of me.

- I feel empty sometimes—like life doesn't have much meaning.

- I have very high expectations of others in terms of how giving they should treat me.

- I have an easier time giving than receiving, but feel resentful when people don't meet my needs.

*As a result of your childhood environment, or if you have
suffered from depression for other reasons, you may have
behaved in some of the following ways as a parent:*

- I expect my child to be there for me in the same way that I was there for my parents.

- I'm so worried that my child will feel overly burdened that I don't give her enough responsibility.

- I have wanted my child to be reassuring or loving to me in ways that may have been unfair.

- I have expected my child to provide a degree of meaning or excitement to my life that is probably unrealistic.

- I haven't had enough energy to be a good parent at various times in my life and I feel guilty about that.

- I feel afraid of my own dependency and this may have made me afraid of my children's appropriate needs to be dependent.

GUIDELINES FOR THE DEPRESSED PARENT AND FOR CHILDREN RAISED BY DEPRESSED PARENTS

*If you have suffered from chronic depression or were
raised by a depressed parent, the following
guidelines can be helpful in your healing:*

- Prioritize your own needs so that you are not at the bottom of the list. Use the pleasure and meaning of these experiences to develop and enliven your inner world.

- It's possible that your depression made it hard for you to be the kind of parent that you wanted to be. If that's the case, work to make amends to your children for whatever ways they felt overlooked by you. Don't punish yourself for the past. Practice the fine art of making amends while not criticizing yourself.

- Work to forgive yourself for whatever ways you made the same mistakes as your parent.

- Use self-talk to counter the self-criticism that stems from your feelings of guilt.

- Get support and stimulation outside of your family in order to help you feel more alive and resourceful.

- If you struggle with depression, consider medication and psychotherapy.

OVERLY CONTROLLING PARENTS

Greg and Melinda lost their first child to a rare disease when he was two years old. When LuAnn was born, they felt blessed, though worried that the same fate would befall her. As a result of losing their first child, they became overly protective of Georgia, and rarely let her spend time outside of the house, even when she became a teenager. As she approached college age, her parents intensified their restrictions in anticipation of the pending separation of her moving away.

Georgia had a quiet and shy temperament that caused her to be compliant to her parents' restrictions. However, when she became an adult she was so fearful of being controlled in relationships that she avoided romantic involvements. Much to her parents' dismay, she limited contact with them out of fear that she would get sucked back into their control if she spent time with them. When she finally got married and had children, her parenting bordered on neglectful because she was so keen to avoid her children feeling controlled in the ways that she did.

Controlling Parents Questionnaire

If you grew up with controlling parents, some of the following statements may be true for you.

Circle the ones that apply:

- I can feel easily controlled.

- I can be a very controlling person.

- I feel easily cornered in relationships.

- I don't like people being dependent on me.

- I can easily feel like people are needy.

- I have a great need for independence.

As a result of this childhood environment, or if you have other anxieties about being controlled, you may have made some of the following mistakes as a parent.

Circle the statements that most closely mirror your experience:

- I have been possessive and controlling of my child in the same way that my parents were with me.

- Because my own parents were needy, I may have disliked some of the ways that my child needed my time or attention.

- I have adopted a "my way or the highway" approach to my parenting as a way to maintain my feelings of independence.

- I have given my children way too much independence because I was worried about making them feel controlled in the same ways that I did growing up.

Healing Exercise
for Parents Raised by Controlling Parents

- If you have been too lax in your supervision, consider reversing that direction if your children still live at home. Teenagers feel unprotected if they're not provided any limits or structure.

- Pay more attention to their complaints about how restrictive or demanding you are. Consider changing your standards. Being overly controlling with teenagers is a recipe for disaster. See chapter 8 for specific recommendations.

- We're sometimes the most uncomfortable when our children are expressing healthy aspects of their needs that we had to suppress in our own childhoods. Use your discomfort at your children's needs as a vehicle for self-discovery.

NEGLECTFUL PARENTS

Children who have been neglected often grow up feeling alone, scared, and unimportant. They sometimes have a hard time taking themselves seriously enough to launch a successful adult life. As one mother said, "I raised myself because I had to. Both of my parents were drug addicts and I couldn't count on them for anything. Half the time, there wasn't any food in the house because they were spending all of their money staying high. It's taken me years of therapy to feel like I deserve to have any kind of a life."

Questionnaire for People Raised by Neglectful Parents

Circle the statements that most closely mirror your experience:

- I have a hard time maintaining any momentum in my life.

- I often feel alone, afraid, and unimportant.

- I'm always surprised when people take an interest in me.

- I am often tempted to behave in ways that are self-sabotaging or hurtful to me.

As a result of this childhood environment, you may have behaved in some of the following ways as a parent:

- I have neglected my children in some of the same ways that I was neglected.

- My desire to not neglect my children has made me overly involved with them.

- It's hard for me to believe that I have any value to my children.

- It's been hard for me to take the time and energy that I need to be a good parent.

Healing Exercise for Those Raised by Neglectful Parents

- Make a commitment to do something meaningful and nurturing for yourself on a daily basis.

- If you have a hard time valuing yourself, consider getting into individual or group therapy so that you can gain a healthier and more positive self -perception.

- If you were neglectful of your children, directly acknowledge that to them and make amends.

- If you have been overly involved, work to tolerate the anxiety that comes when you give your children more independence. You may need help from friends or other family members to calibrate an appropriate level of parental involvement.

CRITICAL, REJECTING, OR ABUSIVE PARENTS

Children raised in environments filled with chaos, threats, or abuse often bring considerable fears of abandonment and mistrust into their adult lives. Like Colette, they may carry a great deal of confusion about their degree of entitlement to set limits on their children's mistreatment of them.

Questionnaire
for People Raised by Critical, Rejecting,
or Abusive Parents

If you grew up with critical, rejecting, or abusive parents, some of the following statements may be true for you.

Circle the ones that most closely mirror your experience:

- You often interpret criticism or annoyance from your children as an act of betrayal or cause for war.

- You blame your children for creating feelings of fear, depression, or anger in you, for which they may have little or no responsibility.

- You get your children to reject you as a way to prove that your parents were right to mistreat you—and that you don't deserve to be loved or cared about.

- You are overly controlling of your children as a way to make yourself feel safer.

- You are overly protective of your children because you experienced the world as dangerous or hostile.

Healing Exercise for Those Raised
by Critical, Rejecting, or Abusive Parents

- Decrease your children's potential to make you feel scared or intimidated by using the assertiveness techniques provided throughout this book.

- Make sure that you have enough support in your life so that you don't take your child's criticisms, rejection, or mistreatment to heart.

- Work to soothe yourself when you feel scared by using self-talk, affirmations, and relaxation techniques.

- Use positive self-talk as a way to insulate yourself against your child's accusations. Your self-esteem should not live or die on the basis of how your children treat you. Strive to see yourself as being more resilient than you believe yourself to be.

- Take responsibility for the ways you participate in the negativity with your child. Work to disengage or re-route the interactions once they turn negative.

- Identify the ways that you mistreat your children in the same way that you felt mistreated. Make amends to them for the ways that you have hurt them in the past.

- Write a letter to your parents or other significant people who abused you in the past. Tell them that they were wrong to hurt you when you were the most in need of guidance and support. Let them know how you suffered as a child or adult because of their treatment. Get in touch with your feelings of anger, as this will help you fight against your internalized messages from them. You can decide later whether or not to send the letter.

- Don't blame your children for standing in the way of your happiness. Make a list of what you need in your life to be happy and go after those things.

MANAGING YOUR STRESS LEVEL

Gaining control over your stress is key to your healing and eventual serenity. The following questions are posed to help you evaluate your current level of stress and your style of managing it.

What is your current coping style in response to stress?

For example, do you *internalize? Externalize? Distract yourself? Neglect yourself?*

What are your current stressors in addition to your child?

- Financial
- Marital or other family stressors such as dealing with aging parents or relationships with siblings
- Career
- Depression or anxiety unrelated to parenting
- Housing
- Health
- _____
- _____
- _____

What is your current support system?

- Friends

- Spouse or partner

- Religion or religious institution

- Psychotherapist

- Outside family members such as parents, siblings, grand-parents, cousins

- Co-workers

Identify the areas where you experience stress.

Make a commitment to reduce it through psychotherapy, medication, meditation, yoga, exercise, affirmations, increased time with friends, or increased spiritual practice.

Our experiences as children can make us less prepared for the often-unforeseen struggles of parenting. Knowing how your childhood has affected you is a powerful tool for healing from the ways you feel hurt by your children. As you discover the foundation for some of your feelings and reactions, you can become more self-forgiving. In addition, you can experience a greater freedom in how you act and feel about your children and everyone else in your life.

AFTERWORD

*In the depth of winter, I finally learned that
there was within me an invincible summer.*

Albert Camus

In the last forty years, the countries with the greatest amount of wealth have experienced the greatest increase in depression. During a time when people are more than ever able to purchase the products and experiences that promise happiness and fulfillment, dissatisfaction is at an all-time high. This is because the promise of these material and emotional goods are based on experiences that are fleeting and require little investment of self. The bumper sticker that says "He who dies with the most toys wins" is worse than foolish.

There is currently a movement in the field of psychology to reverse that trend through practice of the venerable principles of compassion, forgiveness, gratitude, and optimism. I value this movement and have made these principles the foundation of my book.

Let's review them:

THE ESSENTIAL PRINCIPLES

Your healing will be strengthened as you continue to:

- Fearlessly take responsibility for whatever ways that you have contributed to the problems in your relationship with your child or your children

- Make amends for the ways that you were wrong

- Move toward forgiving your child for how he or she hurt you in the past or in the present (this doesn't mean condoning or excusing bad behavior, or minimizing your hurt)

- Move toward forgiving yourself for your mistakes as a parent

- Develop compassion for your child

- Develop compassion for yourself

- Move anger, guilt, shame, and regret into the background of your life and move hope, gratitude, and optimism into the foreground

- Develop an identity and life story based on your strengths and achievements as a parent and individual, instead of a story about your suffering or failures

- Get and maintain support from friends, family, or your faith

- Give something back to society

Of all the principles, I believe that experiencing gratitude and seeking support are the most important. As Cicero wrote, "Gratitude is not only the greatest of virtues, but the parent of all of the others." And it's through support that we develop compassion to forgive ourselves and to forgive others. It's through support that we learn we're not alone in our suffering. And it is through support that we are reminded of all that we have, for which to be grateful.

It is my deepest wish that my book brought you some measure of comfort. I wrote *When Parents Hurt* because I know what it's like to struggle with many of the issues discussed here. I can guarantee you that there will be days when you feel happy, hopeful, and clear, only to have them followed by days when you feel sad, hopeless, and confused. Practicing the principles of this book will help make your days of confusion fewer, and your days of clarity greater.

When I was going through my difficulties with my daughter, I had two friends whom I called all of the time. I chose those friends because they were going through similar challenges with one of their children and could easily relate. It isn't mandatory that your support group has similar struggles, but it helps. For this reason, I have set up a place on my Web site at www.whenparentshurt.com for you to contact other parents who are dealing with the same issues. I hope that this can become part of your community and becomes a place for you to receive support, comfort, and hope. And e-mail me, because I'd love to hear from you.

Joshua Coleman
San Francisco

ACKNOWLEDGMENTS

I am blessed by having many, many wonderful people who helped me with this book. My excellent agent, Faith Hamlin, has been the perfect combination of intellectual peer, comrade, and strategist. She worked hard with me to balance out the many versions of my book proposal before she found a great home for it at HarperCollins, and I am forever indebted to her for that.

I am extremely fortunate to have worked with the fabulous editor Toni Sciarra, who is whip smart, meticulous, and hilarious. It was Toni's idea to make my book one that was both broad and solution-based for the many people who are struggling with the themes addressed here. She was right.

I also want to thank the wonderful team at Collins: Joe Tessitore, president of Collins; Mary Ellen O'Neill, publisher, Collins Lifestyle/ Wellness; production and manufacturing manager, Karen Lumley; Georgia Morrissey, art director; Jessica Heslin, design director; Diane Aronson, copy chief; Marina Padakis, senior production editor; Angie Lee, marketing director; Shelby Meizlik, publicity director; George Bick, sales director; and not least, associate editor Anne Cole.

Special thanks to my gifted friend and colleague, psychologist Jamie Edmund, Ph.D., for contributing her expertise on children and families. Also, a special thanks to my friend Danelle Morton for generously making frequent suggestions on both the proposal and the manuscript. Thanks also to my friend Hal Cox for his suggestions on the scientific material. My book is much stronger for all of their contributions.

Several scholars agreed to discuss the concepts in my book: Historian Stephanie Coontz at Evergreen State University and historian Steven Mintz at the University of Houston helped me to place the topic of my book within a social and cultural context through their books and generous correspondence. Larry McCallum at Augustana College provided his insights on the problems with excessive parental preoccupation with children's self-esteem. Kathryn Asbury at Kings College in London helped me understand the importance of non-shared environmental influences on child development. Katherine Conger at the University of California, Davis, helped me clarify the sometimes-contradictory findings on siblings. Special thanks to historian Peter Stearns for his book, *Anxious Parents: A History of Modern Childrearing in America.*

I am very grateful to the many parents who volunteered to be interviewed for this book and for their willingness to share their stories with me. Their contributions have made this book a real and living entity.

There were numerous friends and colleagues who volunteered to discuss the manuscript or read versions of the manuscript for clarity and accessibility. In alphabetical order they are: Nell Barrett, Kenny Bender, Janet Beverly, Jessica Broitman, Barbara Flores, Jessica Flynn, Melody Matthews Lowman, Marilyn Middleton, Karen Schwartzman, and Heidi Swillinger.

I am lucky to have friends, brothers, and parents who are supportive to me in every way imaginable.

Thanks to my three wonderful children, Misha, Max, and Daniel, for being the three wonderful people that you are.

Last and never least, love and thanks to my wife of nineteen years, Ellie Schwartzman, child psychologist, friend, and confidante. She generously read every single rewrite of every single chapter, and, just as important, refrained from complaining as entropy became the defining characteristic of our home office space. I'm going to go clean it up right now. Honest.

WHEN A FAMILY MAN THINKS TWICE

JOSHUA COLEMAN
San Francisco Chronicle
SUNDAY SECTION, FATHER'S DAY, 2000

You get married. And at some point you don't know if the marriage is going to work. And since it's your first marriage, you feel discouraged and hopeless and start believing that your marriage looks nothing like the ones on TV or in *Us Weekly*. And you think how nice it would be to have a marriage like that, built on friendship, hiking, and an active sex life.

And since it's a marriage with children, you don't know what it feels like to be divorced with children, but figure it might not be that bad. It's a tradeoff. And people say everything in life is a tradeoff, so there must be something worthwhile about tradeoffs.

And you start thinking about it after you leave the movie theater because your marriage once looked like the movie marriage, at least when you were first dating. Or maybe the movie is realistic, with lots of alienated, confused adults, but even those movies feature somebody who's falling in love, like the two teenagers in *American Beauty*. And so you compare your marriage to the teenagers in *American Beauty* and wonder how you got as far off the track as Kevin Spacey, and do you need to get a GTO and start smoking pot again to find yourself, even if you're smart enough to date somebody your own age instead of your daughter's friend?

And maybe you realize that the same actors you're comparing your marriage to on the screen are having as much trouble in their marriages off the screen as you are having in yours at home. And so you stop comparing yourself to their happy on-screen marriages, and compare yourself to them as happy divorced actors who have their kids part-time and live in LA or New York or on their ranches in Montana.

And at the playground, watching your kids go down the slide with your wife, you end up sitting by a divorced father. And if you've never been divorced, you won't see his loneliness as he stretches his legs and watches and waves at his children because he looks like you when you wave and smile at yours playing on the swings or that circular spinning thing that makes you nauseous when you have the poor judgment to get on it. And you don't see that this very same child on the swing set saying look at me look at me will have to be returned to her mother's house like a videotape by six because that was the time agreed to in the agreement. And you may not know the sadness he feels returning that child to her mother as she closes the door to him like a vault while his kid waves, sad, bewildered, or worse, happy to be back with her mom and now oblivious of him, her father.

And you, who walks in and out of your home every day with your wife and kids, can't know what it's like to sit in your car and watch the place you lived in as family, knowing your child is in there, laughing, talking loudly, or waving briefly at you from the window like she does when her uncle leaves. And since you are married and wake up every day to your child's loud laughter and endless questions and requests and frustrations and hurts, you can't contemplate the deadwood barrenness of a house deprived of that sound. And you wouldn't know that going home to that silence, a silence you craved many times while married, is a silence found more often on hillsides after a large-scale fire.

And being married, you and your wife may have just put your child to bed with Harry Potter or *The Little Engine That Could* or other magical children's stories that teach the value of never giving up and struggling against the odds. And as the evening goes on, you end up in one of those god-awful fights with her that leave you feeling alone, and why should you have to put up with this as hard as you work and try. And it's hard to feel like nobody else has it as bad or understands what you feel except perhaps the woman you've begun to have an affair with who always says the right thing and makes you feel good about yourself, which, of course, you deserve. And the sex with the woman you're having an affair with is unbelievable because sex is always unbelievable in affairs or else why would anybody bother.

And since you're a married father who goes on vacations with his kids and helps them with their soccer, homework, or playground politics, you may underestimate the feelings of seeing your child walk out of the house you once lived in as family, holding the hand of your ex-wife's new husband. Perhaps you're surprised by the stab of betrayal when you hear your child refer to your ex-wife's new husband as "my other daddy." And even though you've had enough psychotherapy to start a clinic on both coasts, you watch yourself get mad and hurt and state that she Does not, Can not, and Will not have another daddy because that is a position only you can fill and if she ever brings up that phrase again, something really bad is going to happen to somebody, you're just not sure who.

And you begin to wonder if anything is worth this kind of pain. Is anything worth having your baby, your child, your self, handed to you and ripped back out like an assembly line robot on a killing spree, week after week after week after week? And friends and family and professionals say it will get better over time and it does get better because you eventually get better at finding new and improved ways to blind and numb yourself. And people will tell you this change is called growth. And you know that must mean growth is highly overrated.

And you always swore you would be a great dad and you have been but you better set your sorry ass down with divorce and give thanks for every other weekend or summer visitation or some other version of fatherhood that has nothing to do with family and everything to do with an arrangement so dubious only a court can invent it. And maybe when your kids grow up and go off to college or move out you'll feel better. But then maybe you won't. Maybe their new independence will just free them up to see your limitations even more clearly.

And though you would never do it, you come to understand those lost fathers, marginalized through their own mistakes or a lousy arrangement, moving miles away and rarely calling, leaving their kids bobbing and drifting like toys thrown from the back of a moving boat.

And how these fathers get struck dead and dumb years later when there's an angry and betrayed call from a child who's now a teenager or an adult. And how these dads stumble out an excuse that tries to be an apology but ends up blaming the child and the ex-wife, and leaves the kid glad the father wasn't around in the first place no wonder mom wanted out.

And maybe you'd never let it get to that point and you do need to leave your marriage. Maybe the smoking stacked years of hurt and resentment are sooting the air you and your family breathe and no priest or rabbi or therapist can ever reverse it because you already tried all that. And you end up falling in love with someone new because she reminds you of all the qualities you love best; those of your children, your closest friends and—you hate to admit it but yeah—those of your ex-wife.

And then, whether it's the right thing or the wrong thing, better or worse, you look back. And at some point, your kids ask when you and mom are going to live together again. And though they eventually stop asking, they won't stop hoping. And they carry that hope the way you carry your love for them—soft, constant, and close to the surface. And no matter how awful it was to be married and how grateful you are to be out, and how much getting out was the right decision, some part of you may always wonder, was there something else I could have done? Something?

NOTES

TWO: GETTING IT WRONG ABOUT PARENTS

10 *While parents are expected to love all of their children equally*: Aldous, J., Klaus, E., Klein, J., The understanding heart: Aging parents and their favorite children. *Child Development* (1985) 56(2): 303–16.

10 *A child who radiates affection and love:* Harris, Judith Rich. *The Nurture Assumption: Why Children Turn Out the Way They Do* (New York: Touchstone, 1999), 29; Reiss, D., Neiderhiser, J. M., Hetherington, E. M., and Plomin, R. *The Relationship Code: Deciphering Genetic and Social Influences on Adolescent Development* (Cambridge, MA: Harvard University Press, 2000). On page 377, the authors cite a study by van den Boom and Hokesma where the following was reported: "Compared with children with easier temperaments, irritable children appeared to turn off their mothers: they got less visual and physical contact and their mothers showed less emotional involvement with them, even though they tried to soothe them more often. Indeed, even when these fussy babies showed some positive behavior, their inured mothers seemed not to notice." van den Boom, D. C., and Hokesma, J. B., The effect of infant irritability on mother-infant interaction: A growth curve analysis. *Developmental Psychology* (1994) 4:581–90.

10 *Difficulties with children of any stripe*: Hetherington found that a difficult temperament in children and teens may elicit aversive responses from parents: Hetherington, E. M., The role of individual differences and family relationships in children's coping with divorce and remarriage. In P. A. Cowan and E. M. Hetherington, eds., *Family Transitions* (Hillsdale, NJ: Lawrence Erlbaum, 1991), 165–94. Also see Reiss et al., *The Relationship Code*, 5: "The same genetic factors that influence antisocial behavior in adolescents are those that influence the amount of harsh parenting they receive."

10   *Research psychologist Diana Baumrind*: Baumrind, D., Rearing competent chil-
     dren. In W. Damon, ed., *Child Development Today and Tomorrow* (San Francisco:
     Jossey-Bass, 1989), 349–78; Baumrind, D., The influence of parenting style on
     adolescent competence and substance use. *Journal of Early Adolescence* (1991)
     11(1): 56–95.

11   *Part of what makes parenting so confusing*: Siblings are treated differently by their
     parents and by their siblings. Even when parental treatment seems to be simi-
     lar, siblings may experience it very differently: Dunn, Judith, and Plomin,
     Robert. *Separate Lives: Why Siblings Are So Different* (New York: Basic Books,
     1990), 41. See also J. R. Harris, *The Nurture Assumption*, 47–49, where Harris
     argues that research like Baumrind's doesn't adequately control for child-to-
     parent effects. See also Jenkins, J. M, Dunn, J., O'Connor, T. G., Rashbash, J.,
     and Behnke P., Change in maternal perception of sibling negativity: Within
     and between family influences. *Journal of Family Psychology* (2005) 19(4): 633–42;
     Shebloski, B., Conger, K. J., and Widaman, K. F., Reciprocal links among dif-
     ferential parenting, perceived partiality, and self-worth: A three-wave longitu-
     dinal study. *Journal of Family Psychology* (2005) 19(4): 633–42.

15   *New findings in the field of behavioral genetics*: Dunn and Plomin, *Separate Lives*.
     See also Plomin, R., and Asbury, K., Nature and nurture: Genetic and environ-
     mental influences on behavior, *The ANNALS of the American Academy of Political
     and Social Science* (2005) 600(1): 86–98, where they describe the molecular ge-
     netic research that is beginning to identify specific DNA sequences responsible
     for genetic influence on common behavioral disorders such as mental illness
     and on behavioral dimensions of personality. As they write, "The most impor-
     tant implication of this research for social scientists is that as multiple QTLs
     (quantitative trait loci) of small effect size for a particular trait are identified,
     they can be aggregated in a 'QTL set' that can then be used as a genetic risk
     index in the same way that environmental risk indices such as socioeconomic
     status or education are used."

15   *The recent findings in child development*: Stern, Daniel. *The Interpersonal World of
     the Infant: A View from Psychoanalysis and Developmental Psychology* (New York:
     Basic Books, 2000), 25.

16   *For example, we now know*: Scarr, S., and McCartney, K., How people make their
     own environments: A theory of genotype → environment effects. *Child Devel-
     opment* (1983) 54: 424–35; Reiss et al., *The Relationship Code*, 245. Researchers
     refer to these as "evocative gene-environment correlations." Both studies dis-
     cuss how genetic influences in childhood can cause a child to behave in a
     matter that evokes rejecting behavior from family, school, and peers. These ef-
     fects may persist in the child's development even if the cause of that behavior
     is genetically switched off later in life.

16 *How do the genes of the parent*: Reiss et al., *The Relationship Code*, 243. Genetic influences have been associated with antisocial behavior, cognitive agency, social responsibility, depression, and autonomous functioning.

16 *How do the siblings respond*: Dunn and Plomin, *Separate Lives*, 79; Shebloski, Conger, and Widaman (2005).

16 *Which peer group does the child choose:* Harris, J. R., The Nurture Assumption, 133.

17 *What is the economic status of the parents*: Mayhew, K. P., and Lempers, J., The relation among financial strain, parenting, parent self-esteem and adolescent self-esteem. *The Journal of Early Adolescence* (1998) 18(2): 145–72.

17 *How much institutional and governmental:* Coontz, Stephanie. *The Way We Really Are: Coming to Terms with America's Changing Families* (New York: Basic Books, 1997), 40–41.

18 *It took control of your pituitary gland:* Hardy, Sara Blaffer. *Mother Nature: Maternal Instincts and How They Shape the Human Species* (New York: Ballantine, 1999); Haig, D., Genetic conflicts of human pregnancy. *Quarterly Review of Biology* (1993) 68: 495–532.

18 *But sometimes it goes awry*: Barker, D. J. P., Bull, A. R., Osmond, C., and Simmonds, S.J., Fetal and placental size and risk of hypertension in adult life. *BMJ*, v. 301(6746), Aug 4, 1990.

18 *From the very beginning*: Stern, *The Interpersonal World*, 30.

18 *Infants as young as one year*: Izard, C. E., Fantauzzo, C. A., Castle, J. M., Haynes, O. M., Rayias, M. F., and Putnam, P. H., The ontogeny and significance of infants' facial expressions in the first 9 months of life. *Developmental Psychology* (1995) 31(6): 997–1013; Zahn-Waxler, C., and Radke-Yarrow, M., The origins of empathic concern. *Motivation and Emotion* (1990) 14(2): 107–130.

18 *By the age of thirty-six months*: Dunn and Plomin, *Separate Lives*, 72.

19 *As evolutionary biologist Robert Trivers writes*: Trivers, R. L., Parent-offspring conflict. *American Zoologist* (1974) 14:249–64, in Hardy, *Mother Nature*, pp. 429–30.

THREE: PARENTAL GUILT

28 *Prior to the second half*: Stearns, Peter N. *Anxious Parents: A History of Modern Childrearing in America* (New York: University Press, 2003).

31   *Studies have shown*: Luskin, Fred. *Forgive for Good: A Proven Prescription for Health and Happiness* (New York: HarperCollins, 2002), 42.

FOUR: A CHILD'S VIEW

40   *It is crucial to understand*: Behavioral geneticists refer to the different experiences that people can have in a family both within and outside of that family as nonshared experiences. As Asbury, Dunn, and Plomin write, "To that extent they can either represent objectively nonshared experiences or differential responses to an ostensibly shared environment such as socioeconomic status, parental divorce, or even a family holiday." Asbury, K., Dunn J. F., and Plomin, R., Birthweight-discordance and differences in early parenting relate to monozygotic twin differences in behaviour problems and academic achievement at age 7. *Developmental Science* 9(2): F10–F19, 2006; Reiss et al., *The Relationship Code* (p. 407), write that in adolescence, "the nonshared environment is the predominant environmental influence on individual differences."

40   *This is why siblings*: Dunn and Plomin, *Separate Lives*, 108.

40   *Rashomon*: Sato, Tadao. *Rashomon*. Ed. Donald Richie (New Brunswick, NJ: Rutgers, Tadao, 1987).

40   *In Michael Dorris's novel*: Dorris, Michael. *A Yellow Raft in Blue Water* (New York: Warner Books, 1998).

40   *Amy Tan's novel*: Tan, Amy. *The Joy Luck Club* (New York: Ivy Books, 1990).

41   *Why do they behave in this way*: Expanding on a Freudian concept of "turning passive into active," psychoanalyst Joseph Weiss believed that people sometimes seek to master unconscious conflicts when they treat others in ways similar to how they have been treated. For a discussion of this phenomena see Foreman, S., The significance of turning passive into active in control mastery theory. *Journal of Psychotherapy Practice and Research* (1996) 5: 106–21.

43   *Whereas the family once existed*: Coontz, Stephanie. *The Way We Never Were: American Families and the Nostalgia Trap* (New York: Basic Books, 1992), 277–278.

43   *The problem with this culture*: Mintz, Steven. *Huck's Raft: A History of American Childhood* (Cambridge, MA: Harvard University Press, 2004), 4.

44   *Stanford University psychologist*: Luskin, *Forgive for Good*, 17.

44   *Luskin's research and the research of others*: Seligman, Martin. *Authentic Happiness: Using the New Positive Psychology to Realize Your Potential for Lasting Fulfillment* (New York: Free Press, 2002), 70; Ostir, G., Markides, K., Black, S., and Good-

win, J., Emotional wellbeing predicts subsequent functional independence and survival. *Journal of the American Geriatrics Society* (2000) 48: 473–78.

45 *Forgiveness doesn't mean*: Luskin, *Forgive for Good*, vii.

46 *Luskin and other researchers*: See Weiss, Joseph, *How Psychotherapy Works: Process and Technique* (New York: The Guilford Press, 1993); Seligman, *Authentic Happiness*, 95.

49 *Seligman's research*: Seligman, *Authentic Happiness*, 76.

52 *Seligman and other researchers*: Beck, Aaron. *Love Is Never Enough: How Couples Can Overcome Misunderstandings, Resolve Conflicts, and Solve Relationship Problems Through Cognitive Therapy* (New York: Harper and Row, 1988); Burns, David. *Feeling Good: The New Mood Therapy* (New York: Wholecare, 1999).

53 *Researchers have found*: Emmons, R. A., and Crumpler, C. A., Gratitude as a human strength. *Journal of Social and Clinical Psychology* (2000) 19(11): 56–69; McCullough, M. E., Emmons, R. A., and Tsang, J., The grateful disposition: A conceptual and empirical topography. *Journal of Personality and Social Psychology* (2002) 82: 112–27; Emmons, R. A., McCullough, M. E., and Tsang, J., The assessment of gratitude. In S. Lopez and C. R. Snyder, eds., *Handbook of Positive Psychology Assessment* (Washington D.C.: American Psychological Association, 2003), 327–42.

53 *Loyola University researchers*: Bryant, Fred, and Veroff, Joseph. *Savoring: A New Model of Positive Experience* (New York: Lawrence Erlbaum Associates, 2006).

FIVE: BRAVE NEW PARENTS

61 *Here's an example*: "Reality Check," *Parenting Magazine*, July 2005.

63 *Because of the likelihood of divorce*: Ehrensaft, Diane. *Spoiling Childhood: How Well-Meaning Parents Are Giving Children Too Much—But Not What They Need* (New York: Guilford Press, 1997), 10.

63 *As a result, many parents*: Coleman, Joshua. *The Marriage Makeover: Finding Happiness in Imperfect Harmony* (New York: St. Martin's Press, 2004), 18.

63 *Aside from economics*: Aquilino, W., Predicting parents' experiences with coresident adult children. *Journal of Family Issues* (1991) 12: 323–42. Aquilino found, however, that the older the adult child, the more negative were the effects of coresidence on the parents' lives.

63 *The democratic climate*: Coltrane, Scott. *Family Man: Fatherhood, Housework, and Gender Equity* (New York: Oxford University Press, 1996), 33.

64   *By the mid–30s*: Mintz, *Huck's Raft*, 219.

64   *While parenting advice has existed*: Stearns, *Anxious Parents*, 39.

64   *Sigmund Freud was one of the most*: Freud, Sigmund. "Inhibitions, Symptoms, and Anxiety," in *The Complete Works of Sigmund Freud: The Standard Edition* 20 (London: Hogarth Press, 1926), 77–175. See also Stearns, *Anxious Parents*, 41.

64   *In 1928 behaviorist John Watson*: Watson, John. *Psychological Care of Infant and Child* (New York: Norton, 1928), cited in Stearns, *Anxious Parents*, 18. See Stearns, 67–70, for how behaviorism affected parenting attitudes, and also Coontz, *The Way We Never Were*, 214–15.

65   *Watson's ideas had*: Mintz, *Huck's Raft*, 58; Harris, Ian. *The Mind of John Locke: A Study of Political Theory in Its Intellectual Setting* (Cambridge: Cambridge University Press, 1995).

65   *Dr. Benjamin Spock*: Spock, Benjamin. *The Common Sense Book of Baby and Child Care* (New York: Pocket Books, 1946), quoted in Mintz, *Huck's Raft*, 279.

65   *As historian Steven Mintz*: Mintz, *Huck's Raft*, 279.

65   *While Spock's perspective*: Stearns, *Anxious Parents*, 213.

66   *With the notable exceptions*: Mintz, *Huck's Raft*, 27–37. In discussing how the attitudes of the Quakers were more affection-based, Mintz writes (p. 49), "More than any earlier group of English immigrant, the Quakers extolled a family life centered on the affection and companionship between a husband and wife and the love, care, and emotional support of their children. Unlike the Puritans, the Quakers emphasized equality over hierarchy, gentle guidance over strict discipline, and early autonomy for children." He also notes (p. 35) that the goal of Native American parents was to instill courage, pride, and independence.

66   *During the twentieth century*: Stearns writes in *Anxious Parents*, p. 72, "All these strictures, positive and negative alike were compatible with the new beliefs about children's vulnerability and the potential for parental excess … They blended with other disciplinary changes, such as the desire of growing number of fathers to be pals with their kids, rather than courts of last resort, and the concomitant effort to blend greater disciplinary obligations with the assumptions of motherhood."

66   *The emphasis on helping children*: Ibid., 108. Stearns notes that "the self-esteem movement was affected by the American economy shifting toward service sector functions that required social skills where sociability and school performance became increasingly linked."

66   *Parents began to feel terrified*: Ibid., 108–109.

66 *As of 2001*: Marano, Estroff Hara, "A Nation of Wimps," *Psychology Today*, Nov./Dec. 2004.

66 *Some California schools*: Stearns, *Anxious Parents*, 117.

67 *The influential child psychologist*: Bettelheim, Bruno. *The Empty Fortress* (New York: Free Press, 1967).

67 *Gregory Bateson's theory*: Bateson, Gregory. *Steps to an Ecology of Mind* (New York: Ballantine, 1980).

67 *Anthropologist Margaret Mead*: Mead, Margaret. Preface to Ruth Benedict's *Patterns of Culture*, 2nd ed. (Boston: Houghton Mifflin, 1959).

68 *The hazards of electricity*: Stearns, *Anxious Parents*, 35–37.

68 *As historian Peter Stearns*: Ibid., 37.

68 *For example, Stearns*: Ibid., 177.

68 *In 1945*: Mintz, *Huck's Raft*, 282.

69 *Maybe because in 1982*: Stearns, *Anxious Parents*, 35.

70 *Perhaps this is because*: Ibid., 35.

70 *The media and some*: Jenkins, Philip. *Concepts of the Child Molester in Modern America* (Cambridge, MA: Yale University Press, 1998).

71 *In the short period*: Mintz, *Huck's Raft*, 347–48.

71 *The fact that the United States*: *Statistical Abstract of the United States: The National Data Book*, 122nd edition (US Dept of Commerce/US Census Bureau, 2002). For more on changes in the nature of children's play, see Chamberlin, J., Childhood revisited: Through longitudinal research, Roger Hart seeks to inform debate on the changing nature of childhood play. *Monitor on Psychology*, March 2006 (Vol. 37).

71 *They also feel*: Stearns, *Anxious Parents*, 163.

73 *This is a major*: Ehrensaft, *Spoiling Childhood*, 11–12.

73 *As Mintz writes, " ... the most important*: Mintz, *Huck's Raft*, 282.

73 *Historian Stephanie Coontz observes*: Coontz, *The Way We Really Are*, 15.

73 *In the United States*: Mintz, S. "How we all became Jewish mothers," *National Post*, February 17, 2006.

74 *Girls between the ages*: Stearns, *Anxious Parents*, 185.

74 *A newspaper recently*: Carter, C. "Cookie Monster Eating Less," *San Francisco Chronicle*, April 7, 2005.

74 *As divorce rates*: Stearns, *Anxious Parents*, 108–109.

75 *This was fueled*: Hackstaff, Karla B. *Marriage in a Culture of Divorce* (Philadelphia: Temple, 1999), 36.

75 *While divorce has been*: Amato, Paul R., and Booth, Alan. *A Generation at Risk* (Cambridge, MA: Harvard University Press, 1997), 115.

75 *As historian Coontz*: Coontz, *The Way We Never Were*, 226.

75 *Economic stressors*: Mayhew, K. P., and Lempers, J., The relation among financial strain, parenting, parent self-esteem and adolescent self-esteem. *The Journal of Early Adolescence* (1998) 18(2): 145–72.

SIX: CONFRONTING PARENTAL SHAME

77 *The more you know about*: Nathanson, Donald, *Shame and Pride: Affect, Sex and the Birth of the Self* (New York, NY: Norton, 1992), 31.

81 *Marriage researcher John Gottman*: Gottman, John. *Why Marriages Succeed or Fail … And How You Can Make Yours Last* (New York: Simon and Schuster, 1994), 58.

81 *Psychiatrist and researcher*: Kiecolt-Glaser, J. K., and Newton, T. L., Marriage and health: His and hers. *Psychological Bulletin* (2001) 127: 472–503.

83 *University of Pennsylvania sociologist*: Marano, "A Nation of Wimps."

83 *The consolidation of identity*: Erikson, Erik. *Identity and the Life Cycle* (New York: Norton, 1994).

84 *This is part of what psychoanalyst*: Jung, Carl G. *The Archetypes and the Collective Unconscious*. In *Collected Works of C. G. Jung*, vol. 9, part 1 (Princeton: Princeton University Press, 1981).

84 *Writer Hara Estroff Marano*: Marano, "A Nation of Wimps."

84 *In addition, years eighteen to twenty-five*: Marano, E. H., "Crisis on the Campus," *Psychology Today*, May 2002.

86 *Psychiatrist and shame researcher*: Nathanson, *Shame and Pride*, 7.

86 *As Judith Rich Harris*: Harris, J. R., "How Can We Tell Which Teen Will Kill?" *Los Angeles Times*, March 8, 2001.

86 *Nathanson describes it similarly*: Nathanson, *Shame and Pride*, 365.

87   *This theory of mind*: Baron-Cohen, S., The extreme male brain theory of autism. *TRENDS in Cognitive Sciences* (2002), 6 (6).

87   *It is through empathic reflection*: Lewis, Thomas, Amini, Fari, and Lannon, Richard. *A General Theory of Love* (New York: Random House, 2000), 207.

88   *Despite the fact*: Thompson, L., and Walker, A. J., Gender in families: Women and men in marriage, work and parenthood. *Journal of Marriage and the Family*, Nov. 1989, 845–71.

88   *As psychologist Diane Ehrensaft*: Ehrensaft, *Spoiling Childhood*, 190.

89   *Another quote from Jung*: Jung, *The Archetypes and the Collective Unconscious*, 172.

90   *Nathanson suggests*: Nathanson, *Shame and Pride*, 115.

SEVEN: WHERE DID THIS KID COME FROM?

96   *In part, these separate*: Dunn and Plomin, *Separate Lives*, 8.

96   *Personality traits known to*: Pinker, Stephen. *The Blank Slate: The Modern Denial of Human Nature* (New York: Viking, 2003), 375.

96   *Because of these differences*: J. R. Harris, in *The Nurture Assumption*, p. 28, cites the following study: "When adolescent twins were asked how much affection or rejection they had received from their parents, identical twins were more likely than fraternal twins to give matching reports ... But if one fraternal twin reported that her parents made her feel loved, the other might say either that she also felt loved, *or that she felt rejected*" (italics added).

96   *The genetic differences*: Ibid., 119.

97   *In fact, vulnerability*: Dunn and Plomin, *Separate Lives*, 10.

98   *As psychologist Daniel Shaw*: "How Your Siblings Make You Who You Are," *TIME*, July 2006.

98   *For example, older siblings*: Dunn and Plomin, *Separate Lives*, 64.

98   *In several studies*: Ibid., 75. For example, in one study, 61 percent of mothers stated that they felt more affectionate toward their younger child, who was, on average, six years old; only 10 percent said that they felt more affection toward their older child. However, family sociologist Katherine Conger concluded from her observational research that most parents gave preferential treatment to the older child. *TIME*, "How Your Siblings."

98   *In two studies of preschoolers*: Dunn and Plomin, *Separate Lives*, 72.

98 *Charles Dickens wrote*: Writer Henry James apparently felt diminished by the intelligence and writings of his brother, William James. Dunn and Plomin, *Separate Lives*, 95.

99 *An aggressive child*: Reiss et al., *The Relationship Code*, 155. In another place, Reiss says, "Even as genes are calling forth particular reactions, they're also reaching out for particular kinds of experience. That's because each person's DNA codes for a certain type of nervous system: one that feels alarm at new situations, one that craves strong sensations, or one that is sluggish and slow to react." Quoted in A. M. Paul, "The Gene Responsibility," *Psychology Today*, Jan./Feb. 1998.

99 *In a recent study*: Shebloski, Conger, and Widaman, "Reciprocal Links," 633–42.

99 *As Conger said*: Katherine Conger, personal communication, Oct. 1, 2006.

100 *In child psychiatrist*: Greenspan, Stanley. *The Challenging Child: Understanding, Raising, and Enjoying the Five "Difficult" Types of Children* (Cambridge, MA: Perseus, 1995), 136.

101 *Aggressive/defiant temperaments*: Ibid., 125.

102 *They like rough-and-tumble*: Ibid., 237.

102 *Authoritarian parents*: Baumrind, "The influence of parenting style," 56–95.

103 *In some cultures*: Harris, J. R., *Socialization, personality development, and the child's environments*: Comment on Vandell. *Developmental Psychology* (Nov. 2000) 36: 6.

103 *As David Lykken, a behavioral geneticist*: Paul, A. M., "The Gene Responsibility," *Psychology Today*, Jan./Feb. 1998.

105 *Set clear limits*: Sells, Scott. *Parenting Your Out-of-Control Teenager* (New York: St. Martin's Press, 2001), 45.

107 *However, not all sensitive*: Greenspan, *The Challenging Child*, 38.

112 *Studies show that ongoing*: Weissman, M., Warner, V., and Wickramaratne, P., Offspring of depressed parents: Ten years later. *Archives of General Psychiatry* (1997) 54: 932–40.

114 *Long work hours, low pay*: Coontz, *The Way We Really Are*, 129.

114 *Or, as historian Stephanie Coontz*: Ibid., 147.

115 *Men often respond*: Pleck, J. H., Paternal involvement: Levels, sources, and consequences. In *The Role of the Father in Child Development*, 3rd ed., Lamb (New York: Wiley & Sons, 1997).

EIGHT: TAKING IT PERSONALLY

124 *There is evidence*: Seligman, *Authentic Happiness*, 117.

124 *In 1820 girls*: Coontz, *The Way We Really Are*, 14. Steven Mintz writes, "The first published use of the word teenager occurred in September 1941 when a columnist in *Popular Science Monthly* remarked about a young person: 'I never knew teen-agers could be so serious.'" Mintz, *Huck's Raft*, 252.

126 *Most teens feel*: Riera, Mike. *Uncommon Sense for Parents with Teenagers* (New York: Celestial Arts, 2004), 24.

129 *In psychologist Scott Sells's*: Sells, *Parenting Your Out-of-Control Teenager*. I am indebted to Scott Sells for many of the strategies offered in this chapter.

130 *"Any time you say ..."*: Ibid., 99.

132 *During this conversation*: Ibid., 194.

132 *Adolescent expert Mike Riera*: Riera, *Uncommon Sense*, 24.

126 *Well-meaning parents exhibit*: Sells, *Parenting Your Out-of-Control Teenager*, 98.

136 *A recent study*: Dissell, R., "When Children Are the Abusers," *Cleveland Plain Dealer*, August 28, 2006.

137 *Why Is My Teen Violent?*: Sells, *Parenting Your Out-of-Control Teenager*, 217.

142 *This arrangement may put*: "Teens Skilled at Manipulating Divorced Parents," http://www.medicineonline.com, June 23, 2004.

143 *The stresses created during*: Riera, *Uncommon Sense*, 100.

143 *Some psychological illnesses*: Reiss et al., *The Relationship Code*, 240.

143 *However, some illnesses*: Ibid., 96.

NINE: DIVORCE WOUNDS

147 *"When A Family Man Thinks Twice"*: Coleman, Joshua D. "When a family man thinks twice," *San Francisco Chronicle*, Sunday June 18, 2000.

148 *As marital researcher*: Hetherington, E. Mavis, and Kelly, John. *For Better or For Worse: Divorce Reconsidered* (New York: W.W. Norton, 2002), 2.

148 *Divorce often means*: Aquilino, W. S., Later life parental divorce and widowhood: Impact on young adults' assessment of parent-child relations. *Journal of Marriage and the Family* (Nov. 1994) 56: 908–22; Booth, A., and Amato, P. R., Parental marital quality, parental divorce, and relations with parents. *Journal of Marriage and the Family* (Feb. 1994) 56(1): 21–34.

148 *Children may be induced*: Marquadt, Elizabeth. *Between Two Worlds: The Inner Lives of Children of Divorce* (New York: Crown, 2005), 93.

152 *Studies show that a father's*: Amato and Booth, *A Generation at Risk*, 74; Cooney, T. M., Young adults' relations with parents: The influence of recent parental divorce. *Journal of Marriage and the Family* (Feb. 1994) 56(1): 45–56.

152 *In general, mothers appear*: Hetherington and Kelly, *For Better or For Worse*; Kaufman, G.; Uhlenberg, P., Effects of life course transitions on the quality of relationships between adult children and their parents. *Journal of Marriage and the Family* (1998) 60(4): 924–38.

152 *While a maturely handled divorce*: Marquadt, *Between Two Worlds*, 38.

153 *Studies show that one*: Allen, S. M., and Hawkins, A. J., Maternal gatekeeping: Mothers' beliefs and behaviors that inhibit greater father involvement in family work. *Journal of Marriage and the Family* (1999) 61: 199–212; Belsky, J., Youngblade, L., Rovine, M., and Volling, B., Patterns of marital change and parent-child interaction. *Journal of Marriage and Family* (1991) 53: 487–98; Fagan, J.; Barnett, M., The relationship between maternal gatekeeping, paternal competence, mothers' attitudes about the father role, and father involvement. *Journal of Family Issues* (2003) 24(8): 1020–43; De Luccie, M. F., Mothers as gatekeepers: A model of maternal mediators of father involvement. *Journal of Genetic Psychology* (1995) 156(1): 115–31.

154 *Because boys can feel*: Hetherington and Kelly, *For Better or For Worse*, 149.

154 *Studies show that women's feelings*: Ibid., 13.

154 *Only 25 percent of fathers*: Ibid., 121.

155 *These dynamics may explain*: Ibid., 193.

156 *This isn't to say that stepfathers*: Ibid., 191; Visher, Emily B., and Visher, John S. *Stepfamilies: Myths and Realities* (New York: Citadel, 1979).

156 *This is why divorce*: Hetherington and Kelly, *For Better or For Worse*, 74.

156 *Perhaps this is why 60 percent*: Ibid., 175.

157 *Having a psychologically healthy parent*: Amato and Booth, *A Generation at Risk*; Neighbors B., Forehand R., and McVicar, D., Resilient adolescents and interparental conflict. *American Journal of Orthopsychiatry* (1993) 63: 462–71.

158 *"I've learned not to …"*: Pollack, Rachel, "Grandparents Struggle to Hang On after Divorce," *St. Petersburg Times*, Aug. 29, 2006.

164 *"I felt like talking about the divorce …"*: Marquadt, *Between Two Worlds*, 129.

TEN: PROBLEM MARRIAGES AND TROUBLED SPOUSES

176 *For those who worry*: Hetherington, *For Better or For Worse*, 121.

177 *In fact, most of the time*: Amato, P. R., Loomis, L., and Booth, A., Parental divorce, parental marital conflict, and offspring well-being during early adulthood. *Social Forces* (1995) 73: 895–916; Jekielek, S. M., Parental conflict, marital disruption, and children's emotional well-being. *Social Forces* (1998) 76: 905–35.

177 *Even without yelling*: Amato and Booth, *A Generation at Risk*; Reiss et al., *The Relationship Code*, 96; Booth and Amato, "Parental marital quality."

181 *Marital researcher John Gottman*: Gottman, *Why Marriages Succeed or Fail*, 57.

183 *Researchers Alan Booth*: Booth and Amato, "Parental marital quality."

194 *A large study found*: Hetherington, *For Better or for Worse*, 41.

ELEVEN: FAILURE TO LAUNCH

208 *Current studies in neurology*: Teicher, M., "The neurobiology of child abuse," *Scientific American*, March 2002, p. 70.

208 *As children, they are more likely*: Ibid.; Miller, Alice. *For Your Own Good: Hidden Cruelty in Child-Rearing and the Roots of Violence* (New York: Noonday Press, 1990); Cummings, E. M., and Cummings, J. L., A process-oriented approach to children's coping with adult's angry behavior. *Developmental Review* (1988) 8: 296–321.

209 *Their distrust in others*: Bass, Ellen, and Davis, Laura. *The Courage to Heal: A Guide for Women Survivors of Child Sexual Abuse* (New York: Collins, 1994); Widom C. S., Posttraumatic stress disorder in abused and neglected children grown up. *American Journal of Psychiatry* (1999) 156(8): 1223–29.

215 *The research of William Aquilino*: Aquilino, W., Predicting parents' experiences with coresident adult children. *Journal of Family Issues* (1991) 12: 323–42.

216 *She may develop beliefs*: Engel, Lewis, and Ferguson, Tom. *Imaginary Crimes* (Boston: Houghton Mifflin Company, 1990).

TWELVE: ALL GROWN UP

229 *Adults who suffer*: *Diagnostic and Statistical Manual of Mental Disorders* (2000), American Psychiatric Press.

229 *Studies show that having a child*: Pillemer, K., and Suitor, J., Will I ever escape my children's problems? Effects of adult children's problems on elderly parents. *Journal of Marriage and Family* (Aug. 1991) 53: 585–94. These researchers found that among women, having a problem child was a more powerful predictor than marital status or educational level in terms of predicting depression in the parent. See also Judith Cook, Who mothers the chronically mentally ill? *Family Relations* (1988) 37: 42–49.

231 *As discussed in chapter 9*: Cicirelli, V., A comparison of helping behavior to elderly parents of adult children with intact and disrupted marriages. *Gerontologist* (1983) 23: 619–25; Aquilino, W. S., Impact of childhood family disruption on young adults' relationship with parents. *Journal of Marriage and the Family* (1994) 56: 296–313.

232 *Studies show that children*: Amato, Loomis, and Booth, "Parental divorce"; Cummings, E. M., and Cummings, J. L., "A process-oriented approach"; Emery, R. E., Interparental conflict and the children of discord and divorce. *Psychological Bulletin* (1982) 92: 310–30.

232 *In addition, mothers*: Doherty, W. J., Responsible fathering: An overview and conceptual framework. *Journal of Marriage and the Family* (1998) 60: 277–92; Pleck, J. H., Paternal involvement: Levels, sources, and consequences. In *The Role of the Father in Child Development*, 3rd ed., Lamb, (New York: Wiley & Sons, 1997).

232 *Parents in high-conflict marriages*: Amato, Loomis, and Booth, "Parental divorce," 115.

235 *A study by the Institute*: Lacar, M., "The Bank of Mom and Dad," *The New York Times*, April 9, 2006.

240 *John Gottman has shown*: Gottman, John. *The Seven Principles for Making Marriage Work* (New York: Crown Publishing, 1999).

251 *University of Wisconsin*: Ellison, K., "Mastering Your Own Mind," *Psychology Today*, Sept./Oct. 2006.

251 *As writer Katherine Ellison*: Ibid.

252 *As the Dalai Lama*: Ibid.

THIRTEEN: ADDRESSING THE LONG REACH OF THE PAST

254 *English psychoanalyst*: Winnicott, Donald. *The Child, the Family, and the Outside World* (New York: Addison Wesley, 1992).

263 *They rear children*: Flett, G. L., and Hewitt, P. L. *Perfectionism: Theory, research and treatment* (Washington, D.C.: American Psychological Association, 2002); Haring, M., and Hewitt, P. L., Perfectionism, coping, and quality of intimate relationships *Journal of Marriage and the Family* (2003) 65(1): 143–58.

266 *Studies show that children*: Murray, L. P., Cooper, P. J., and Stein, A., Postnatal depression and infant development. *British Medical Journal* (1991): 978–79; Lewis, Amini, and Lannon, *General Theory of Love.*

269 *If you grew up with controlling*: Bourne, Edmund J. *The Anxiety and Phobia Workbook* (Oakland, CA: New Harbinger Publications, 2000).

270 *Children who have been neglected*: Engel and Ferguson, *Imaginary Crimes.*

AFTERWORD

277 *In the depth of winter*: Lottman, Herbert. *Camus: A Biography* (Corte Madera, CA: Gingko Press, 1997).

277 *In the last forty years*: Seligman, *Authentic Happiness*, 117.

INDEX